Mrs. Oliphant

Jeanne D'Arc: Her Life And Death

© 2025, Mrs. Margaret Oliphant (domaine public)
Édition : BoD · Books on Demand, 31 avenue Saint-Rémy, 57600 Forbach, bod@bod.fr
Impression : Libri Plureos GmbH, Friedensallee 273, 22763 Hamburg (Allemagne)
ISBN : 978-2-3225-1698-8
Dépôt légal : Avril 2025

Jeanne D'Arc: Her Life And Death

By
Mrs. Oliphant

JEANNE D'ARC

CHAPTER I — FRANCE IN THE FIFTEENTH CENTURY. 1412-1423.

It is no small effort for the mind, even of the most well-informed, how much more of those whose exact knowledge is not great (which is the case with most readers, and alas! with most writers also), to transport itself out of this nineteenth century which we know so thoroughly, and which has trained us in all our present habits and modes of thought, into the fifteenth, four hundred years back in time, and worlds apart in every custom and action of life. What is there indeed the same in the two ages? Nothing but the man and the woman, the living agents in spheres so different; nothing but love and grief, the affections and the sufferings by which humanity is ruled and of which it is capable. Everything else is changed: the customs of life, and its methods, and even its motives, the ruling principles of its continuance. Peace and mutual consideration, the policy which even in its selfish developments is so far good that it enables men to live together, making existence possible,—scarcely existed in those days. The highest ideal was that of war, war no doubt sometimes for good ends, to redress wrongs, to avenge injuries, to make crooked things straight—but yet always war, implying a state of affairs in which the last thing that men thought of was the golden rule, and the highest attainment to be looked for was the position of a protector, doer of justice, deliverer of the oppressed. Our aim now that no one should be oppressed, that every man should have justice as by the order of nature, was a thing unthought of. What individual help did feebly for the sufferer then, the laws do for us now, without fear or favour: which is a much greater thing to say than that the organisation of modern life, the mechanical helps, the comforts, the easements of the modern world, had no existence in those days. We are often told that the poorest peasant in our own time has aids to existence that had not been dreamt of for princes in the Middle Ages. Thirty years ago the world was mostly of opinion that the balance was entirely on our side, and that in everything we were so much better off than our fathers, that comparison was impossible. Since then there have been many revolutions of opinion, and we think it is now the general conclusion of wise men, that one period has little to boast itself of against another, that one form of civilisation replaces another without improving upon it, at least to the extent which appears on the surface. But yet the general prevalence of peace, interrupted only by occasional wars, even when we recognise a certain large and terrible utility in war itself, must always make a difference incalculable between the condition of the nations now, and then.

It is difficult, indeed, to imagine any concatenation of affairs which could reduce a country now to the condition in which France was in the beginning of the fifteenth century. A strong and splendid kingdom, to which in early ages one great man had given the force and supremacy of a united nation, had fallen into a disintegration which seems almost incredible when regarded in the light of that warm flame of nationality which now illumines, almost above all others, the French nation. But Frenchmen were not Frenchmen, they were Burgundians, Armagnacs, Bretons, Provençaux five hundred years ago. The interests of one part of the kingdom were not those of the other. Unity had no existence. Princes of the same family were more furious enemies to each other, at the head of their respective fiefs and provinces, than the traditional foes of their race; and instead of meeting an invader with a united force of patriotic resistance, one or more of these subordinate rulers was sure to side with the invader and to execute greater atrocities against his own flesh and blood than anything the alien could do.

When Charles VII. of France began, nominally, his reign, his uncles and cousins, his nearest kinsmen, were as determinedly his opponents, as was Henry V. of England, whose frank object was to take the crown from his head. The country was torn in pieces with different causes and cries. The English were but little farther off from the Parisian than was the Burgundian, and the English king was only a trifle less French than were the members of the royal family of France. These circumstances are little taken into consideration in face of the general history, in which a careless reader sees nothing but the two nations pitted against each other as they might be now, the French united in one strong and distinct nationality, the three kingdoms of Great Britain all welded into one. In the beginning of the fifteenth century the Scots fought on the French side, against their intimate enemy of England, and if there had been any unity in Ireland, the Irish would have done the same. The advantages and disadvantages of subdivision were in full play. The Scots fought furiously against the English—and when the latter won, as was usually the case, the Scots contingent, whatever bounty might be shown to the French, was always exterminated. On the other side the Burgundians, the Armagnacs, and Royalists met each other almost more fiercely than the latter encountered the English. Each country was convulsed by struggles of its own, and fiercely sought its kindred foes in the ranks of its more honest and natural enemy.

When we add to these strange circumstances the facts that the French King, Charles VI., was mad, and incapable of any real share either in the internal government of his country or in resistance to its invader: that his only son, the Dauphin, was no more than a foolish boy, led by incompetent councillors, and even of doubtful legitimacy, regarded with hesitation and uncertainty by many, everybody being willing to believe the worst of his mother, especially after the treaty of Troyes in which she virtually gave him up: that the King's brothers or cousins at the head of their respective fiefs were all seeking their own advantage, and that some of them, especially the Duke of Burgundy, had cruel wrongs to avenge: it will be more easily understood that France had reached a period of depression and apparent despair which no principle of national elasticity or new spring of national impulse was present to amend. The extraordinary aspect of whole districts in so strong and populous a country, which disowned the native monarch, and of towns and castles innumerable which were held by the native nobility in the name of a foreign king, could scarcely have been possible under other circumstances. Everything was out of joint. It is said to be characteristic of the nation that it is unable to play publicly (as we say) a losing game; but it is equally characteristic of the race to forget its humiliations as if they had never been, and to come out intact when the fortune of war changes, more French than ever, almost unabashed and wholly uninjured, by the catastrophe which had seemed fatal.

If we had any right to theorise on such a subject—which is a thing the French themselves above all other men love to do,—we should be disposed to say, that wars and revolutions, legislation and politics, are things which go on over the head of France, so to speak—boilings on the surface, with which the great personality of the nation if such a word may be used, has little to do, and cares but little for; while she herself, the great race, neither giddy nor fickle, but unusually obstinate, tenacious, and sober, narrow even in the unwavering pursuit of a certain kind of well-being congenial to her—goes steadily on, less susceptible to temporary humiliation than many peoples much less excitable on the surface, and always coming back into sight when the commotion is over, acquisitive, money-making, profit-loving, uninjured in any essential particular by the most terrific of convulsions. This of course is to be said more or less of every country, the strain of common life being always, thank God, too strong for every temporary commotion—but it is true in a special way of France:—witness the extraordinary manner in which in our own time, and under our own eyes, that wonderful country righted herself after the tremendous misfortunes of the Franco-German war, in which for a moment not only her prestige, her honour, but her money and credit seemed to be lost.

It seems rather a paradox to point attention to the extraordinary tenacity of this basis of French character, the steady prudence and solidity which in the end always triumph over the light heart and light head, the excitability and often rash and dangerous élan, which are popularly supposed to be the chief distinguishing features of France—at the very moment of beginning such a fairy tale, such a wonderful embodiment of the visionary and ideal, as is the story of Jeanne d'Arc. To call it a fairy tale is, however, disrespectful: it is an angelic revelation, a vision made into flesh and blood, the dream of a woman's fancy, more ethereal, more impossible than that of any man—even a poet:—for the man, even in his most uncontrolled imaginations, carries with him a certain practical limitation of what can be—whereas the woman at her highest is absolute, and disregards all bounds of possibility. The Maid of Orleans, the Virgin of France, is the sole being of her kind who has ever attained full expression in this world. She can neither be classified, as her countrymen love to classify, nor traced to any system of evolution as we all attempt to do nowadays. She is the impossible verified and attained. She is the thing in every race, in every form of humanity, which the dreaming girl, the visionary maid, held in at every turn by innumerable restrictions, her feet bound, her actions restrained, not only by outward force, but by the law of her nature, more effectual still,—has desired to be. That voiceless poet, to whom what can be is nothing, but only what should be if miracle could be attained to fulfil her trance and rapture of desire—is held by no conditions, modified by no circumstances; and miracle is all around her, the most credible, the most real of powers, the very air she breathers. Jeanne of France is the very flower of this passion of the imagination. She is altogether impossible from beginning to end of her, inexplicable, alone, with neither rival nor even second in the one sole ineffable path: yet all true as one of the oaks in her wood, as one of the flowers in her garden, simple, actual, made of the flesh and blood which are common to us all.

And she is all the more real because it is France, impure, the country of light loves and immodest passions, where all that is sensual comes to the surface, and the courtesan is the queen of ignoble fancy, that has brought forth this most perfect embodiment of purity among the nations. This is of itself one of those miracles which captivate the mind and charm the imagination, the living paradox in which the soul delights. How did she come out of that stolid peasant race, out of that distracted and ignoble age, out of riot and license and the fierce thirst for gain, and failure of every noble faculty? Who can tell? By the grace of God, by the inspiration of heaven, the only origins in which the student of nature, which is over nature, can put any trust. No evolution, no system of development, can explain Jeanne. There is but one of her and no more in all the astonished world.

With the permission of the reader I will retain her natural and beautiful name. To translate it into Joan seems quite unnecessary. Though she is the finest emblem to the world in general of that noble, fearless, and spotless Virginity which is one of the finest inspirations of the mediæval mind, yet she is inherently French, though France scarcely was in her time: and national, though as yet there were rather the elements of a nation than any indivisible People in that great country. Was not she herself one of the strongest and purest threads of gold to draw that broken race together and bind it irrevocably, beneficially, into one?

It is curious that it should have been from the farthest edge of French territory that this national deliverer came. It is a commonplace that a Borderer should be a more hot partisan of his own country against the other from which but a line divides him in fact, and scarcely so much in race—than the calmer inhabitant of the midland country who knows no such press of constant antagonism; and Jeanne is another example of this well known fact. It is even a question still languidly discussed whether Jeanne and her family were actually on one side of the line or the other. "Il faut opter," says M. Blaze de Bury, one of her latest biographers, as if the peasant household of 1412 had inhabited an Alsatian cottage in 1872. When the line is drawn so closely, it is difficult to determine, but Jeanne herself does not ever seem to have entertained a moment's doubt on the subject, and she after all is the best authority. Perhaps Villon was thinking more of his rhyme than of absolute fact when he spoke of "Jeanne la bonne Lorraine." She was born on the 5th of January, 1412, in the village of Domremy, on the banks of the Meuse, one of those little grey hamlets, with its little church tower, and remains of a little chateau on the soft elevation of a mound not sufficient for the name of hill—which are scattered everywhere through those level countries, like places which have never been built, which have grown out of the soil, of undecipherable antiquity—perhaps, one feels, only a hundred, perhaps a thousand years old—yet always inhabitable in all the ages, with the same names lingering about, the same surroundings, the same mild rural occupations, simple plenty and bare want mingling together with as little difference of level as exists in the sweeping lines of the landscape round.

The life was calm in so humble a corner which offered nothing to the invader or marauder of the time, but yet was so much within the universal conditions of war that the next-door neighbour, so to speak, the adjacent village of Maxey, held for the Burgundian and English alliance, while little Domremy was for the King. And once at least when Jeanne was a girl at home, the family were startled in their quiet by the swoop of an armed party of Burgundians, and had to gather up babies and what portable property they might have, and flee across the frontier, where the good Lorrainers received and sheltered them, till they could go back to their village, sacked and pillaged and devastated in the meantime by the passing storm. Thus even in their humility and inoffensiveness the Domremy villagers knew what war and its miseries were, and the recollection would no doubt be vivid among the children, of that half terrible, half exhilarating adventure, the fright and excitement of personal participation in the troubles, of which, night and day, from one quarter or another, they must have heard.

Domremy had originally belonged to the Abbey of St. Remy at Rheims—the ancient church of which, in its great antiquity, is still an interest and a wonder even in comparison with the amazing splendour of the cathedral of that place, so rich and ornate, which draws the eyes of the visitor to itself, and its greater associations. It is possible that this ancient connection with Rheims may have brought the great ceremony for which it is ever memorable, the consecration of the kings of France, more distinctly before the musing vision of the village girl; but I doubt whether such chance associations are ever much to be relied upon. The village was on the high-road to Germany; it must have been therefore in the way of news, and of many rumours of what was going on in the centres of national life, more than many towns of importance. Feudal bands, a rustic Seigneur with his little troop, going out for their forty days' service, or returning home after it, must have passed along the banks of the lazy Meuse many days during the fighting season, and indeed throughout the year, for garrison duty would be as necessary in winter as in summer; or a wandering pair of friars who had seen strange sights must have passed with their wallets from the neighbouring convents, collecting the day's provision, and leaving news and gossip behind, such as flowed to these monastic hostelries from all quarters—tales of battles, and anecdotes of the Court, and dreadful stories of English atrocities, to stir the village and rouse ever generous sentiment and stirring of national indignation. They are said by Michelet to have been no man's vassals, these outlying hamlets of Champagne; the men were not called upon to follow their lord's banner at a day's notice, as were the sons of other villages. There is no appearance even of a lord at all upon this piece of Church land, which was, we are told, directly held under the King, and would only therefore be touched by a general levy en masse—not even perhaps by that, so far off were they, and so near the frontier, where a reluctant man-at-arms could without difficulty make his escape, as the unwilling conscript sometimes does now.

There would seem to have been no one of more importance in Domremy than Jacques d'Arc himself and his wife, respectable peasants, with a little money, a considerable rural property in flocks and herds and pastures, and a good reputation among their kind. He had three sons working with their father in the peaceful routine of the fields; and two daughters, of whom some authorities indicate Jeanne as the younger, and some as the elder. The cottage interior, however, appears more clearly to us than the outward aspect of the family life. The daughters were not, like the children of poorer peasants, brought up to the rude outdoor labours of the little farm. Painters have represented Jeanne as keeping her father's sheep, and even the early witnesses say the same; but it is contradicted by herself, who ought to know best—(except in taking her turn to herd them into a place of safety on an alarm). If she followed the flocks to the fields, it must have been, she says, in her childhood, and she has no recollection of it. Hers was a more sheltered and safer lot. The girls were brought up by their mother indoors in all the labours of housewifery, but also in the delicate art of needlework, so much more exquisite in those days than now. Perhaps Isabeau, the mistress of the house, was of convent training, perhaps some ancient privilege in respect to the manufacture of ornaments for the altar, and church vestments, was still retained by the tenants of what had been Church lands. At all events this, and other kindred works of the needle, seems to have been the chief occupation to which Jeanne was brought up.

The education of this humble house seems to have come entirely from the mother. It was natural that the children should not know A from B, as Jeanne afterward said; but no one did, probably, in the village nor even on much higher levels than that occupied by the family of Jacques d'Arc. But the children at their mother's knee learned the Credo, they learned the simple universal prayers which are common to the wisest and simplest, which no great savant or poet could improve, and no child fail to understand: "Our Father, which art in Heaven," and that "Hail, Mary, full of grace," which the world in that day put next. These were the alphabet of life to the little Champagnards in their rough woollen frocks and clattering sabots; and when the house had been set in order,—a house not without comfort, with its big wooden presses full of linen, and the pot au feu hung over the cheerful fire,— came the real work, perhaps embroideries for the Church, perhaps only good stout shirts made of flax spun by their own hands for the father and the boys, and the fine distinctive coif of the village for the women. "Asked if she had learned any art or trade, said: Yes, that her mother had taught her to sew and spin, and so well, that she did not think any woman in Rouen could teach her anything." When the lady in the ballad makes her conditions with the peasant woman who is to bring up her boy, her "gay goss hawk," and have him trained in the use of sword and lance, she undertakes to teach the "turtle-doo," the woman child substituted for him, "to lay gold with her hand." No doubt Isabeau's child learned this difficult and dainty art, and how to do the beautiful and delicate embroidery which fills the treasuries of the old churches.

And while they sat by the table in the window, with their shining silks and gold thread, the mother made the quiet hours go by with tale and legend—of the saints first of all—and stories from Scripture, quaintly interpreted into the costume and manners of their own time, as one may still hear them in the primitive corners of Italy: mingled with incidents of the war, of the wounded man tended in the village, and the victors all flushed with triumph, and the defeated with trailing arms and bowed heads, riding for their lives: perhaps little epics and tragedies of the young knight riding by to do his devoir with his handful of followers all spruce and gay, and the battered and diminished remnant that would come back. And then the Black Burgundians, the horrible English ogres, whose names would make the children shudder! No God-den had got so far as Domremy; there was no personal knowledge to soften the picture of the invader. He was unspeakable as the Turk to the imagination of the French peasant, diabolical as every invader is.

This was the earliest training of the little maid before whom so strange and so great a fortune lay. Autre personne que sadite mère ne lui apprint—any lore whatsoever; and she so little—yet everything that was wanted—her prayers, her belief, the happiness of serving God, and also man; for when any one was sick in the village, either a little child with the measles, or a wounded soldier from the wars, Isabeau's modest child—no doubt the mother too—was always ready to help. It must have been a family de bien, in the simple phrase of the country, helpful, serviceable, with charity and aid for all. An honest labourer, who came to speak for Jeanne at the second trial, held long after her death, gave his incontestable evidence to this. "I was then a child," he said, "and it was she who nursed me in my illness." They were all more or less devout in those days, when faith was without question, and the routine of church ceremonial was followed as a matter of course; but few so much as Jeanne, whose chief pleasure it was to say her prayers in the little dark church, where perhaps in the morning sunshine, as she made her early devotions, there would blaze out upon her from a window, a Holy Michael in shining armour, transfixing the dragon with his spear, or a St. Margaret dominating the same emblem of evil with her cross in her hand. So, at least, the historians conjecture, anxious to find out some reason for her visions; and there is nothing in the suggestion which is unpleasing. The little country church was in the gift of St. Remy, and some benefactor of the rural curé might well have given a painted window to make glad the hearts of the simple people. St. Margaret was no warrior-saint, but she overcame the dragon with her cross, and was thus a kind of sister spirit to the great archangel.

Sitting much of her time at or outside the cottage door with her needlework, in itself an occupation so apt to encourage musing and dreams, the bells were one of Jeanne's great pleasures. We know a traveller, of the calmest English temperament and sobriety of Protestant fancy, to whom the midday Angelus always brings, he says, a touching reminder—which he never neglects wherever he may be—to uncover the head and lift up the heart; how much more the devout peasant girl softly startled in the midst of her dreaming by that call to prayer. She was so fond of those bells that she bribed the careless bell-ringer with simple presents to be more attentive to his duty. From the garden where she sat with her work, the cloudy foliage of the bois de chêne, the oak wood, where were legends of fairies and a magic well, to which her imagination, better inspired, seems to have given no great heed, filled up the prospect on one side. At a later period, her accusers attempted to make out that she had been a devotee of these nameless woodland spirits, but in vain. No doubt she was one of the procession on the holy day once a year, when the curé of the parish went out through the wood to the Fairies' Well to say his mass, and exorcise what evil enchantment might be there. But Jeanne's imagination was not of the kind to require such stimulus. The saints were enough for her; and indeed they supplied to a great extent the fairy tales of the age, though it was not of love and fame and living happy ever after, but of sacrifice and suffering and valorous martyrdom that their glory was made up.

We hear of the woods, the fields, the cottages, the little church and its bells, the garden where she sat and sewed, the mother's stories, the morning mass, in this quiet preface of the little maiden's life; but nothing of the highroad with its wayfarers, the convoys of provisions for the war, the fighting men that were coming and going. Yet these, too, must have filled a large part in the village life, and it is evident that a strong impression of the pity of it all, of the distraction of the country and all the cruelties and miseries of which she could not but hear, must have early begun to work in Jeanne's being, and that while she kept silence the fire burned in her heart. The love of God, and that love of country which has nothing to say to political patriotism but translates itself in an ardent longing and desire to do "some excelling thing" for the benefit and glory of that country, and to heal its wounds—were the two principles of her life. We have not the slightest indication how much or how little of this latter sentiment was shared by the simple community about her; unless from the fact that the Domremy children fought with those of Maxey, their disaffected neighbours, to the occasional effusion of blood. We do not know even of any volunteer from the village, or enthusiasm for the King. The district was voiceless, the little clusters of cottages fully occupied in getting their own bread, and probably like most other village societies, disposed to treat any military impulse among their sons as mere vagabondism and love of adventure and idleness.

Nothing, so far as anyone knows, came near the most unlikely volunteer of all, to lead her thoughts to that art of war of which she knew nothing, and of which her little experience could only have shown her the horrors and miseries, the sufferings of wounded fugitives and the ruin of sacked houses. Of all people in the world, the little daughter of a peasant was the last who could have been expected to respond to the appeal of the wretched country. She had three brothers who might have served the King, and there was no doubt many a stout clodhopper about, of that kind which in every country is the fittest material for fighting, and "food for powder." But to none of these did the call come. Every detail goes to increase the profound impression of peacefulness which fills the atmosphere—the slow river floating by, the roofs clustered together, the church bells tinkling their continual summons, the girl with her work at the cottage door in the shadow of the apple trees. To pack the little knapsack of a brother or a lover, and to convoy him weeping a little way on his road to the army, coming back to the silent church to pray there, with the soft natural tears which the uses of common life must soon dry—that is all that imagination could have demanded of Jeanne. She was even too young for any interposition of the lover, too undeveloped, the French historians tell us with their astonishing frankness, to the end of her short life, to have been moved by any such thought. She might have poured forth a song, a prayer, a rude but sweet lament for her country, out of the still bosom of that rustic existence. Such things have been, the trouble of the age forcing an utterance from the very depths of its inarticulate life. But it was not for this that Jeanne d'Arc was born.

CHAPTER II — DOMREMY AND VAUCOULEURS. 1424-1429.

In the year 1424, the year in which, after the battle of Agincourt, France was delivered over to Henry V., an extraordinary event occurred in the life of this little French peasant. We have not the same horror of that treaty, naturally, as have the French. Henry V. is a favourite of our history, probably not so much for his own merit as because of that master-magician, Shakespeare, who of his supreme good pleasure, in the exercise of that voluntary preference, which even God himself seems to show to some men, has made of that monarch one of the best beloved of our hearts. Dear to us as he is, in Eastcheap as at Agincourt, and more in the former than the latter, even our sense of the disgraceful character of that bargain, le traité infâme of Troyes, by which Queen Isabeau betrayed her son, and gave her daughter and her country to the invader, is softened a little by our high estimation of the hero. But this is simple national prejudice; regarded from the French side, or even by the impartial judgment of general humanity, it was an infamous treaty, and one which might well make the blood boil in French veins.

We look at it at present, however, through the atmosphere of the nineteenth century, when France is all French, and when the royal house of England has no longer any French connection. If George III., much more George II., on the basis of his kingdom of Hanover, had attempted to make himself master of a large portion of Germany, the situation would have been more like that of Henry V. in France than anything we can think of now. It is true the kings of England were no longer dukes of Normandy—but they had been so within the memory of man: and that noble duchy was a hereditary appanage of the family of the Conqueror; while to other portions of France they had the link of temporary possession and inheritance through French wives and mothers; added to which is the fact that Jean sans Peur of Burgundy, thirsting to avenge his father's blood upon the Dauphin, would have been probably a more dangerous usurper than Henry, and that the actual sovereign, the unfortunate, mad Charles VI., was in no condition to maintain his own rights.

There is little evidence, however, that this treaty, or anything so distinct in detail, had made much impression on the outlying borders of France. What was known there, was only that the English were victorious, that the rightful King of France was still uncrowned and unacknowledged, and that the country was oppressed and humiliated under the foot of the invader. The fact that the new King was not yet the Lord's anointed, and had never received the seal of God, as it were, to his commission, was a fact which struck the imagination of the village as of much more importance than many greater things—being at once more visible and matter-of-fact, and of more mystical and spiritual efficacy than any other circumstance in the dreadful tale.

Jeanne was in the garden as usual, seated, as we should say in Scotland, at "her seam," not quite thirteen, a child in all the innocence of infancy, yet full of dreams, confused no doubt and vague, with those impulses and wonderings —impatient of trouble, yearning to give help—which tremble on the chaos of a young soul like the first lightening of dawn upon the earth. It was summer, and afternoon, the time of dreams. It would be easy in the employment of legitimate fancy to heighten the picturesqueness of that quiet scene—the little girl with her favourite bells, the birds picking up the crumbs of brown bread at her feet. She was thinking of nothing, most likely, in a vague suspense of musing, the wonder of youth, the awakening of thought, as yet come to little definite in her child's heart—looking up from her work to note some passing change of the sky, a something in the air which was new to her. All at once between her and the church there shone a light on the right hand, unlike anything she had ever seen before; and out of it came a voice equally unknown and wonderful. What did the voice say? Only the simplest words, words fit for a child, no maxim or mandate above her faculties—"Jeanne, sois bonne et sage enfant; va souvent à l'église." Jeanne, be good! What more could an archangel, what less could the peasant mother within doors, say? The little girl was frightened, but soon composed herself. The voice could be nothing but sacred and blessed which spoke thus. It would not appear that she mentioned it to anyone. It is such a secret as a child, in that wavering between the real and unreal, the world not realised of childhood, would keep, in mingled shyness and awe, uncertain, rapt in the atmosphere of vision, within her own heart.

It is curious how often this wonderful scene has been repeated in France, never connected with so high a mission, but yet embracing the same circumstances, the same situation, the same semi-angelic nature of the woman-child. The little Bernadette of Lourdes is almost of our own day; she, too is one who puts the scorner to silence. What her visions and her voices were, who can say? The last historian of them is not a man credulous of good or moved towards the ideal; yet he is silent, except in a wondering impression of the sacred and the true, before the little Bearnaise in her sabots; and, notwithstanding the many sordid results that have followed and all that sad machinery of expected miracle through which even, repulsive as it must always be, a something breaks forth from time to time which no man can define and account for except in ways more incredible than miracle—so is the rest of the world. Why has this logical, sceptical, doubting country, so able to quench with an epigram, or blow away with a breath of ridicule the finest vision—become the special sphere and birthplace of these spotless infant-saints? This is one of the wonders which nobody attempts to account for. Yet Bernadette is as Jeanne, though there are more than four hundred years between.

After what intervals the vision returned we are not told, nor in what circumstances. It seems to have come chiefly out-of-doors, in the silence and freedom of the fields or garden. Presently the heavenly radiance shaped itself into some semblance of forms and figures, one of which, clearer than the others, was like a man, but with wings and a crown on his head and the air "d'un vrai prud' homme"; a noble apparition before whom at first the little maid trembled, but whose majestic, honest regard soon gave her confidence. He bade her once more to be good, and that God would help her; then he told her the sad story of her own suffering country, la pitié qui estoit au royaume de France. Was it the pity of heaven that the archangel reported to the little trembling girl, or only that which woke with the word in her own childish soul? He has chosen the small things of this world to confound the great. Jeanne's young heart was full of pity already, and of yearning over the helpless mother-country which had no champion to stand for her. "She had great doubts at first whether it was St. Michael, but afterwards when he had instructed her and shown her many things, she believed firmly that it was he."

It was this warrior-angel who opened the matter to her, and disclosed her mission. "Jeanne," he said, "you must go to the help of the King of France; and it is you who shall give him back his kingdom." Like a still greater Maid, trembling, casting in her mind what this might mean, she replied, confused, as if that simple detail were all: "Messire, I am only a poor girl; I cannot ride or lead armed men." The vision took no notice of this plea. He became minute in his directions, indicating exactly what she was to do. "Go to Messire de Baudricourt, captain of Vaucouleurs, and he will take you to the King. St. Catherine and St. Margaret will come and help you." Jeanne was overwhelmed by this exactness, by the sensation of receiving direct orders. She cried, weeping and helpless, terrified to the bottom of her soul—What was she that she should do this? a little girl, able to guide nothing but her needle or her distaff, to lend her simple aid in nursing a sick child. But behind all her fright and hesitation, her heart was filled with the emotion thus suggested to her— the immeasurable pitié que estoit au royaume de France. Her heart became heavy with this burden. By degrees it came about that she could think of nothing else; and her little life was confused by expectations and recollections of the celestial visitant, who might arrive upon her at any moment, in the midst perhaps of some innocent play, or when she sat sewing in the garden before her father's humble door.

After a while the vrai prud' homme came seldom; other figures more like herself, soft forms of women, white and shining, with golden circlets and ornaments, appeared to her in the great halo of the light; they bowed their heads, naming themselves, as to a sister spirit, Catherine, and the other Margaret. Their voices were sweet and soft with a sound that made you weep. They were both martyrs, encouraging and strengthening the little martyr that was to be. "A lady is there in the heavens who loves thee": Virgil could not say more to rouse the flagging strength of Dante. When these gentle figures disappeared, the little maid wept in an anguish of tenderness, longing if only they would take her with them. It is curious that though she describes in this vague rapture the appearance of her visitors, it is always as "mes voix" that she names them—the sight must always have been more imperfect than the message. Their outlines and their lovely faces might shine uncertain in the excess of light; but the words were always plain. The pity for France that was in their hearts spread itself into the silent rural atmosphere, touching every sensitive chord in the nature of little Jeanne. It was as if her mother lay dying there before her eyes.

Curious to think how little anyone could have suspected such meetings as these, in the cottage hard by, where the weary ploughmen from the fields would come clamping in for their meal, and Dame Isabeau would call to the child, even sharply perhaps now and then, to leave that all-absorbing needlework and come in and help, as Martha called Mary fourteen hundred years before; and where the priest, mumbling his mass of a cold morning in the little church, would smile indulgent on the faithful little worshipper when it was done, sure of seeing Jeanne there whoever might be absent. She was a shy girl, blushing and drooping her head when a stranger spoke to her, red and shame-faced when they laughed at her in the village as a dévote before her time; but with nothing else to blush about in all her simple record.

Neither to her parents, nor to the curé when she made her confession, does she seem to have communicated these strange experiences, though they had lasted for some time before she felt impelled to act upon them, and could keep silence no longer. She was but thirteen when the revelations began and she was seventeen when at last she set forth to fulfil her mission. She had no guidance from her voices, she herself says, as to whether she should tell or not tell what had been communicated to her; and no doubt was kept back by her shyness, and by the dreamy confusion of childhood between the real and unreal. One would have thought that a life in which these visions were of constant recurrence would have been rapt altogether out of wholesome use and wont, and all practical service. But this does not seem for a moment to have been the case. Jeanne was no hysterical girl, living with her head in a mist, abstracted from the world. She had all the enthusiasms even of youthful friendship, other girls surrounding her with the intimacy of the village, paying her visits, staying all night, sharing her room and her bed. She was ready to be sent for by any poor woman that needed help or nursing, she was always industrious at her needle; one would love to know if perhaps in the Trésor at Rheims there was some stole or maniple with flowers on it, wrought by her hands. But the Trésor at Rheims is nowadays rather vulgar if truth must be told, and the bottles and vases for the consecration of Charles X., that pauvre sire, are more thought of than relics of an earlier age.

At length, however, one does not know how, the secret of her double life came out. No doubt long brooding over these voices, long intercourse with such celestial visitors, and the mission continually pressed upon her—meaningless to the child at first, a thing only to shed terrified tears over and wonder at— ripened her intelligence so that she came at last to perceive that it was practicable, a thing to be done, a charge to be obeyed. She had this before her, as a girl in ordinary circumstances has the new developments of life to think of, and how to be a wife and mother. And the news brought by every passer-by would prove doubly interesting, doubly important to Jeanne, in her daily growing comprehension of what she was called upon to do. As she felt the current more and more catching her feet, sweeping her on, overcoming all resistance in her own mind, she must have been more and more anxious to know what was going on in the distracted world, more and more touched by that great pity which had awakened her soul. And all these reports were of a nature to increase that pity till it became overwhelming. The tales she would hear of the English must have been tales of cruelty and horror; not so many years ago what tales did not we hear of German ferocity in the French villages, perhaps not true at all, yet making their impression always; and it was more probable in that age that every such story should be true. Then the compassion which no one can help feeling for a young man deprived of his rights, his inheritance taken from him, his very life in danger, threatened by the stranger and usurper, was deepened in every particular by the fact that it was the King, the very impersonation of France, appointed by God as the head of the country, who was in danger. Everything that Jeanne heard would help to swell the stream.

Thus she must have come step by step—this extraordinary, impossible suggestion once sown in her dreaming soul—to perceive a kind of miraculous reasonableness in it, to see its necessity, and how everything pointed towards such a deliverance. It would have seemed natural to believe that the prophecies of the countryside which promised a virgin from an oak grove, a maiden from Lorraine, to deliver France, might have affected her mind, did we not have it from her own voice that she had never heard that prophecy; but the word of the blessed Michael, so often repeated, was more than an old wife's tale; and the child's alarm would seem to have died away as she came to her full growth. And Jeanne was no ethereal spirit lost in visions, but a robust and capable peasant girl, fearing little, and full of sense and determination, as well as of an inspiration so far above the level of the crowd. We hear with wonder afterwards that she had the making of a great general in her untutored female soul,—which is perhaps the most wonderful thing in her career,—and saw with the eye of an experienced and able soldier, as even Dunois did not always see it, the fit order of an attack, the best arrangement of the forces at her command. This I honestly avow is to me the most incredible point in the story. I am not disturbed by the apparition of the saints; there is in them an ineffable appropriateness and fitness against which the imagination, at least, has not a word to say. The wonder is not, to the natural mind, that such interpositions of heaven come, but that they come so seldom. But that Jacques d'Arc's daughter, the little girl over her sewing, whose only fault was that she went to church too often, should have the genius of a soldier, is too bewildering for words to say. A poet, yes, an inspiring influence leading on to miraculous victory; but a general, skilful with the rude artillery of the time, divining the better way in strategy,—this is a wonder beyond the reach of our faculties; yet according to Alençon, Dunois, and other military authorities, it was true.

We have little means of finding out how it was that Jeanne's long musings came at last to a point at which they could be hidden no longer, nor what it was which induced her at last to select the confidant she did. No doubt she must have been considering and weighing the matter for a long time before she fixed upon the man who was her relation, yet did not belong to Domremy, and was safer than a townsman for the extraordinary revelations she had to make. One of her neighbours, her gossip, Gerard of Epinal, to whose child she was godmother, had perhaps at one moment seemed to her a likely helper. But he belonged to the opposite party. "If you were not a Burgundian," she said to him once, "there is something I might tell you." The honest fellow took this to mean that she had some thought of marriage, the most likely and natural supposition. It was at this moment, when her heart was burning with her great secret, the voices urging her on day by day, and her power of self-constraint almost at an end, that Providence sent Durand Laxart, her uncle by marriage, to Domremy on some family visit. She would seem to have taken advantage of the opportunity with eagerness, asking him privately to take her home with him, and to explain to her father and mother that he wanted her to take care of his wife. No doubt the girl, devoured with so many thoughts, would have the air of requiring "a change" as we say, and that the mother would be very ready to accept for her an invitation which might bring back the brightness to her child. Laxart was a peasant like the rest, a prud' homme well thought of among his people. He lived in Burey le Petit, near to Vaucouleurs, the chief place of the district, and Jeanne already knew that it was to the captain of Vaucouleurs that she was to address herself. Thus she secured her object in the simplest and most natural way.

Yet the reader cannot but hold his breath at the thought of what that amazing revelation must have been to the homely, rustic soul, her companion, communicated as they went along the common road in the common daylight. "She said to the witness that she must go to France to the Dauphin, to make him to be crowned King." It must have been as if a thunderbolt had fallen at his feet when the girl whom he had known in every development of her little life, thus suddenly disclosed to him her secret purpose and determination. All her simple excellence the good man knew, and that she was no fantastic chatterer, but truly une bonne douce fille, bold in nothing but kindness, with nothing to blush for but the fault of going too often to church. "Did you never hear that France should be made desolate by a woman and restored by a maid?" she said; and this would seem to have been an unanswerable argument. He had, henceforth, nothing to do but to promote her purpose as best he could in every way.

It would not seem at all unlikely to this good man that the Archangel Michael, if Jeanne's revelation to him went so far, should have named Robert de Baudricourt, the chief of the district, captain of the town and its forces, the principal personage in all the neighbourhood, as the person to whom Jeanne's purpose was to be revealed, but rather a guarantee of St. Michael himself, familiar with good society; and the Seigneur must have been more or less in good intelligence with his people, not too alarming to be referred to, even on so insignificant a subject as the vagaries of a country girl—though these by this time must have begun to seem something more than vagaries to the half-convinced peasant. And it was no doubt a great relief to his mind thus to put the decision of the question into the hands of a man better informed than himself. Laxart proceeded to Vaucouleurs upon his mission, shyly yet with confidence. He would seem to have had a preliminary interview with Baudricourt before introducing Jeanne. The stammering countryman, the bluff, rustic noble and soldier, cheerfully contemptuous, receiving, with a loud laugh into all the echoes, the extraordinary demand that he should send a little girl from Domremy to the King, to deliver France, come before us like a picture in the countryman's simple words. Robert de Baudricourt would scarcely hear the story out. "Box her ears," he said, "and send her home to her mother." The little fool! What did she know of the English, those brutal, downright fighters, against whom no élan was sufficient, who stood their ground and set up vulgar posts around their lines, instead of trusting to the rush of sudden valour, and the tactics of the tournament! She deliver France! On a much smaller argument and to put down a less ambition, the half serious, half amused adviser has bidden a young fanatic's ears to be boxed on many an unimportant occasion, and has often been justified in so doing. There would be a half hour of gaiety after poor Laxart, crestfallen, had got his dismissal. The good man must have turned back to Jeanne, where she waited for him in courtyard or antechamber, with a heavy heart. No boxing of ears was possible to him. The mere thought of it was blasphemy. This was on Ascension Day the 13 May, 1428.

Jeanne, however, was not discouraged by M. de Baudricourt's joke, and her interview with him changed his views completely. She appears indeed from the moment of setting out from her father's house to have taken a new attitude. These great personages of the country before whom all the peasants trembled, were nothing to this village maid, except, perhaps, instruments in the hand of God to speed her on her way if they could see their privileges—if not, to be swept out of it like straws by the wind. It had no doubt been hard for her to leave her father's house; but after that disruption what did anything matter? And she had gone through five years of gradual training of which no one knew. The tears and terror, the plea, "I am a poor girl; I cannot even ride," of her first childlike alarm had given place to a profound acquaintance with the voices and their meaning. They were now her familiar friends guiding her at every step; and what was the commonplace burly Seigneur, with his roar of laughter, to Jeanne? She went to her audience with none of the alarm of the peasant. A certain young man of Baudricourt's suite, Bertrand de Poulengy, another young D'Artagnan seeking his fortune, was present in the hall and witnessed the scene. The joke would seem to have been exhausted by the time Jeanne appeared, or her perfect gravity and simplicity, and beautiful manners —so unlike her rustic dress and village coif—imposed upon the Seigneur and his little court. This is how the story is told, twenty-five years after, by the witness, then an elderly knight, recalling the story of his youth.

"She said that she came to Robert on the part of her Lord, that he should send to the Dauphin, and tell him to hold out, and have no fear, for the Lord would send him succour before the middle of Lent. She also said that France did not belong to the Dauphin but to her Lord; but her Lord willed that the Dauphin should be its King, and hold it in command, and that in spite of his enemies she herself would conduct him to be consecrated. Robert then asked her who was this Lord? She answered, 'The King of Heaven.' This being done (the witness adds) she returned to her father's house with her uncle, Durand Laxart of Burey le Petit."

This brief and sudden preface to her career passed over and had no immediate effect; indeed but for Bertrand we should have been unable to separate it from the confused narrative to which all these witnesses brought what recollection they had, often without sequence or order, Durand himself taking no notice of any interval between this first visit to Vaucouleurs and the final one. The episode of Ascension Day appears like the formal sommation of French law, made as a matter of form before the appellant takes action on his own responsibility; but Baudricourt had probably more to do with it than appears to be at all certain from the after evidence. One of the persons present, at all events, young Poulengy above mentioned, bore it in mind and pondered it in his heart.

Meantime, Jeanne returned home—the strangest home-going,—for by this time her mission and her aspirations could no longer be hid, and rumour must have carried the news almost as quickly as any modern telegraph, to startle all the echoes of the village, heretofore unaware of any difference between Jeanne and her companions save the greater goodness to which everybody bears testimony. No doubt, it must have reached Jacques d'Arc's cottage even before she came back with the kind Durand, a changed creature, already the consecrated Maid of France, La Pucelle, apart from all others. The French peasant is a hard man, more fierce in his terror of the unconventional, of having his domestic affairs exposed to the public eye, or his family disgraced by an exhibition of anything unusual either in act or feeling, than almost any other class of beings. And it is evident that he took his daughter's intention according to the coarsest interpretation, as a wild desire for adventure and intention of joining herself to the roving troopers, the soldiers always hated and dreaded in rural life. He suddenly appears in the narrative in a fever of apprehension, with no imaginative alarm or anxiety about his girl, but the fiercest suspicion of her, and dread of disgrace to ensue. We do not know what passed when she returned, further than that her father had a dream, no doubt after the first astounding explanation of the purpose that had so long been ripening in her mind. He dreamed that he saw her surrounded by armed men, in the midst of the troopers, the most evident and natural interpretation of her purpose, for who could divine that she meant to be their leader and general, on a level not with the common men-at-arms, but of princes and nobles? In the morning he told his dream to his wife and also to his sons. "If I could think that the thing would happen that I dreamed, I would wish that she should be drowned; and if you would not do it, I should do it with my own hands." The reader remembers with a shudder the Meuse flowing at the foot of the garden, while the fierce peasant, mad with fear lest shame should be coming to his family, clenched his strong fist and made this outcry of dismay.

No doubt his wife smoothed the matter over as well as she could, and, whatever alarms were in her own mind, hastily thought of a feminine expedient to mend matters, and persuaded the angry father that to substitute other dreams for these would be an easier way. Isabeau most probably knew the village lad who would fain have had her child, so good a housewife, so industrious a workwoman, and always so friendly and so helpful, for his wife. At all events there was such a one, too willing to exert himself, not discouraged by any refusal, who could be egged up to the very strong point of appearing before the bishop at Toul and swearing that Jeanne had been promised to him from her childhood. So timid a girl, they all thought, so devout a Catholic, would simply obey the bishop's decision and would not be bold enough even to remonstrate, though it is curious that with the spectacle of her grave determination before them, and sorrowful sense of that necessity of her mission which had steeled her to dispense with their consent, they should have expected such an expedient to arrest her steps. The affair, we must suppose, had gone through all the more usual stages of entreaty on the lover's part, and persuasion on that of the parents, before such an attempt was finally made. But the shy Jeanne had by this time attained that courage of desperation which is not inconsistent with the most gentle nature; and without saying anything to anyone, she too went to Toul, appeared before the bishop, and easily freed herself from the pretended engagement, though whether with any reference to her very different destination we are not told.

These proceedings, however, and the father's dreams and the remonstrances of the mother, must have made troubled days in the cottage, and scenes of wrath and contradiction, hard to bear. The winter passed distracted by these contentions, and it is difficult to imagine how Jeanne could have borne this had it not been that the period of her outset had already been indicated, and that it was only in the middle of Lent that her succour was to reach the King. The village, no doubt, was almost as much distracted as her father's house to hear of these strange discussions and of the incredible purpose of the bonne douce fille, whose qualities everybody knew and about whom there was nothing eccentric, nothing unnatural, but only simple goodness, to distinguish her above her neighbours. In the meantime her voices called her continually to her work. They set her free from the ordinary yoke of obedience, always so strong in the mind of a French girl. The dreadful step of abandoning her home, not to be thought of under any other circumstances, was more and more urgently pressed upon her. Could it indeed be saints and angels who ordained a step which was outside of all the habits and first duties of nature? But we have no reason to believe that this nineteenth-century doubt of her visitors, and of whether their mandates were right, entered into the mind of a girl who was of her own period and not of ours. She went on steadfastly, certain of her mission now, and inaccessible either to remonstrance or appeal.

It was towards the beginning of Lent, as Poulengy tells us, that the decision was made, and she left home finally, to go "to France" as is always said. But it seems to have been in January that she set out once more for Vaucouleurs, accompanied by her uncle, who took her to the house of some humble folk they knew, a carter and his wife, where they lodged. Jeanne wore her peasant dress of heavy red homespun, her rude heavy shoes, her village coif. She never made any pretence of ladyhood or superiority to her class, but was always equal to the finest society in which she found herself, by dint of that simple good faith, sense, and seriousness, without excitement or exaggeration, and radiant purity and straightforwardness which were apparent to all seeing eyes. By this time all the little world about knew something of her purpose and followed her every step with wonder and quickly rising curiosity: and no doubt the whole town was astir, women gazing at their doors, all on her side from the first moment, the men half interested, half insolent, as she went once more to the chateau to make her personal appeal. Simple as she was, the bonne douce fille was not intimidated by the guard at the gates, the lounging soldiers, the no doubt impudent glances flung at her by these rude companions. She was inaccessible to alarms of that kind—which, perhaps, is one of the greatest safeguards against them even in more ordinary cases. We find little record of her second interview with Baudricourt. The Journal du Siège d'Orleans and the Chronique de la Pucelle both mention it as if it had been one of several, which may well have been the case, as she was for three weeks in Vaucouleurs. It is almost impossible to arrange the incidents of this interval between her arrival there and her final departure for Chinon on the 23d February, during which time she made a pilgrimage to a shrine of St. Nicolas and also a visit to the Duke of Lorraine. It is clear, however, that she must have repeated her demand with such stress and urgency that the Captain of Vaucouleurs was a much perplexed man. It was a very natural idea then, and in accordance with every sentiment of the time that he should suspect this wonderful girl, who would not be daunted, of being a witch and capable of bringing an evil fate on all who crossed her. All thought of boxing her ears must ere this have departed from his mind. He hastened to consult the curé, which was the most reasonable thing to do. The curé was as much puzzled as the Captain. The Church, it must be said, if always ready to take advantage afterwards of such revelations, has always been timid, even sceptical about them at first. The wisdom of the rulers, secular and ecclesiastic, suggested only one thing to do, which was to exorcise, and perhaps to overawe and frighten, the young visionary. They paid a joint and solemn visit to the carter's house, where no doubt their entrance together was spied by many eager eyes; and there the priest solemnly taking out his stole invested himself in his priestly robes and exorcised the evil spirits, bidding them come out of the girl if they were her inspiration. There seems a certain absurdity in this sudden assault upon the evil one, taking him as it were by surprise: but it was not ridiculous to any of the performers, though Jeanne no doubt looked on with serene and smiling eyes. She remarked afterwards to her hostess, that the curé had done wrong, as he had already heard her in confession.

Outside, the populace were in no uncertainty at all as to her mission. A little mob hung about the door to see her come and go, chiefly to church, with her good hostess in attendance, as was right and seemly, and a crowd streaming after them who perhaps of their own accord might have neglected mass, but who would not, if they could help it, lose a look at the new wonder. One day a young gentleman of the neighbourhood was passing by, and amused by the commotion, came through the crowd to have a word with the peasant lass. "What are you doing here, ma mie?" the young man said. "Is the King to be driven out of the kingdom, and are we all to be made English?" There is a tone of banter in the speech, but he had already heard of the Maid from his friend, Bertrand, and had been affected by the other's enthusiasm. "Robert de Baudricourt will have none of me or my words," she replied, "nevertheless before Mid-Lent I must be with the King, if I should wear my feet up to my knees; for nobody in the world, be it king, duke, or the King of Scotland's daughter, can save the kingdom of France except me alone: though I would rather spin beside my poor mother, and this is not my work: but I must go and do it, because my Lord so wills it." "And who is your Seigneur?" he asked. "God," said the girl. The young man was moved, he too, by that wind which bloweth where it listeth. He stretched out his hands through the gaping crowd and took hers, holding them between his own, to give her his pledge: and so swore by his faith, her hands in his hands, that he himself would conduct her to the King. "When will you go?" he said. "Rather to-day than to-morrow," answered the messenger of God.

This was the second convert of La Pucelle. The peasant bonhomme first, the noble gentleman after him; not to say all the women wherever she went, the gazing, weeping, admiring crowd which now followed her steps, and watched every opening of the door which concealed her from their eyes. The young gentleman was Jean de Novelonpont, "surnamed Jean de Metz": and so moved was he by the fervour of the girl, and by her strong sense of the necessity of immediate operations, that he proceeded at once to make preparations for the journey. They would seem to have discussed the dress she ought to wear, and Jeanne decided for many obvious reasons to adopt the costume of a man—or rather boy. She must, one would imagine have been tall, for no remark is ever made on this subject, as if her dress had dwarfed her, which is generally the case when a woman assumes the habit of a man: and probably with her peasant birth and training, she was, though slim, strongly made and well knit, besides being at the age when the difference between boy and girl is sometimes but little noticeable.

In the meantime Baudricourt had not been idle. He must have been moved by the sight of Jeanne, at least to perceive a certain gravity in the business for which he was not prepared; and her composure under the curé's exorcism would naturally deepen the effect which her own manners and aspect had upon all who were free of prejudice. Another singular event, too, added weight to her character and demand. One day after her return from Lorraine, February 12th, 1429, she intimated to all her surroundings and specially to Baudricourt, that the King had suffered a defeat near Orleans, which made it still more necessary that she should be at once conducted to him. It was found when there was time for the news to come, that this defeat, the Battle of the Herrings, so-called, had happened as she said, at the exact time; and such a strange fact added much to the growing enthusiasm and excitement. Baudricourt is said by Michelet to have sent off a secret express to the Court to ask what he should do; but of this there seems to be no direct evidence, though likelihood enough. The Court at Chinon contained a strong feminine element, behind the scenes. And it might be found that there were uses for the enthusiast, even if she did not turn out to be inspired. No doubt there were many comings and goings at this period which can only be traced confusedly through the depositions of Jeanne's companions twenty-five years after. She had at least two interviews with Baudricourt before the exorcism of the curé and his consequent change of procedure towards her. Then, escorted by her uncle Laxart, and apparently by Jean de Metz, she had made a pilgrimage to a shrine of St. Nicolas, as already mentioned, on which occasion, being near Nancy, she was sent for by the Duke of Lorraine, then lying ill at his castle in that city, who had a fancy to consult the young prophetess, sorceress—who could tell what she was?—on the subject apparently of his illness. He was the son of Queen Yolande of Anjou, who was mother-in-law to Charles VII., and it would no doubt be thought of some importance to secure his good opinion. Jeanne gave the exalted patient no light on the subject of his health, but only the (probably unpleasing) advice to flee from the wrath of God and to be reconciled with his wife, from whom he was separated. He too, however, was moved by the sight of her and her straightforward, undeviating purpose. He gave her four francs, Durand tells us,—not much of a present,—which she gave to her uncle, and which helped to buy her outfit. Probably he made a good report of her to his mother, for shortly after her return to Vaucouleurs (I again follow Michelet who ought to be well informed) a messenger from Chinon arrived to take her to the King. In the councils of that troubled Court, perhaps, the idea of a prodigy and miraculous leader, though she was nothing but a peasant girl, would be not without attraction, a thing to conjure withal, so far as the multitude were concerned.

Anyhow from any point of view, in the hopeless condition of affairs, it was expedient that nothing which gave promise of help, either real or visionary, should lightly be rejected. There was much anxiety no doubt in the careless Court still dancing and singing in the midst of calamity, but the reception of the ambitious peasant would form an exciting incident at least, if nothing more important and notable.

Thus the whole anxious world of France stirred round that youthful figure in the little frontier town, repeating with many an alteration and exaggeration the sayings of Jeanne, and those popular superstitions about the Maid from Lorraine which might be so naturally applied to her. It would seem, indeed, that she had herself attached some importance to this prophecy, for both her uncle Laxart and her hostess at Vaucouleurs report that she asked them if they had heard it: which question "stupefied" the latter, whose mind evidently jumped at once to the conviction that the prophecy was fulfilled. Not in Domremy itself, however, were these things considered with the same awe-stricken and admiring faith. Nothing had softened the mood of Jacques d'Arc. It was a shame to the village prud' homme to think of his daughter away from all the protection of home, living among men, encountering the young Seigneurs who cared for no maiden's reputation, hearing the soldiers' rude talk, exposed to their insults, or worse still to their kindness. Probably even now he thought of her as surrounded by troopers and men-at-arms, instead of the princes and peers with whom henceforth Jeanne's lot was to be cast; but in the former case there would have perhaps been less to fear than in the latter. Anyhow, Jeanne's communications with her family were more painful to her than had been the jeers of Baudricourt or the exorcism of the curé. They sent her angry orders to come back, threats of parental curses and abandonment. We may hope that the mother, grieved and helpless, had little to do with this persecution. The woman who had nourished her children upon saintly legend and Scripture story could scarcely have been hard upon the child, of whom she, better than any, knew the perfect purity and steadfast resolution. One of the little household at least, revolted by the stern father's fury, perhaps secretly encouraged by the mother, broke away and joined his sister at a later period. But we hear, during her lifetime, little or nothing of Pierre.

Much time, however, was passed in these preliminaries. The final start was not made till the 23d February, 1429, when the permission is supposed to have come by the hands of Colet de Vienne, the King's messenger, who attended by a single archer, was to be her escort. It is possible that he had no mission to this effect, but he certainly did escort her to Chinon. The whole town gathered before the house of Baudricourt to see her depart. Baudricourt, however, does not seem to have provided any guard for her. Jean de Metz, who had so chivalrously pledged himself to her service, with his friend De Poulengy, equally ready for adventure, each with his servant, formed her sole protectors. Jean de Metz had already sent her the clothes of one of his retainers, with the light breastplate and partial armour that suited it; and the townspeople had subscribed to buy her a further outfit, and a horse which seems to have cost sixteen francs—not so small a sum in those days as now. Laxart declares himself to have been responsible for this outlay, though the money was afterwards paid by Baudricourt, who gave Jeanne a sword, which some of her historians consider a very poor gift: none, however, of her equipments would seem to have been costly. The little party set out thus, with a sanction of authority, from the Captain's gate, the two gentlemen and the King's messenger at the head of the party with their attendants, and the Maid in the midst. "Go: and let what will happen," was the parting salutation of Baudricourt. The gazers outside set up a cry when the decisive moment came, and someone, struck with the feeble force which was all the safeguard she had for her long journey through an agitated country—perhaps a woman in the sudden passion of misgiving which often follows enthusiasm,—called out to Jeanne with an astonished outcry to ask how she could dare to go by such a dangerous road. "It was for that I was born," answered the fearless Maid. The last thing she had done had been to write a letter to her parents, asking their pardon if she obeyed a higher command than theirs, and bidding them farewell.

The French historians, with that amazement which they always show when they find a man behaving like a gentleman towards a woman confided to his honour, all pause with deep-drawn breath to note that the awe of Jeanne's absolute purity preserved her from any unseemly overture, or even evil thought, on the part of her companions. We need not take up even the shadow of so grave a censure upon Frenchmen in general, although in the far distance of the fifteenth century. The two young men, thus starting upon a dangerous adventure, pledged by their honour to protect and convey her safely to the King's presence, were noble and generous cavaliers, and we may well believe had no evil thoughts. They were not, however, without an occasional chill of reflection when once they had taken the irrevocable step of setting out upon this wild errand. They travelled by night to escape the danger of meeting bands of Burgundians or English on the way, and sometimes had to ford a river to avoid the town, where they would have found a bridge. Sometimes, too, they had many doubts, Bertrand says, perhaps as to their reception at Chinon, perhaps even whether their mission might not expose them to the ridicule of their kind, if not to unknown dangers of magic and contact with the Evil One, should this wonderful girl turn out no inspired virgin but a pretender or sorceress. Jean de Metz informs us that she bade them not to fear, that she had been sent to do what she was now doing; that her brothers in paradise would tell her how to act, and that for the last four or five years her brothers in paradise and her God had told her that she must go to the war to save the kingdom of France. This phrase must have struck his ear, as he thus repeats it. Her brothers in paradise! She had not apparently talked of them to anyone as yet, but now no one could hinder her more, and she felt herself free to speak. A great calm seems to have been in her soul. She had at last begun her work. How it was all to end for her she neither foresaw nor asked; she knew only what she had to do. When they ventured into a town she insisted on stopping to hear mass, bidding them fear nothing. "God clears the way for me," she said; "I was born for this," and so proceeded safe, though threatened with many dangers. There is something that breathes of supreme satisfaction and content in her repetition of those words.

CHAPTER III — BEFORE THE KING. FEB.-APRIL, 1429.

Jeanne and her little party were eleven days on the road, but do not seem to have encountered any special peril. They lodged sometimes in the security of a convent, sometimes in a village hostel, pursuing the long and tedious way across the great levels of midland France, which has so few features of beauty except in the picturesque towns with their castles and churches, which the escort avoided. At length they paused in the village of Fierbois not far from Chinon where the Court was, in order to announce their arrival and ask for an audience, which was not immediately accorded. Charles held his Court with incredible gaiety and folly, in the midst of almost every disaster that could overtake a king, in the castle of Chinon on the banks of the Vienne. The situation and aspect of this noble building, now in ruins, is wonderfully like that of Windsor Castle. The great walls, interrupted and strengthened by huge towers, stretch along a low ridge of rocky hill, with the swift and clear river, a little broader and swifter than the Thames, flowing at its foot. The red and high-pitched roofs of the houses clustered between the castle hill and the stream, give a point of resemblance the more. The large and ample dwelling, defensible, but with no thought of any need of defence, a midland castle surrounded by many a level league of wealthy country, which no hostile force should ever have power to get through, must have looked like the home of a well-established royalty. There was no sound or sight of war within its splendid enclosure. Noble lords and gentlemen crowded the corridors; trains of gay ladies, attendant upon two queens, filled the castle with fine dresses and gay voices. There had been but lately a dreadful and indeed shameful defeat, inflicted by a mere English convoy of provisions upon a large force of French and Scottish soldiers, the former led by such men as Dunois, La Hire, Xaintrailles, etc., the latter by the Constable of Scotland, John Stuart—which defeat might well have been enough to subdue every sound of revelry: yet Charles's Court was ringing with music and pleasantry, as if peace had reigned around.

It may be believed that there were many doubts and questions how to receive this peasant from the fields, which prevented an immediate reply to her demand for an audience. From the first, de la Tremoille, Charles's Prime Minister and chief adviser, was strongly against any encouragement of the visionary, or dealings with the supernatural; but there would no doubt be others, hoping if not for a miraculous maid, yet at least for a passing wonder, who might kindle enthusiasm in the country and rouse the ignorant with hopes of a special blessing from Heaven. The gayer and younger portion of the Court probably expected a little amusement, above all, a new butt for their wit, or perhaps a soothsayer to tell their fortunes and promise good things to come. They had not very much to amuse them, though they made the best of it. The joys of Paris were very far off; they were all but imprisoned in this dull province of Touraine; nobody knew at what moment they might be forced to leave even that refuge. For the moment here was a new event, a little stir of interest, something to pass an hour. Jeanne had to wait two days in Chinon before she was granted an audience, but considering the carelessness of the Court and the absence of any patron that was but a brief delay.

The chamber of audience is now in ruins. A wild rose with long, arching, thorny branches and pale flowers, straggles over the greensward where once the floor was trod by so many gay figures. From the broken wall you look sheer down upon the shining river; one great chimney, which at that season must have been still the most pleasant centre of the large, draughty hall, shows at the end of the room, with a curious suggestion of warmth and light which makes ruin more conspicuous. The room must have been on the ground floor almost level with the soil towards the interior of the castle, but raised to the height of the cliffs outside. It was evening, an evening of March, and fifty torches lighted up the ample room; many noble personages, almost as great as kings, and clothed in the bewildering splendour of the time, and more than three hundred cavaliers of the best names in France filled it to overflowing. The peasant girl from Domremy in the hose and doublet of a servant, a little travel-worn after her tedious journey, was led in by one of those splendid seigneurs, dazzled with the grandeur she had never seen before, looking about her in wonder to see which was the King—while Charles, perhaps with boyish pleasure in the mystification, perhaps with a little half-conviction stealing over him that there might be something more in it, stood among the smiling crowd.

The young stranger looked round upon all those amused, light-minded, sceptical faces, and without a moment's hesitation went forward and knelt down before him. "Gentil Dauphin," she said, "God give you good life." "But it is not I that am the King; there is the King," said Charles. "Gentil Prince, it is you and no other," she said; then rising from her knee: "Gentil Dauphin, I am Jeanne the Maid. I am sent to you by the King of Heaven to tell you that you shall be consecrated and crowned at Rheims, and shall be lieutenant of the King of Heaven, who is King of France." The little masquerade had failed, the jest was over. There would be little more laughing among the courtiers, when they saw the face of Charles grow grave. He took the new-comer aside, perhaps to that deep recess of the window where in the darkening night the glimmer of the clear, flowing river, the great vault of sky would still be visible dimly, outside the circle of the blazing interior with all its smoky lights.

Charles VII. of France was, like many of his predecessors, a pauvre Sire enough. He had thought more of his amusements than of the troubles of his country; but a wild and senseless gaiety will sometimes spring from despair as well as from lightness of heart; and after all, the dread responsibility, the sense that in all his helplessness and inability to do anything he was still the man who ought to do all, would seem to have moved him from time to time. A secret doubt in his heart, divulged to no man, had added bitterness to the conviction of his own weakness. Was he indeed the heir of France? Had he any right to that sustaining confidence which would have borne up his heart in the midst of every discouragement? His very mother had given him up and set him aside. He was described as the so-called Dauphin in treaties signed by Charles and Isabeau his parents. If anyone knew, she knew; and was it possible that more powerful even than the English, more cruel than the Burgundians, this stain of illegitimacy was upon him, making all effort vain? There is no telling where the sensitive point is in any man's heart, and little worthy as was this King, the story we are here told has a thrill of truth in it. It is reported by a certain Sala, who declares that he had it from the lips of Charles's favourite and close follower, the Seigneur de Boisi, a courtier who, after the curious custom of the time, shared even the bed of his master. This was confided to Boisi by the King in the deepest confidence, in the silence of the wakeful night:

"This was in the time of the good King Charles, when he knew not what step to take, and did nothing but think how to redeem his life: for as I have told you he was surrounded by enemies on all sides. The King in this extreme thought, went in one morning to his oratory all alone; and there he made a prayer to our

Lord, in his heart, without pronouncing any words, in which he asked of Him devoutly that if he were indeed the true heir, descended from the royal House of France, and that justly the kingdom was his, that He would be pleased to guard and defend him, or at the worst to give him grace to escape into Spain or Scotland, whose people, from all antiquity, were brothers-in-arms, friends and allies of the kings of France, and that he might find a refuge there."

Perhaps there is some excuse for a young man's endeavour to forget himself in folly or even in dissipation when his secret thoughts are so despairing as these.

It was soon after this melancholy moment that the arrival of Jeanne took place. The King led her aside, touched as all were, by her look of perfect sincerity and good faith; but it is she herself, not Charles, who repeats what she said to him. "I have to tell you," said the young messenger of God, "on the part of my Lord (Messire) that you are the true heir of France and the son of the King; He has sent me to conduct you to Rheims that you may receive your consecration and your crown,"—perhaps here, Jeanne caught some look which she did not understand in his eyes, for she adds with, one cannot but think a touch of sternness—"if you will."

Was it a direct message from God in answer to his prayer, uttered within his own heart, without words, so that no one could have guessed that secret? At least it would appear that Charles thought so: for how should this peasant maid know the secret fear that had gnawed at his heart? "When thou wast in the garden under the fig-tree I saw thee." Great was the difference between the Israelite without guile and the troubled young man, with whose fate the career of a great nation was entangled; but it is not difficult to imagine what the effect must have been on the mind of Charles when he was met by this strange, authoritative statement, uttered like all that Jeanne said, de la part de Dieu.

The impression thus made, however, was on Charles alone, and he was surrounded by councillors, so much the more pedantic and punctilious as they were incapable, and placed amidst pressing necessities with which in themselves they had no power to cope. It may easily be allowed, also, that to risk any hopes still belonging to the hapless young King on the word of a peasant girl was in itself, according to every law of reason, madness and folly. She would seem to have had the women on her side always and at every point. The Church did not stir, or else was hostile; the commanders and military men about, regarded with scornful disgust the idea that an enterprise which they considered hopeless should be confided to an ignorant woman—all with perfect reason we are obliged to allow. Probably it was to gain time—yet without losing the aid of such a stimulus to the superstitious among the masses —and to retard any rash undertaking—that it was proposed to subject Jeanne to an examination of doctors and learned men touching her faith and the character of her visions, which all this time had been of continual recurrence, yet charged with no further revelation, no mystic creed, but only with the one simple, constantly repeated command.

Accordingly, after some preliminary handling by half a dozen bishops, Jeanne was taken to Poitiers—where the university and the local parliament, all the learning, law, and ecclesiastical wisdom which were on the side of the King, were assembled—to undergo this investigation. It is curious that the entire history of this wildest and strangest of all visionary occurrences is to be found in a series of processes at law, each part recorded and certified under oath; but so it is. The village maid was placed at the bar, before a number of acute legists, ecclesiastics, and statesmen, to submit her to a not-too-benevolent cross-examination. Several of these men were still alive at the time of the Rehabilitation and gave their recollections of this examination, though its formal records have not been preserved. A Dominican monk, Aymer, one of an order she loved, addressed her gravely with the severity with which that institution is always credited. "You say that God will deliver France; if He has so determined, He has no need of men-at-arms." "Ah!" cried the girl, with perhaps a note of irritation in her voice, "the men must fight; it is God who gives the victory." To another discomfited Brother, Jeanne, exasperated, answered with a little roughness, showing that our Maid, though gentle as a child to all gentle souls, was no piece of subdued perfection, but a woman of the fields, and lately much in the company of rough-spoken men. He was of Limoges, a certain Brother Seguin, "bien aigre homme," and disposed apparently to weaken the trial by questions without importance: he asked her what language her celestial visitors spoke? "Better than yours," answered the peasant girl. He could not have been, as we say in Scotland, altogether "an ill man," for he acknowledged that he spoke the patois of his district, and therefore that the blow was fair. But perhaps for the moment he was irritated too. He asked her, a question equally unnecessary, "do you believe in God?" to which with more and more impatience she made a similar answer: "Better than you do." There was nothing to be made of one so well able to defend herself. "Words are all very well," said the monk, "but God would not have us believe you, unless you show us some sign." To this Jeanne made an answer more dignified, though still showing signs of exasperation, "I have not come to Poitiers to give signs," she said; "but take me to Orleans—I will then show the signs I am sent to show. Give me as small a band as you please, but let me go."

The situation of Orleans was at the time a desperate one. It was besieged by a strong army of English, who had built a succession of towers round the city, from which to assail it, after the manner of the times. The town lies in the midst of the plain of the Loire, with not so much as a hillock to offer any advantage to the besiegers. Therefore these great works were necessary in face of a very strenuous resistance, and the possibility of provisioning the besieged, which their river secured. The English from their high towers kept up a disastrous fire, which, though their artillery was of the rudest kind, did great execution. The siege was conducted by eminent generals. The works were of themselves great fortifications, the assailants numerous, and strengthened by the prestige of almost unbroken success; there seemed no human hope of the deliverance of the town unless by an overwhelming army, which the King's party did not possess, or by some wonderful and utterly unexpected event. Jeanne had always declared the destruction of the English and the relief of Orleans to be the first step in her mission.

Besides the formal and official examination of her faith and character, held at Poitiers, private inquests of all kinds were made concerning of the claims of the miraculous maid. She was visited by every curious person, man or woman, in the neighbourhood, and plied with endless questions, so that her simple personal story, and that of her revelations—mes voix, as she called them—became familiarly known from her own report, to the whole country round about. The women pressed a question specially interesting—for no doubt, many a good mother half convinced otherwise, shook her head at Jeanne's costume—Why she wore the dress of a man? for which the Maid gave very good reasons: in the first place because it was the only dress for fighting, which, though so far from her desires or from the habits of her life, was henceforward to be her work; and also because in her strange circumstances, constrained as she was to live among men, she considered it safest for herself —statements which evidently convinced the minds of the questioners. It was, no doubt, good policy to make her thus widely and generally known, and the result was a daily growing enthusiasm for her and belief in her, in all classes. The result of the formal process was that the doctors could find nothing against her, and they reluctantly allowed that the King might lawfully take what advantage he could of her offered services.

Jeanne was then brought back to Chinon, where she was lodged in one of the great towers still standing, though no special room is pointed out as hers. And there she was subjected to another process, more penetrating still than the interrogations of the graver tribunals. The Queens and their ladies and all the women of the Court took her in hand. They inquired into her history in every subtle and intimate feminine way, testing her innocence and purity; and once more she came out triumphant. The final judgment was given as follows: "After hearing all these reports, the King taking into consideration the great goodness that was in the Maid, and that she declared herself to be sent by God, it was by the said Seigneur and his council determined that from henceforward he should make use of her for his wars, since it was for this that she was sent."

It was now necessary to equip Jeanne for her service. She had a maison, an état majeur, or staff, formed for her, the chief of which, Jean d'Aulon, already distinguished and worthy of such a trust never left her thenceforward until the end of her active career. Her chaplain, Jean Pasquerel, also followed her fortunes faithfully. Charles would have given her a sword to replace the probably indifferent weapon given her by Baudricourt at Vaucouleurs; but Jeanne knew where to find the sword destined for her. She gave orders that someone should be sent to Fierbois, the village at which she had paused on her way to Chinon, to fetch a sword which would be found there buried behind the high altar of the church of St. Catherine. To make this as little miraculous as possible, we are told by some historians that it was common for knights to be buried with their arms, and that Jeanne, in her visit to this church, where she heard three masses in succession to make up for the absence of constant religious services on her journey—had probably seen some tomb or other token that such an interment had taken place. However, as we are compelled to receive the far greater miracle of Jeanne herself and her work, without explanation, it is foolish to take the trouble to attempt any explanation of so small a matter as this. The sword in fact was found, by the clergy of the church, and was by them cleaned and polished and put in a scabbard of crimson velvet, scattered over with fleur-de-lys in gold, for her use. Her standard, which she considered of the greatest importance was made apparently at Tours. It was of white linen, fringed with silk and embroidered with a figure of the Saviour holding a globe in His hands, while an angel knelt at either side in adoration. Jhesus' Maria was inscribed at the foot. A repetition of this banner, which must have been re-copied from age to age is to be seen now at Tours. Having indicated the exact device to be emblazoned upon the banner, as dictated to her by her saints,—Margaret and Catherine—Jeanne announced her intention of carrying it herself, a somewhat surprising office for one who was to act as a general. But it was the command of her heavenly guides. "Take the standard on the part of God, and carry it boldly," they had said. She had, besides, a simple, half-childish intention of her own in this, which she explained shame-faced—she had no wish to use her sword though she loved it, and would kill no man. The banner was a more safe occupation, and saved her from all possibility of blood-shedding; it must however, have required the robust arm of a peasant to sustain the heavy weight.

It will show how long a time all these examinations and preparations had taken when we read that Jeanne set out from Blois, where she had passed some time in military preparations, only on the 27th day of April; nearly two whole months had thus been taken up in testing her truth, and arranging details, trifling and unnecessary in her eyes:—a period which had been passed in great anxiety by the people of Orleans, with the huge bastilles of the English—three of which were named Paris, Rouen, and London—towering round them, their provisions often intercepted, all the business of life come to a standstill, and the overwhelming responsibility upon them of being almost the last barrier between the invader and the final subjugation of France. It is strange to add that, judging by ordinary rules, the garrison of Orleans ought to have been quite sufficient in itself in numbers and science of war, to have beaten and dispersed the English force which had thus succeeded in shutting them in; there were many notable captains among them, with Dunois, known as the Bastard of Orleans, one of the most celebrated and brave of French generals, at their head. Dunois was in no way inferior to the generals of the English army; he was popular, beloved by the people and soldiers alike, and though illegitimate, of the House of Orleans, one of the native seigneurs of the place. The wonder is how he and his officers permitted the building of these towers, and the shutting in of the town which they were quite strong enough to protect. But it was a losing game which they were playing, a part which does not suit the genius of the nation; and the superstition in favour of the English who had won so many battles with all the disadvantages on their side,— cutting the finest armies to pieces—was strong upon the imagination of the time. It seemed a fate which no valour or skill upon the side of the French could avert. Dunois, himself an unlikely person, one would have thought, to yield the honour of the fight to a woman, seems to have perceived that without a strong counter-motive, not within the range of ordinary methods, the situation was beyond hope.

Accordingly, on the 27th or 28th of April, Jeanne set out at the head of her little army, accompanied by a great number of generals and captains. She had been equipped by the Queen of Sicily (with a touch of that keen sense of decorative effect which belonged to the age) in white armour inlaid with silver —all shining like her own St. Michael himself, a radiance of whiteness and glory under the sun—armed de toutes pièces sauve la teste, her uncovered head rising in full relief from the dazzling breastplate and gorget. This is the description given of her by an eye-witness a little later. The country is flat as the palm of one's hand. The white armour must have flashed back the sun for miles and miles of the level road, to the eyes which from the height of any neighbouring tower watched the party setting out. It is all fertile now, the richest plain, and even then, corn and wine must have been in full bourgeon, the great fresh greenness of the big leaves coming out upon such low stumps of vine as were left in the soil; but the devastated country was in those days covered with a wild growth like the macchia of Italian wilds, which half hid the movements of the expedition. They went by the Loire to Tours, where Jeanne had been assigned a dwelling of her own, with the estate of a general; and from thence to Blois, where they had to wait for some days while the convoy of provisions, which they were to convey to Orleans, was being prepared. And there Jeanne fulfilled one of the preliminary duties of her mission. She had informed her examiners at Poitiers that she had been commanded to write to the English generals before attacking them, appealing to them de la part de Dieu, to give up their conquests, and leave France to the French. The letter which we quote would seem to have been dictated by her at Poitiers, probably to the confessor who now formed part of her suite and who attended her wherever she went:

JHESUS MARIA.

King of England, and you Duke of Bedford calling yourself Regent of France, you, William de la Poule, Comte de Sulford, John, Lord of Talbot, and you Thomas, Lord of Scales, who call yourself lieutenants of the said Bedford, listen to the King of Heaven: Give back to the Maid who is here sent on the part of God the King of Heaven, the keys of all the good towns which you have taken by violence in His France. She is ready to make peace if you will hear reason and be just towards France and pay for what you have taken. And you archers, brothers-in-arms, gentles and others who are before the town of Orleans, go in peace on the part of God; if you do not so you will soon have news of the Maid who will see you shortly to your great damage. King of England, if you do not this, I am captain in this war, and in whatsoever place in France I find your people I will make them go away. I am sent here on the part of God the King of Heaven to push you all forth of France. If you obey I will be merciful. And be not strong in your own opinion, for you do not hold the kingdom from God the Son of the Holy Mary, but it is held by Charles the true heir, for God, the King of Heaven so wills, and it is revealed by the Maid who shall enter Paris in good company. If you will not believe this news on the part of God and the Maid, in whatever place you may find yourselves we shall make our way there, and make so great a commotion as has not been in France for a thousand years, if you will not hear reason. And believe this, that the King of Heaven will send more strength to the Maid than you can bring against her in all your assaults, to her and to her good men-at-arms. You, Duke of Bedford, the Maid prays and requires you to destroy no more. If you act according to reason you may still come in her company where the French shall do the greatest work that has ever been done for Christianity. Answer then if you will still continue against the city of Orleans. If you do so you will soon recall it to yourself by great misfortunes. Written the Saturday of Holy Week (22 March, 1429).

Jeanne had by this time made a wonderful moral revolution in her little army; most likely she had not been in the least aware what an army was, until this moment; but frank and fearless, she had penetrated into every corner, and it was not in her to permit those abuses at which an ordinary captain has to smile. The pernicious and shameful crowd of camp followers fled before her like shadows before the day. She stopped the big oaths and unthinking blasphemies which were so common, so that La Hire, one of the chief captains, a rough and ready Gascon, was reduced to swear by his bâton, no more sacred name being permitted to him. Perhaps this was the origin of the harmless swearing which abounds in France, meaning probably just as much and as little as bigger oaths in careless mouths; but no doubt the soldiers' language was very unfit for gentle ears. Jeanne moved among the wondering ranks, all radiant in her silver armour and with her virginal undaunted countenance, exhorting all those rude and noisy brothers to take thought of their duties here, and of the other life that awaited them. She would stop the march of the army that a conscience-stricken soldier might make his confession, and desired the priests to hear it if necessary without ceremony, or church, under the first tree. Her tender heart was such that she shrank from any man's death, and her hair rose up on her head, as she said, at the sight of French blood shed—although her mission was to shed it on all sides for a great end. But the one thing she could not bear was that either Frenchmen or Englishmen should die unconfessed, "unhouseled, disappointed, unannealed." The army went along attended by songs of choristers and masses of priests, the grave and solemn music of the Church accompanied strangely by the fanfares and bugle notes. What a strange procession to pass along the great Loire in its spring fulness, the raised banners and crosses, and that dazzling white figure, all effulgence, reflected in the wayward, quick flowing stream!

La Hire, who is like a figure out of Dumas, and indeed did service as a model to that delightful romancer, had come from Orleans to escort Jeanne upon her way, and Dunois met her as she approached the town. There could not be found more unlikely companions than these two, to conduct to a great battle the country maid who was to carry the honours of the day from them both, and make men fight like heroes, who under them did nothing but run away. The candour and true courage of such leaders in circumstances so extraordinary, are beyond praise, for it was an offence both to their pride and skill in their profession, had she been anything less than the messenger of God which she claimed to be; and these rude soldiers were not men to be easily moved by devout imaginations. There would seem, however, even in the case of the greater of the two, to have arisen a strange friendship and mutual understanding between the famous man of war and the peasant girl. Jeanne, always straightforward and simple, speaks to him, not with the downcast eyes of her humility, but as an equal, as if the great Dunois had been a prud' homme of her own degree. There is no appearance indeed that the Maid allowed herself to be overborne now by any shyness or undue humility. She speaks loudly, so as to be heard by those fighting men, taking something of their own brief and decisive tone, often even impatient, as one who would not be put aside either by cunning or force.

Her meeting with Dunois makes this at once evident. She had been deceived in the manner of her approach to Orleans, her companions, among whom there were several field-marshals and distinguished leaders, taking advantage of her ignorance of the place to lead her by the opposite bank of the river instead of that on which the English towers were built, which she desired to attack at once. This was the beginning of a long series of deceits and hostile combinations, by which at every step of her way she was met and retarded; but it turned, as these devices generally did, to the discomfiture of the adverse captains. She crossed the river at Chécy above Orleans, to meet Dunois who had come so far to meet her. It will be seen by the conversation which she held with him on his first appearance, how completely Jeanne had learnt to assert herself, and how much she had overcome any fear of man. "Are you the Bastard of Orleans?" she said. "I am; and glad of your coming," he replied. "Is it you who have had me led to this side of the river and not to the bank on which Talbot is and his English?" He answered that he and the wisest of the leaders had thought it the best and safest way. "The counsel of God, our Lord, is more sure and more powerful than yours," she replied. The expedition, as a matter of fact, had to turn back, and to lose precious time, there being, it is to be presumed, no means of transporting so large a force across the river. The large convoy of provisions which Jeanne brought was embarked in boats while the majority of the army returned to Blois, in order to cross by the bridge.

Jeanne, however, having freely expressed her opinion, adapted herself to the circumstances, though extremely averse to separate herself from her soldiers, good men who had confessed and prepared their souls for every emergency. She finally consented, however, to ride on with Dunois and La Hire. The wind was against the convoy, so that the heavy boats, deeply laden with beeves and corn, had a dangerous and slow voyage before them. "Have patience," cried Jeanne; "by the help of God all will go well"; and immediately the wind changed, to the astonishment and joy of all, and the boats arrived in safety "in spite of the English, who offered no hindrance whatever," as she had predicted. The little party made their way along the bank, and in the twilight of the April evening, about eight o'clock, entered Orleans. The Deliverer, it need not be said, was hailed with joy indescribable. She was on a white horse, and carried, Dunois says, the banner in her hand, though it was carried before her when she entered the town. The white figure in the midst of those darkly gleaming mailed men, would in itself throw a certain glory through the dimness of the night, as she passed the gates and came into view by the blaze of all the torches, and the lights in the windows, over the dark swarming crowds of the citizens. Her white banner waving, her white armour shining, it was little wonder that the throng that filled the streets received the Maid "as if they had seen God descending among them." "And they had good reason," says the Chronicle, "for they had suffered many disturbances, labours, and pains, and, what is worse, great doubt whether they ever should be delivered. But now all were comforted, as if the siege were over, by the divine strength that was in this simple Maid whom they regarded most affectionately, men, women, and little children. There was a marvellous press around her to touch her or the horse on which she rode, so much so that one of the torchbearers approached too near and set fire to her pennon; upon which she touched her horse with her spurs, and turning him cleverly, extinguished the flame, as if she had long followed the wars."

There could have been nothing she resembled so much as St. Michael, the warrior-angel, who, as all the world knew, was her chief counsellor and guide, and who, no doubt, blazed, a familiar figure, from some window in the cathedral to which this his living picture rode without a pause, to give thanks to God before she thought of refreshment or rest. She spoke to the people who surrounded her on every side as she went on through the tumultuous streets, bidding them be of good courage and that if they had faith they should escape from all their troubles. And it was only after she had said her prayers and rendered her thanksgiving, that she returned to the house selected for her—the house of an important personage, Jacques Boucher, treasurer to the Duke of Orleans, not like the humble places where she had formerly lodged. The houses of that age were beautiful, airy and light, with much graceful ornament and solid comfort, the arched and vaulted Gothic beginning to give place to those models of domestic architecture which followed the Renaissance, with their ample windows and pleasant space and breadth. There the table was spread with a joyous meal in honour of this wonderful guest, to which, let us hope, Dunois and La Hire and the rest did full justice. But Jeanne was indifferent to the feast. She mixed with water the wine poured for her into a silver cup, and dipped her bread in it, five or six small slices. The visionary peasant girl cared for none of the dainty meats. And then she retired to the comfort of a peaceful chamber, where the little daughter of the house shared her bed: strange return to the days when Hauvette and Mengette in Domremy lay by her side and talked as girls love to do, through half the silent night. Perhaps little Charlotte, too, lay awake with awe to wonder at that other young head on the pillow, a little while ago shut into the silver helmet, and shining like the archangel's. The état majeur, the Chevalier d'Aulon, Jean de Metz, and Bertrand de Poulengy, who had never left her, first friends and most faithful, and her brother Pierre d'Arc, were lodged in the same house. It was the last night of April, 1429.

CHAPTER IV — THE RELIEF OF ORLEANS. MAY 1-8, 1429.

Next morning there was a council of war among the many leaders now collected within the town. It was the eager desire of Jeanne that an assault should be made at once, in all the enthusiasm of the moment, upon the English towers, without waiting even for the arrival of the little army which she had preceded. But the captains of the defence who had borne the heat and burden of the day, and who might naturally enough be irritated by the enthusiasm with which this stranger had been received, were of a different opinion. I quote here a story, for which I am told there is no foundation whatever, touching a personage who probably never existed, so that the reader may take it as he pleases, with indulgence for the writer's weakness, or indignation at her credulity. It seems to me, however, to express very naturally a sentiment which must have existed among the many captains who had been fighting unsuccessfully for months in defence of the beleaguered city. A certain Guillaume de Gamache felt himself insulted above all by the suggestion. "What," he cried, "is the advice of this hussy from the fields (une péronnelle de bas lieu) to be taken against that of a knight and captain! I will fold up my banner and become again a simple soldier. I would rather have a nobleman for my master than a woman whom nobody knows."

Dunois, who was too wise to weaken the forces at his command by such a quarrel, is said to have done his best to reconcile and soothe the angry captain. This, however, if it was true, was only a mild instance of the perpetual opposition which the Maid encountered from the very beginning of her career and wherever she went. Notwithstanding her victories, she remained through all her career a péronnelle to these men of war (with the noble exception, of course, of Alençon, Dunois, Xaintrailles, La Hire, and others). They were sore and wounded by her appearance and her claims. If they could cheat her, balk her designs, steal a march in any way, they did so, from first to last, always excepting the few who were faithful to her. Dunois could afford to be magnanimous, but the lesser men were jealous, envious, embittered. A péronnelle, a woman nobody knew! And they themselves were belted knights, experienced soldiers, of the best blood of France. It was not unnatural; but this atmosphere of hate, malice, and mortification forms the background of the picture wherever the Maid moves in her whiteness, illuminating to us the whole scene. The English hated her lustily as their enemy and a witch, casting spells and enchantments so that the strength was sucked out of a man's arm and the courage from his heart: but the Frenchmen, all but those who were devoted to her, regarded her with an ungenerous opposition, the hate of men shamed and mortified by every triumph she achieved.

Jeanne was angry, too, and disappointed, more than she had been by all discouragements before. She had believed, perhaps, that once in the field these oppositions would be over, and that her mission would be rapidly accomplished. But she neither rebelled nor complained. What she did was to occupy herself about what she felt to be her business, without reference to any commander. She sent out two heralds, who were attached to her staff, and therefore at her personal disposal, to summon once more Talbot and Glasdale

(Classidas, as the French called him) de la part de Dieu to evacuate their towers and return home. It would seem that in her miraculous soul she had a visionary hope that this appeal might be successful. What so noble, what so Christian, as that the one nation should give up, of free-will, its attempt upon the freedom and rights of another, if once the duty were put simply before it— and both together joining hands, march off, as she had already suggested, to do the noblest deed that had ever yet been done for Christianity? That same evening she rode forth with her little train; and placing herself on the town end of the bridge (which had been broken in the middle), as near as the breach would permit to the bastille, or fort of the Tourelles, which was built across the further end of the bridge, on the left side of the Loire—called out to the enemy, summoning them once more to withdraw while there was time. She was overwhelmed, as might have been expected, with a storm of abusive shouts and evil words, Classidas and his captains hurrying to the walls to carry on the fierce exchange of abuse. To be called dairy-maid and péronnellewas a light matter, but some of the terms used were so cruel that, according to some accounts, she betrayed her womanhood by tears, not prepared apparently for the use of such foul weapons against her. The Journal du Siège declares, however, that she was "aucunement yrée" (angry), but answered that they lied, and rode back to the city.

The next Sunday, the 1st of May, Dunois, alarmed by the delay of his main body, set out for Blois to meet them, and we are told that Jeanne accompanied him to the special point of danger, where the English from their fortifications might have stopped his progress, and took up a position there, along with La Hire, between the expedition and the enemy. But in the towers not a man budged, not a shot was fired. It was again a miracle, and she had predicted it. The party of Dunois marched on in safety, and Jeanne returned to Orleans, once more receiving on the breeze some words of abuse from the defenders of those battlements, which sent forth no more dangerous missile, and replying again with her summons, "Retournez de la par Dieu à Angleterre." The townsfolk watched her coming and going with an excitement impossible to describe; they walked by the side of her charger to the cathedral, which was the end of every progress; they talked to her, all speaking together, pressing upon her—and she to them, bidding them to have no fear. "Messire has sent me," she said again and again. She went out again, Wednesday, 4th May, on the return of Dunois, to meet the army, with the same result, that they entered quietly, the English not firing a shot.

On this same day, in the afternoon, after the early dinner, there happened a wonderful scene. Jeanne, it appeared, had fallen asleep after her meal, no doubt tired with the expedition of the morning, and her chief attendant, D'Aulon, who had accompanied Dunois to fetch the troops from Blois, being weary after his journey, had also stretched himself on a couch to rest. They were all tired, the entry of the troops having been early in the morning, a fact of which the angry captains of Orleans, who had not shared in that expedition, took advantage to make a secret sortie unknown to the new chiefs. All at once the Maid awoke in agitation and alarm. Her "voices" had awakened her from her sleep. "My council tell me to go against the English," she cried; "but if to assail their towers or to meet Fastolfe I cannot tell." As she came to the full command of her faculties her trouble grew. "The blood of our soldiers is flowing," she said; "why did they not tell me? My arms, my arms!" Then she rushed down stairs to find her page amusing himself in the tranquil afternoon, and called to him for her horse. All was quiet, and no doubt her attendants thought her mad: but D'Aulon, who knew better than to contradict his mistress, armed her rapidly, and Luis, the page, brought her horse to the door. By this time there began to rise a distant rumour and outcry, at which they all pricked their ears. As Jeanne put her foot in the stirrup she perceived that her standard was wanting, and called to the page, Louis de Contes, above, to hand it to her out of the window. Then with the heavy flag-staff in her hand she set spurs to her horse, her attendants one by one clattering after her, and dashed onward "so that the fire flashed from the pavement under the horse's feet."

Jeanne's presentiment was well-founded. There had been a private expedition against the English fort of St. Loup carried out quietly to steal a march upon her—Gamache, possibly, or other malcontents of his temper, in the hope perhaps of making use of her prestige to gain a victory without her presence. But it had happened with this sally as with many others which had been made from Orleans; and when Jeanne appeared outside the gate which she and the rest of the followers after her had almost forced—coming down upon them at full gallop, her standard streaming, her white armour in a blaze of reflection, she met the fugitives flying back towards the shelter of the town. She does not seem to have paused or to have deigned to address a word to them, though the troop of soldiers and citizens who had snatched arms and flung themselves after her, arrested and turned them back. Straight to the foot of the tower she went, Dunois startled in his turn, thundering after her. It is not for a woman to describe, any more than it was for a woman to execute such a feat of war. It is said that she put herself at the head of the citizens, Dunois at the head of the soldiers. One moment of pity and horror and heart-sickness Jeanne had felt when she met several wounded men who were being carried towards the town. She had never seen French blood shed before, and the dreadful thought that they might die unconfessed, overwhelmed her soul; but this was but an incident of her breathless gallop to the encounter. To isolate the tower which was attacked was the first necessity, and then the conflict was furious—the English discouraged, but fighting desperately against a mysterious force which overwhelmed them, at the same time that it redoubled the ardour of every Frenchman. Lord Talbot sent forth parties from the other forts to help their companions, but these were met in the midst by the rest of the army arriving from Orleans, which stopped their course. It was not till evening, "the hour of Vespers," that the bastille was finally taken, with great slaughter, the Orleanists giving little quarter. During these dreadful hours the Maid was everywhere visible with her standard, the most marked figure, shouting to her men, weeping for the others, not fighting herself so far as we hear, but always in the front of the battle. When she went back to Orleans triumphant, she led a band of prisoners with her, keeping a wary eye upon them that they might not come to harm.

The next day, May 5th, was the Feast of the Ascension, and it was spent by Jeanne in rest and in prayer. But the other leaders were not so devout. They held a crowded and anxious council of war, taking care that no news of it should reach the ears of the Maid. When, however, they had decided upon the course to pursue they sent for her, and intimated to her their decision to attack only the smaller forts, which she heard with great impatience, not sitting down, but walking about the room in disappointment and anger. It is difficult for the present writer to follow the plans of this council or to understand in what way Jeanne felt herself contradicted and set aside. However it was, the fact seems certain that their plan failed at first, the English having themselves abandoned one of the smaller forts on the right side of the river and concentrated their forces in the greater ones of Les Augustins and Les Tourelles on the left bank. For all this, reference to the map is necessary, which will make it quite clear. It was Classidas, as he is called, Glasdale, the most furious enemy of France, and one of the bravest of the English captains who held the former, and for a moment succeeded in repulsing the attack. The fortune of war seemed about to turn back to its former current, and the French fell back on the boats which had brought them to the scene of action, carrying the Maid with them in their retreat. But she perceived how critical the moment was, and reining up her horse from the bank, down which she was being forced by the crowd, turned back again, closely followed by La Hire, and at once, no doubt, by the stouter hearts who only wanted a leader—and charging the English, who had regained their courage as the white armour of the witch disappeared, and were in full career after the fugitives—drove them back to their fortifications, which they gained with a rush, leaving the ground strewn with the wounded and dying. Jeanne herself did not draw bridle till she had planted her standard on the edge of the moat which surrounded the tower.

Michelet is very brief concerning this first victory, and claims only that "the success was due in part to the Maid," although the crowd of captains and men-at-arms where by themselves quite sufficient for the work, had there been any heart in them. But this was true to fact in almost every case: and it is clear that she was simply the heart, which was the only thing wanted to those often beaten Frenchmen; where she was, where they could hear her robust young voice echoing over all the din, they were as men inspired; when the impetus of their flight carried her also away, they became once more the defeated of so many battles. The effect upon the English was equally strong; when the back of Jeanne was turned, they were again the men of Agincourt; when she turned upon them, her white breastplate blazing out like a star, the sunshine striking dazzling rays from her helmet, they trembled before the sorceress; an angel to her own side, she was the very spirit of magic and witchcraft to her opponents. Classidas, or which captain soever of the English side it might happen to be, blaspheming from the battlements, hurled all the evil names of which a trooper was capable, upon her, while she from below summoned them, in different tones of appeal and menace, calling upon them to yield, to go home, to give up the struggle. Her form, her voice are always evident in the midst of the great stone bullets, the cloth-yard shafts that were flying—they were so near, the one above, the other below, that they could hear each other speak.

On the 7th of May the fort of Les Augustins on the left bank was taken. It will be seen by reference to the map, that this bastille, an ancient convent, stood at some distance from the river, in peaceful times a little way beyond the bridge, and no doubt a favourite Sunday walk from the city. The bridge was now closed up by the frowning bulk of the Tourelles built upon it, with a smaller tower or "boulevard" on the left bank communicating with it by a drawbridge. When Les Augustins was taken, the victorious French turned their arms against this boulevard, but as night had fallen by this time, they suspended the fighting, having driven back the English, who had made a sally in help of Les Augustins. Here in the dark, which suited their purpose, another council was held. The captains decided that they would now pursue their victory no further, the town being fully supplied with provisions and joyful with success, but that they would await the arrival of reinforcements before they proceeded further; probably their object was solely to get rid of Jeanne, to conclude the struggle without her, and secure the credit of it. The council was held in the camp within sight of the fort, by the light of torches; after she had been persuaded to withdraw, on account of a slight wound in her foot from a calthrop, it is said. This message was sent after her into Orleans. She heard it with quiet disdain. "You have held your council, and I have had mine," she said calmly to the messengers; then turning to her chaplain, "Come to me to-morrow at dawn," she said, "and do not leave me; I shall have much to do. My blood will be shed. I shall be wounded to-morrow," pointing above her right breast. Up to this time no weapon had touched her; she had stood fast among all the flying arrows, the fierce play of spear and sword, and had taken no harm.

In the morning early, at sunrise, she dashed forth from the town again, though the generals, her hosts, and all the authorities who were in the plot endeavoured to detain her. "Stay with us, Jeanne," said the people with whom she lodged—official people, much above the rank of the Maid—"stay and help us to eat this fish fresh out of the river." "Keep it for this evening," she said, "and I shall return by the bridge and bring you some Goddens to have their share." She had already brought in a party of the Goddens on the night before to protect them from the fury of the crowd. The peculiarity of this promise lay in the fact that the bridge was broken, and could not be passed, even without that difficulty, without passing through the Tourelles and the boulevard which blocked it at the other end. At the closed gates another great official stood by, to prevent her passing, but he was soon swept away by the flood of enthusiasts who followed the white horse and its white rider. The crowd flung themselves into the boats to cross the river with her, horse and man. Les Tourelles stood alone, black and frowning across the shining river in its early touch of golden sunshine, on the south side of the Loire, the lower tower of the boulevard on the bank blackened with the fire of last night's attack, and the smoking ruins of Les Augustins beyond. The French army, whom Orleans had been busy all night feeding and encouraging, lay below, not yet apparently moving either for action or retreat. Jeanne plunged among them like a ray of light, D'Aulon carrying her banner; and passing through the ranks, she took up her place on the border of the moat of the boulevard. Her followers rushed after with that élan of desperate and uncalculating valour which was the great power of the French arms. In the midst of the fray the girl's clear voice, assez voix de femme, kept shouting encouragements, de la part de Dieu always her war-cry. "Bon coeur, bonne espérance," she cried—"the hour is at hand." But after hours of desperate fighting the spirit of the assailants began to flag. Jeanne, who apparently did not at any time take any active part in the struggle, though she exposed herself to all its dangers, seized a ladder, placed it against the wall, and was about to mount, when an arrow struck her full in the breast. The Maid fell, the crowd closed round; for a moment it seemed as if all were lost.

Here we have over again in the fable our friend Gamache. It is a pretty story, and though we ask no one to take it for absolute fact, there is no reason why some such incident might not have occurred. Gamache, the angry captain who rather than follow a péronnelle to the field was prepared to fold his banner round its staff, and give up his rank, is supposed to have been the nearest to her when she fell. It was he who cleared the crowd from about her and raised her up. "Take my horse," he said, "brave creature. Bear no malice. I confess that I was in the wrong." "It is I that should be wrong if I bore malice," cried Jeanne, "for never was a knight so courteous" (chevalier si bien apprins). She was surrounded immediately by her people, the chaplain whom she had bidden to keep near her, her page, all her special attendants, who would have conveyed her out of the fight had she consented. Jeanne had the courage to pull the arrow out of the wound with her own hand,—"it stood a hand breadth out" behind her shoulder—but then, being but a girl and this her first experience of the sort, notwithstanding her armour and her rank as General-in-Chief, she cried with the pain, this commander of seventeen. Somebody then proposed to charm the wound with an incantation, but the Maid indignant, cried out, "I would rather die." Finally a compress soaked in oil was placed upon it, and Jeanne withdrew a little with her chaplain, and made her confession to him, as one who might be about to die.

But soon her mood changed. She saw the assailants waver and fall back; the attack grew languid, and Dunois talked of sounding the retreat. Upon this she got to her feet, and scrambled somehow on her horse. "Rest a little," she implored the generals about her, "eat something, refresh yourselves: and when you see my standard floating against the wall, forward, the place is yours." They seem to have done as she suggested, making a pause, while Jeanne withdrew a little into a vineyard close by, where there must have been a tuft of trees, to afford her a little shelter. There she said her prayers, and tasted that meat to eat that men wot not of, which restores the devout soul. Turning back she took her standard from her squire's hand, and planted it again on the edge of the moat. "Let me know," she said, "when the pennon touches the wall." The folds of white and gold with the benign countenance of the Saviour, now visible, now lost in the changes of movement, floated over their heads on the breeze of the May day. "Jeanne," said the squire, "it touches!" "On!" cried the Maid, her voice ringing through the momentary quiet. "On! All is yours!" The troops rose as one man; they flung themselves against the wall, at the foot of which that white figure stood, the staff of her banner in her hand, shouting, "All is yours." Never had the French élan been so wildly inspired, so irresistible; they swarmed up the wall "as if it had been a stair." "Do they think themselves immortal?" the panic-stricken English cried among themselves—panic-stricken not by their old enemies, but by the white figure at the foot of the wall. Was she a witch, as had been thought? was not she indeed the messenger of God? The dazzling rays that shot from her armour seemed like butterflies, like doves, like angels floating about her head. They had thought her dead, yet here she stood again without a sign of injury; or was it Michael himself, the great archangel whom she resembled do much? Arrows flew round her on every side but never touched her. She struck no blow, but the folds of her standard blew against the wall, and her voice rose through all the tumult. "On! Enter! de la part de Dieu! for all is yours."

The Maid had other words to say, "Renty, renty, Classidas!" she cried, "you called me vile names, but I have a great pity for your soul." He on his side showered down blasphemies. He was at the last gasp; one desperate last effort he made with a handful of men to escape from the boulevard by the drawbridge to Les Tourelles, which crossed a narrow strip of the river. But the bridge had been fired by a fire-ship from Orleans and gave way under the rush of the heavily-armed men; and the fierce Classidas and his companions were plunged into the river, where a knight in armour, like a tower falling, went to the bottom in a moment. Nearly thirty of them, it is said, plunged thus into the great Loire and were seen no more.

It was the end of the struggle. The French flag swung forth on the parapet, the French shout rose to heaven. Meanwhile a strange sight was to be seen—the St. Michael in shining armour, who had led that assault, shedding tears for the ferocious Classidas, who had cursed her with his last breath. "J'ai grande pitié de ton âme." Had he but had time to clear his soul and reconcile himself with God!

This was virtually the end of the siege of Orleans. The broken bridge on the Loire had been rudely mended, with a great gouttière and planks, and the people of Orleans had poured out over it to take the Tourelles in flank—the English being thus taken between Jeanne's army on the one side and the citizens on the other. The whole south bank of the river was cleared, not an Englishman left to threaten the richest part of France, the land flowing with milk and honey. And though there still remained several great generals on the other side with strong fortifications to fall back upon, they seem to have been paralysed, and did not strike a blow. Jeanne was not afraid of them, but her ardour to continue the fight dropped all at once; enough had been done. She awaited the conclusion with confidence. Needless to say that Orleans was half mad with joy, every church sounding its bells, singing its song of triumph and praise, the streets so crowded that it was with difficulty that the Maid could make her progress through them, with throngs of people pressing round to kiss her hand, if might be, her greaves, her mailed shoes, her charger, the floating folds of her banner. She had said she would be wounded and so she was, as might be seen, the envious rent of the arrow showing through the white plates of metal on her shoulder. She had said all should be theirs de par Dieu: and all was theirs, thanks to our Lord and also to St. Aignan and St. Euvert, patrons of Orleans, and to St. Louis and St. Charlemagne in heaven who had so great pity of the kingdom of France: and to the Maid on earth, the Heaven-sent deliverer, the spotless virgin, the celestial warrior—happy he who could reach to kiss it, the point of her mailed shoe.

Someone says that she rode through all this half-delirious joy like a creature in a dream,—fatigue, pain, the happy languor of the end attained, and also the profound pity that was the very inspiration of her spirit, for all those souls of men gone to their account without help of Church or comfort of priest— overwhelming her. But next day, which was Sunday, she was up again and eagerly watching all that went on. A strange sight was Orleans on that Sunday of May. On the south side of the Loire, all those half-ruined bastilles smoking and silenced, which once had threatened not the city only but all the south of France; on the north the remaining bands of English drawn up in order of battle. The excitement of the town and of the generals in it, was intense; worn as they were with three days of continuous fighting, should they sally forth again and meet that compact, silent, doubly defiant army, which was more or less fresh and unexhausted? Jeanne's opinion was, No; there had been enough of fighting, and it was Sunday, the holy day; but apparently the French did go out though keeping at a distance, watching the enemy. By orders of the Maid an altar was raised between the two armies in full sight of both sides, and there mass was celebrated, under the sunshine, by the side of the river which had swallowed Classidas and all his men. French and English together devoutly turned towards and responded to that Mass in the pause of bewildering uncertainty. "Which way are their heads turned?" Jeanne asked when it was over. "They are turned away from us, they are turned to Meung," was the reply. "Then let them go, de par Dieu," the Maid replied.

The siege had lasted for seven months, but eight days of the Maid were enough to bring it to an end. The people of Orleans still, every year, on the 8th of May, make a procession round the town and give thanks to God for its deliverance. Henceforth, the Maid was known no longer as Jeanne d'Arc, the peasant of Domremy, but as La Pucelle d'Orléans, in the same manner in which one might speak of the Prince of Waterloo, or the Duc de Malakoff.

CHAPTER V — THE CAMPAIGN OF THE LOIRE. JUNE, JULY, 1429.

The rescue of Orleans and the defeat of the invincible English were news to move France from one end to the other, and especially to raise the spirits and restore the courage of that part of France which had no sympathy with the invaders and to which the English yoke was unaccustomed and disgraceful. The news flew up and down the Loire from point to point, arousing every village, and breathing new heart and encouragement everywhere; while in the meantime Jeanne, partially healed of her wound (on May 9th she rode out in a maillet, a light coat of chain-mail), after a few days' rest in the joyful city which she had saved with all its treasures, set out on her return to Chinon. She found the King at Loches, another of the strong places on the Loire where there was room for a Court, and means of defence for a siege should such be necessary, as is the case with so many of these wonderful castles upon the great French river. Hot with eagerness to follow up her first great success and accomplish her mission, Jeanne's object was to march on at once with the young Prince, with or without his immense retinue, to Rheims where he should be crowned and anointed King as she had promised. Her instinctive sense of the necessities of the position, if we use that language—more justly, her boundless faith in the orders which she believed had been give her from

Heaven, to accomplish this great act without delay, urged her on. She was straitened, if we may quote the most divine of words, till it should be accomplished.

But the Maid, flushed with victory, with the shouts of Orleans still ringing in her ears, the applause of her fellow-soldiers, the sound of the triumphant bells, was plunged all at once into the indolence, the intrigues, the busy nothingness of the Court, in which whispering favourites surrounded a foolish young prince, beguiling him into foolish amusements, alarming him with coward fears. Wise men and buffoons alike dragged him down into that paltry abyss, the one always counselling caution, the other inventing amusements. "Let us eat and drink for to-morrow we die." Was it worth while to lose everything that was enjoyable in the present moment, to subject a young sovereign to toils and excitement, and probable loss, for the uncertain advantage of a vain ceremony, when he might be enjoying himself safely and at his ease, throughout the summer months, on the cheerful banks of the Loire? On the other hand, the Chancellor, the Chamberlains, the Church, all his graver advisers (with the exception of Gerson, the great theologian to whom has been ascribed the authorship of the Imitation of Christ, who is reported to have said, "If France deserts her, and she fails, she is none the less inspired") shook their hands and advised that the way should be quite safe and free of danger before the King risked himself upon it. It was thus that Jeanne was received when, newly alighted from her charger, her shoulder still but half healed, her eyes scarcely clear of the dust and smoke, she found herself once more in the antechamber, wasting the days, waiting in vain behind closed doors, tormented by the lutes and madrigals, the light women and lighter men, useless and contemptible, of a foolish Court. The Maid, in all the energy and impulse of a success which had proved all her claims, had also a premonition that her own time was short, if not a direct intimation, as some believe, to that effect: and mingled her remonstrances and appeals with the cry of warning: "I shall only last a year: take the good of me as long as it is possible."

No doubt she was a very great entertainment to the idle seigneurs and ladies who would try to persuade her to tell them what was to happen to them, she who had prophesied the death of Glasdale and her own wound and so many other things. The Duke of Lorraine on her first setting out had attempted to discover from Jeanne what course his illness would take, and whether he should get better; and all the demoiselles and demoiseaux, the flutterers of the ante-chamber, would be still more likely to surround with their foolish questions the stout-hearted, impatient girl who had acquired a little of the roughness of her soldier comrades, and had never been slow at any time in answering a fool according to his folly; for Jeanne was no meek or sentimental maiden, but a robust and vigorous young woman, ready with a quick response, as well as with a ready blow did any one touch her unadvisedly, or use any inappropriate freedom. At last, one day while she waited vainly outside the cabinet in which the King was retired with a few of his councillors, Jeanne's patience failed her altogether. She knocked at the door, and being admitted threw herself at the feet of the King. To Jeanne he was no king till he had received the consecration necessary for every sovereign of France. "Noble Dauphin," she cried, "why should you hold such long and tedious councils? Rather come to Rheims and receive your worthy crown."

The Bishop of Castres, Christopher de Harcourt, who was present, asked her if she would not now in the presence of the King describe to them the manner in which her council instructed her, when they talked with her. Jeanne reddened and replied: "I understand that you would like to know, and I would gladly satisfy you." "Jeanne," said the King in his turn, "it would be very good if you could do what they ask, in the presence of those here." She answered at once and with great feeling: "When I am vexed to find myself disbelieved in the things I say from God, I retire by myself and pray to God, complaining and asking of Him why I am not listened to. And when I have prayed I hear a voice which says, 'Daughter of God, go, go, go! I will help thee, go!' And when I hear that voice I feel a great joy." Her face shone as she spoke, "lifting her eyes to heaven," like the face of Moses while still it bore the reflection of the glory of God, so that the men were dazzled who sat, speechless, looking on.

The result was that Charles kindly promised to set out as soon as the road between him and Rheims should be free of the English, especially the towns on the Loire in which a great part of the army dispersed from Orleans had taken refuge, with the addition of the auxiliary forces of Sir John Fastolfe, a name so much feared by the French, but at which the English reader can scarcely forbear a smile. That the young King did not think of putting himself at the head of the troops or of taking part in the campaign shows sufficiently that he was indeed a pauvre sire, unworthy his gallant people. Jeanne, however, nothing better being possible, seems to have accepted this mission with readiness, and instantly began her preparations to carry it out. It is here that the young Seigneur Guy de Laval comes in with his description of her already quoted. He was no humble squire but a great personage to whom the King was civil and pleased to show courtesy. The young man writes to ses mères, that is, it seems, his mother and grandmother, to whom, in their distant château, anxiously awaiting news of the two youths gone to the wars, their faithful son makes his report of himself and his brother. The King, he says, sent for the Maid, in order, Sir Guy believes, that he might see her. And afterwards the young man went to Selles where she was just setting out on the campaign.

From Selles, he writes on the 8th June, exactly a month after the deliverance of Orleans:

"I went to her lodging to see her, and she sent for wine and told me we should soon drink wine in Paris. It was a miraculous thing (toute divine) to see her and hear her. She left Selles on Monday at the hour of vespers for Romorantin, the Marshal de Boussac and a great many armed men with her. I saw her mount her horse, all in white armour excepting the head, a little axe in her hand. The great black charger was very restive at her door and would not let her mount. 'Lead him,' she said, 'to the cross which is in front of the church,' and there she mounted, the horse standing still as if he had been bound. Then turning towards the church which was close by she said in a womanly voice (assez voix de femme), 'You priests and people of the Church, make processions and prayers to God for us'; then turning to the road, 'Forward,' she said. Her unfolded standard was carried by a page; she had her little axe in her hand, and by her side rode a brother who had joined her eight days before. The Maid told me in her lodging that she had sent you, grandmother, a small gold ring, which was indeed a very small affair, and that she would fain have sent you something better, considering your recommendation. To-day M. d'Alençon, the Bastard of Orleans, and Gaucourt were to leave Selles, following the Maid. And men are arriving from all parts every day, all with good hope in God who I believe will help us. But money there is none at the Court, so that for the present I have no hope of any help or assistance. Therefore I desire you, Madame ma mère, who have my seal, spare not the land neither in sale nor mortgage . . . . My much honoured ladies and mothers, I pray the blessed Son of God that you have a good life and long; and both of us recommend ourselves to our brother Louis. And we send our greetings to the reader of this letter. Written from Selles, Wednesday, 8th June, 1429. This afternoon are arrived M. de Vendôme, M. de Boussac, and others, and La Hire has joined the army, and we shall soon be at work (on besognera bientôt)— May God grant that it should be according to your desire."

It was with difficulty that the Duc d'Alençon had been got to start, his wife consenting with great reluctance. He had been long a prisoner in England, and had lately been ransomed for a great sum of money; "Was not that a sufficient sacrifice?" the Duchess asked indignantly. To risk once more a husband so costly was naturally a painful thing to do, and why could not Jeanne be content and stay where she was? Jeanne comforted the lady, perhaps with a little good-humoured contempt. "Fear nothing, Madame," she said; "I will bring him back to you safe and sound." Probably Alençon himself had no great desire to be second in command to this country lass, even though she had delivered Orleans; and if he set out at all he would have preferred to take another direction and to protect his own property and province. The gathering of the army thus becomes visible to us; parties are continually coming in; and no doubt, as they marched along, many a little château—and they abound through the country each with its attendant hamlet—gave forth its master or heir, poor but noble, followed by as many men-at-arms, perhaps only two or three, as the little property could raise, to swell the forces with the best and surest of material, the trained gentlemen with hearts full of chivalry and pride, but with the same hardy, self-denying habits as the sturdy peasants who followed them, ready for any privation; with a proud delight to hear that on besognera bientôt—with that St. Michael at their head, and no longer any fear of the English in their hearts.

The first besogne on which this army entered was the siege of Jargeau, June 11th, into which town Suffolk had thrown himself and his troops when the siege of Orleans was raised. The town was strong and so was the garrison, experienced too in all the arts of war, and already aware of the wild enthusiasm by which Jeanne was surrounded. She passed through Orleans on the 10th of June, and had there been joined by various new detachments. The number of her army was now raised, we are told, to twelve hundred lances, which means, as each "lance" was a separate party, about three thousand six hundred men, though the Journal du Siège gives a much larger number; at all events it was a small army with which to decide a quarrel between the two greatest nations of Christendom. Her associates in command were here once more seized by the prevailing sin of hesitation, and many arguments were used to induce her to postpone the assault. It would seem that this hesitation continued until the very moment of attack, and was only put an end to when Jeanne herself impatiently seized her banner from the hand of her squire, and planting herself at the foot of the walls let loose the fervour of the troops and cheered them on to the irresistible rush in which lay their strength. For it was with the commanders, not with the followers, that the weakness lay. The Maid herself was struck on the head by a stone from the battlements which threw her down; but she sprang up again in a moment unhurt. "Sus! Sus! Our Lord has condemned the English—all is yours!" she cried. She would seem to have stood there in her place with her banner, a rallying-point and centre in the midst of all the confusion of the fight, taking this for her part in it, and though she is always in the thick of the combat, never, so far as we are told, striking a blow, exposed to all the instruments of war, but injured by none. The effect of her mere attitude, the steadiness of her stand, under the terrible rain of stone bullets and dreadful arrows, must of itself have been indescribable.

In the midst of the fiery struggle, there is almost a comic point in her watch over Alençon, for whose safety she had pledged herself, now dragging him from a dangerous spot with a cry of warning, now pushing him forward with an encouraging word. On the first of these occasions a gentleman of Anjou, M. de Lude, who took his place in the front was killed, which seems hard upon the poor gentleman, who was probably quite as well worth caring for as Alençon. "Avant, gentil duc," she cried at another moment, "forward! Are you afraid? you know I promised your wife to bring you safe home." Thus her voice keeps ringing through the din, her white armour gleams. "Sus! Sus!" the bold cry is almost audible, sibilant, whistling amid the whistling of the arrows.

Suffolk, the English Bayard, the most chivalrous of knights, was at last forced to yield. One story tells us that he would give up his sword only to Jeanne herself, but there is a more authentic description of his selection of one youth among his assailants whom the quick perceptions of the leader had singled out. "Are you noble?" Suffolk asks in the brevity of such a crisis. "Yes; Guillame Regnault, gentleman of Auvergne." "Are you a knight?" "Not yet." The victor put a knee to the ground before his captive, the vanquished touched him lightly on the shoulder with the sword which he then gave over to him. Suffolk was always the finest gentleman, the most perfect gentle knight of his time.

"Now let us go and see the English of Meung," cried Jeanne, unwearying, as soon as this victory was assured. That place fell easily; it is called the bridge of Meung, in the Chronicle, without further description, therefore presumably the fortress was not attacked—and they proceeded onward to Beaugency. These towns still shine over the plain, along the line of the Loire, visible as far as the eye will carry over the long levels, the great stream linking one to another like pearls on a thread. There is nothing in the landscape now to give even a moment's shelter to the progress of a marching army which must have been seen from afar, wherever it moved; or to veil the shining battlements, and piled up citadels rising here and there, concentrated points and centres of life. The great white Castle of Blois, the darker tower of Beaugency, still stand where they stood when Jeanne and her men drew near, as conspicuous in their elevation of walls and towers as if they had been planted on a mountain top. On more than one occasion during this wonderful progress from victory to victory, the triumphant leaders returned for a day or two to Orleans to tell their good tidings, and to celebrate their success.

And there is but one voice as to the military skill which she displayed in these repeated operations. The reader sees her, with her banner, posted in the middle of the fight, guiding her men with a sort of infallible instinct which adds force to her absolute quick perception of every difficulty and advantage, the unhesitating promptitude, attending like so many servants upon the inspiration which is the soul of all. These are things to which a writer ignorant of war is quite unable to do justice. What was almost more wonderful still was the manner in which the Maid held her place among the captains, most of whom would have thwarted her if they could, with a consciousness of her own superior place, in which there is never the slightest token of presumption or self-esteem. She guarded and guided Alençon with a good-natured and affectionate disdain; and when there was risk of a great quarrel and a splitting of forces she held the balance like an old and experienced guide of men.

This latter crisis occurred before Beaugency on the 15th of June, when the Comte de Richemont, Constable of France, the brother of the Duc de Bretagne, a great nobleman and famous leader, but in disgrace with the King and exiled from the Court, suddenly appeared with a considerable army to join himself to the royalist forces, probably with the hope of securing the leading place. Richemont was no friend to Jeanne; though he apparently asked her help and influence to reconcile him with the King. He seems indeed to have thought it a disgrace to France that her troops should be led, and victories gained by no properly appointed general, but by a woman, probably a witch, a creature unworthy to stand before armed men. It must not be forgotten that even now this was the general opinion of her out of the range of her immediate influence. The English held it like a religion. Bedford, in his description of the siege of Orleans and its total failure, reports to England that the discomfiture of the hitherto always triumphant army was "caused in great part by the fatal faith and vain fear that the French had, of a disciple and servant of the enemy of man, called the Maid, who uses many false enchantments, and witchcraft, by which not only is the number of our soldiers diminished but their courage marvellously beaten down, and the boldness of our enemies increased." Richemont was a sworn enemy of all such. "Never man hated more, all heresies, sorcerers, and sorceresses, than he; for he burned more in France, in Poitou, and Bretagne, than any other of his time." The French generals were divided as to the merits of Richemont and the advantages to be derived from his support. Alençon, the nominal commander, declared that he would leave the army if Richemont were permitted to join it. The letters of the King were equally hostile to him; but on the other hand there were some who held that the accession of the Constable was of more importance than all the Maids in France. It was a moment which demanded very wary guidance. Jeanne, it would seem, did not regard his arrival with much pleasure; probably even the increase of her forces did not please her as it would have pleased most commanders, holding so strongly as she did, to the miraculous character of her own mission and that it was not so much the strength of her troops as the help of God that got her the victory. But it was not her part to reject or alienate any champion of France. We have an account of their meeting given by a retainer of Richemont, which is picturesque enough. "The Maid alighted from her horse, and the Constable also. 'Jeanne,' he said, 'they tell me that you are against me. I know not if you are from God (de la part de Dieu) or not. If you are from God I do not fear you; if you are of the devil, I fear you still less.' 'Brave Constable,' said Jeanne, 'you have not come here by any will of mine; but since you are here you are welcome.'"

Armed neutrality but suspicion on one side, dignified indifference but acceptance on the other, could not be better shown.

These successes, however, had been attended by various escarmouches going on behind. The English, who had been driven out of one town after another, had now drawn together under the command of Talbot, and a party of troops under Fastolfe, who came to relieve them, had turned back as Jeanne proceeded, making various unsuccessful attempts to recover what had been lost. Failing in all their efforts they returned across the country to Genville, and were continuing their retreat to Paris when the two enemies came within reach of each other. An encounter in open field was a new experience of which Jeanne as yet had known nothing. She had been successful in assault, in the operations of the siege, but to meet the enemy hand to hand in battle was what she had never been required to do; and every tradition, every experience, was in favour of the English. From Agincourt to the Battle of the Herrings at Rouvray near Orleans, which had taken place in the beginning of the year (a fight so named because the field of battle had been covered with herrings, the conquerors in this case being merely the convoy in charge of provisions for the English, which Fastolfe commanded), such a thing had not been known as that the French should hold their own, much less attain any victory over the invaders. In these circumstances there was much talk of falling back upon the camp near Beaugency and of retreating or avoiding an engagement; anything rather than hazard one of those encounters which had infallibly ended in disaster. But Jeanne was of the same mind as always, to go forward and fear nothing. "Fall upon them! Go at them boldly," she cried. "If they were in the clouds we should have them. The gentle King will now gain the greatest victory he has ever had."

It is curious to hear that in that great plain of the Beauce, so flat, so fertile, with nothing but vines and cornfields now against the horizon, the two armies at last almost stumbled upon each other by accident, in the midst of the brushwood by which the country was wildly overgrown. The story is that a stag roused by the French scouts rushed into the midst of the English, who were advantageously placed among the brushwood to arrest the enemy on their march; the wild creature terrified and flying before an army blundered into the midst of the others, was fired at and thus betrayed the vicinity of the foe. The English had no time to form or set up their usual defences. They were so taken by surprise that the rush of the French came without warning, with a suddenness which gave it double force. La Hire made the first attack as leader of the van, and there was thus emulation between the two parties, which should be first upon the enemy. When Alençon asked Jeanne what was to be the issue of the fight, she said calmly, "Have you good spurs?" "What! You mean we shall turn our backs on our enemies?" cried her questioner. "Not so," she replied. "The English will not fight, they will fly, and you will want good spurs to pursue them." Even this somewhat fantastic prophecy put heart into the men, who up to this time had been wont to fly and not to fight.

And this was what happened, strange as it may seem. Talbot himself was with the English forces, and many a gallant captain beside: but the men and their leaders were alike broken in spirit and filled with superstitious terrors. Whether these were the forces of hell or those of heaven that came against them no one could be sure; but it was a power beyond that of earth. The dazzled eyes which seemed to see flights of white butterflies fluttering about the standard of the Maid, could scarcely belong to one who thought her a servant of the enemy of men. But she was a pernicious witch to Talbot, and strangely enough to Richemont also, who was on her own side. The English force was thrown into confusion, partly, we may suppose, from the broken ground on which they were discovered, the undergrowth of the wood which hid both armies from each other. But soon that disorder turned into the wildest panic and flight. It would almost seem as if between these two hereditary opponents one must always be forced into this miserable part. Not all the chivalry of France had been able to prevent it at the long string of battles in which they were, before the revelation of the Maid; and not the desperate and furious valour of Talbot could preserve his English force from the infection now. Fastolfe, with the philosophy of an old soldier, deciding that it was vain to risk his men when the field was already lost, rode off with all his band. Talbot fought with desperation, half mad with rage to be thus a second time overcome by so unlikely an adversary, and finally was taken prisoner; while the whole force behind him fled and were killed in their flight, the plain being scattered with their dead bodies.

Jeanne herself made use of those spurs concerning which she had enquired, and carried away by the passion of battle, followed in the pursuit, we are told, until she met a Frenchman brutally ill-using a prisoner whom he had taken, upon which the Maid, indignant, flung herself from her horse, and, seating herself on the ground beside the unfortunate Englishman, took his bleeding head upon her lap and, sending for a priest, made his departure from life at least as easy as pity and spiritual consolation could make it on such a disastrous field. In all the records there is no mention of any actual fighting on her part. She stands in the thick of the flying arrows with her banner, exposing herself to every danger; in moments of alarm, when her forces seem flagging, she seizes and places a ladder against the wall for an assault, and climbs the first as some say; but we never see her strike a blow. On the banks of the Loire the fate of the mail-clad Glasdale, hopeless in the strong stream underneath the ruined bridge, brought tears to her eyes, and now all the excitement of the pursuit vanished in an instant from her mind, when she saw the English man-at-arms dying without the succour of the Church. Pity was always in her heart; she was ever on the side of the angels, though an angel of war and not of peace.

It is perhaps because the numbers engaged were so few that this flight or

"Chasse de Patay," has not taken a more important place in the records of French historians. In general it is only by means of Fontenoy that the amour propre of the French nation defends itself against the overwhelming list of battles in which the English have had the better of it. But this was probably the most complete victory that has ever been gained over the stubborn enemy whom French tactics are so seldom able to touch; and the conquerors were purely French without any alloy of alien arms, except a few Scots, to help them. The entire campaign on the Loire was one of triumph for the French arms, and of disaster for the English. They—it is perhaps a point of national pride to admit it frankly—were as well beaten as heart of Frenchman could desire, beaten not only in the result, but in the conduct of the campaign, in heart and in courage, in skill and in genius. There is no reason in the world why it should not be admitted. But it was not the French generals, not even Dunois, who secured these victories. It was the young peasant woman, the dauntless Maid, who underneath the white mantle of her inspiration, miraculous indeed, but not so miraculous as this, had already developed the genius of a soldier, and who in her simplicity, thinking nothing but of her "voices" and the counsel they gave her, was already the best general of them all.

When Talbot stood before the French generals, no less a person than Alençon himself is reported to have made a remark to him, of that ungenerous kind which we call in feminine language "spiteful," and which is not foreign to the habit of that great nation. "You did not think this morning what would have happened to you before sunset," said the Duc d'Alençon to the prisoner. "It is the fortune of war," replied the English chief.

Once more, however it is like a sudden fall from the open air and sunshine when the victorious army and its chiefs turned back to the Court where the King and his councillors sat idle, waiting for news of what was being done for them. A battle-field is no fine sight; the excitement of the conflict, the great end to be served by it, the sense of God's special protection, even the tremendous uproar of the fight, the intoxication of personal action, danger, and success have, we do not doubt a rapture and passion in them for the moment, which carry the mind away; but the bravest soldier holds his breath when he remembers the after scene, the dead and dying, the horrible injuries inflicted, the loss and misery. However, not even the miserable scene of the Chasse de Patay is so painful as the reverse of the dismal picture, the halls of the royal habitation where, while men died for him almost within hearing of the fiddling and the dances, the young King trifled away his useless days among his idle favourites, and the musicians played, the assemblies were held, and all went on as in the Tuileries. We feel as if we had fallen fathoms deep into the meannesses of mankind when we come back from the bloodshed and the horror outside, to the King's presence within. The troops which had gone out in uncertainty, on an enterprise which might well have proved too great for them, had returned in full flush of triumph, having at last fully broken the spell of the English superiority—which was the greatest victory that could have been achieved: besides gaining the substantial advantage of three important towns brought back to the King's allegiance—only to find themselves as little advanced as before, coming back to the self-same struggle with indolent complaining, indifference, and ingratitude.

Jeanne had given the signs that had been demanded from her. She had delivered Orleans, she cleared the King's road toward the north. She had filled the French forces with an enthusiasm and transport of valour which swept away all the traditions of ill fortune. From every point of view the instant march upon Rheims and the accomplishment of the great object of her mission had not only become practicable, but was the wisest and most prudent thing to do.

But this was not the opinion of the Chancellor of France, the Archbishop of Rheims, and La Tremouille, or of the indolent young King himself, who was very willing to rejoice in the relief from all immediate danger, the restoration of the surrounding country, and even the victory itself, if only they would have left him in quiet where he was, sufficiently comfortable, amused, and happy, without forcing necessary dangers. Jeanne's successes and her unseasonable zeal and the commotion that she and her train of captains made, pouring in, in all the excitement of their triumph, into the midst of the madrigals—seem to have been anything but welcome. Go to Rheims to be crowned? yes, some time when it was convenient, when it was safe. But in the meantime what was more important was to forbid Richemont, whom the Chancellor hated and the King did not love, to come into the presence or to have any share either in warfare or in pageant. This was not only in itself an extremely foolish thing to do, which is always a recommendation, but it was at the same time an excuse for wasting a little precious time. When this was at last accomplished, and Richemont, though deeply wounded and offended, proved himself so much a man of honour and a patriot, that though dismissed by the King he still upheld, if languidly, his cause—there was yet a great deal of resistance to be overcome. Paris though so far off was thrown into great excitement and alarm by the flight at Patay, and the whole city was in commotion fearing an immediate advance and attack. But in Loches, or wherever Charles may have been, it was all taken very easily. Fastolfe, the fugitive, had his Garter taken from him as the greatest disgrace that could be inflicted, for his shameful flight, about the time when Richemont, one of the victors, was being sent off and disgraced on the other side for the crime of having helped to inflict, without the consent of the King, the greatest blow which had yet been given to the English domination! So the Court held on its ridiculous and fatal course.

However the force of public feeling which must have been very frankly expressed by many important voices was too much for Charles and he was at length compelled to put himself in motion. The army had assembled at Gien, where he joined it, and the great wave of enthusiasm awakened by Jeanne, and on which he now moved forth as on the top of the wave, was for the time triumphant. No one dared say now that the Maid was a sorceress, or that it was by the aid of Beelzebub that she cast out devils; but a hundred jealousies and hatreds worked against her behind backs, among the courtiers, among the clergy, strange as that may sound, in sight of the absolute devotion of her mind, and the saintly life she led. So much was this the case still, notwithstanding the practical proofs she had given of her claims, that even persons of kindred mind, partially sharing her inspirations, such as the famous Brother Richard of Troyes, looked upon her with suspicion and alarm— fearing a delusion of Satan. It is more easy perhaps to understand why the archbishops and bishops should have been inclined against her, since, though perfectly orthodox and a good Catholic, Jeanne had been independent of all priestly guidance and had sought no sanction from the Church to her commission, which she believed to be given by Heaven. "Give God the praise; but we know that this woman is a sinner." This was the best they could find to say of her in the moment of her greatest victories; but indeed it is no disparagement to Jeanne or to any saint that she should share with her Master the opprobrium of such words as these.

At last however a reluctant start was made. Jeanne with her "people," her little staff, in which, now, were two of her brothers, a second having joined her after Orleans, left Gien on the 28th of June; and the next day the King very unwillingly set out. There is given a long list of generals who surrounded and accompanied him, three or four princes of the blood, the Bastard of Orleans, the Archbishop of Rheims, marshals, admirals, and innumerable seigneurs, among whom was our young Guy de Laval who wrote the letter to his "mothers" which we have already quoted and whose faith in the Maid we thus know; and our ever faithful La Hire, the big-voiced Gascon who had permission to swear by his bâton, the d'Artagnan of this history. We reckon these names as those of friends: Dunois the ever-brave, Alençon the gentil Duc for whom Jeanne had a special and protecting kindness, La Hire the rough captain of Free Lances, and the graceful young seigneur, Sir Guy as we should have called him had he been English, who was so ready to sell or mortgage his land that he might convey his troop befittingly to the wars. This little group brightens the march for us with their friendly faces. We know that they have but one thought of the warrior maiden in whose genius they had begun to have a wondering confidence as well as in her divine mission. While they were there we feel that she had at least so many who understood her, and who bore her the affection of brothers. We are told that in the progress of the army

Jeanne had no definite place. She rode where she pleased, sometimes in the front, sometimes in the rear. One imagines with pleasure that wherever her charger passed along the lines it would be accompanied by one or other of those valiant and faithful companions.

The first place at which a halt was made was Auxerre, a town occupied chiefly by Burgundians, which closed its gates, but by means of bribes, partly of provisions to be supplied, partly of gifts to La Tremouille, secured itself from the attack which Jeanne longed to lead. Other smaller strongholds on the road yielded without hesitation. At last they came to Troyes, a large and strong place, well garrisoned and confident in its strength, the town distinguished in the history of the time by the treaty made there, by which the young King had been disinherited—and by the marriage of Henry of England with the Princess Catherine of France, in whose right he was to succeed to the throne. It was an ill-omened place for a French king and the camp was torn with dissensions. Should the army march by, taking no notice of it and so get all the sooner to Rheims? or should they pause first, to try their fortune against those solid walls? But indeed it was not the camp that debated this question. The camp was of Jeanne's mind whichever side she took, and her side was always that of the promptest action. The garrison made a bold sortie, the very day of the arrival of Charles and his forces, but had been beaten back: and the King encamped under the walls, wavering and uncertain whether he might not still depart on the morrow, but sending a repeated summons to surrender, to which no attention was paid.

Once more there was a pause of indecision; the King was not bold enough either to push on and leave the city, or to attack it. Again councils of war succeeded each other day after day, discussing the matter over and over, leaving the King each time more doubtful, more timid than before. From these debates Jeanne was anxiously held back, while every silken fool gave his opinion. At last, one of the councillors was stirred by this strange anomaly. He declared among them all, that as it was by the advice of the Maid that the expedition had been undertaken, without her acquiescence it ought not to be abandoned. "When the King set out it was not because of the great puissance of the army he then had with him, or the great treasure he had to provide for them, nor yet because it seemed to him a probable thing to be accomplished; but the said expedition was undertaken solely at the suit of the said Jeanne, who urged him constantly to go forward, to be crowned at Rheims, and that he should find little resistance, for it was the pleasure and will of God. If the said Jeanne is not to be allowed to give her advice now, it is my opinion that we should turn back," said the Seigneur de Treves, who had never been a partisan of or believer in Jeanne. We are told that at this fortunate moment when one of her opponents had thus pronounced in her favour, Jeanne, impatient and restless, knocked at the door of the council chamber as she had done before in her rustic boldness; and then there occurred a brief and characteristic dialogue.

"Jeanne," said the Archbishop of Rheims, taking the first word, probably with the ready instinct of a conspirator to excuse himself from having helped to shut her out, "the King and his council are in great perplexity to know what they should do."

"Shall I be believed if I speak?" said the Maid.

"I cannot tell," replied the King, interposing; "though if you say things that are reasonable and profitable, I shall certainly believe you."

"Shall I be believed?" she repeated.

"Yes," said the King, "according as you speak."

"Noble Dauphin," she exclaimed, "order your people to assault the city of Troyes, to hold no more councils; for, by my God, in three days I will introduce you into the town of Troyes, by love or by force, and false Burgundy shall be dismayed."

"Jeanne," said the Chancellor, "if you could do that in six days, we might well wait."

"You shall be master of the place," said the Maid, addressing herself steadily to the King, "not in six days, but to-morrow."

And then there occurred once more the now habitual scene. It was no longer the miracle it had been to see her dash forward to her post under the walls with her standard which was the signal for battle, to which the impatient troops responded, confident in her, as she in herself. But for the first time we hear how the young general, learning her trade of war day by day, made her preparations for the siege. She was a gunner born, according to all we hear, and was quick to perceive the advantage of her rude artillery though she had never seen one of these bouches de feu till she encountered them at Orleans. The whole army was set to work during the night, knights and men-at-arms alike, to raise—with any kind of handy material, palings faggots, tables, even doors and windows, taken it must be feared from some neighbouring village or faubourg—a mound on which to place the guns. The country as we have said is as flat as the palm of one's hand. They worked all night under cover of the darkness with incredible devotion, while the alarmed townsfolk not knowing what was being done, but no doubt divining something from the unusual commotion, betook themselves to the churches to pray, and began to ponder whether after all it might not be better to join the King whose armies were led by St. Michael himself in the person of his representative, than to risk a siege. Once more the spell of the Maid fell on the defenders of the place. It was witchcraft, it was some vile art. They had no heart to man the battlements, to fight like their brothers at Orleans and Jargeau in face of all the powers of the evil one: the cry of "Sus! Sus!" was like the death-knell in their ears.

While the soldiers within the walls were thus trembling and drawing back, the bishop and his clergy took the matter in hand; they sallied forth, a long procession attended by half the city, to parley with the King. It was in the earliest dawn, while yet the peaceful world was scarcely awake; but the town had been in commotion all night, every visionary person in it seeing visions and dreaming dreams, and a panic of superstition and spiritual terror taking the strength out of every arm. Jeanne was already at her post, a glimmering white figure in the faint and visionary twilight of the morning, when the gates of the city swung back before this tremulous procession. The King, however, received the envoys graciously, and readily promised to guarantee all the rights of Troyes, and to permit the garrison to depart in peace, if the town was given up to him. We are not told whether the Maid acquiesced in this arrangement, though it at once secured the fulfilment of her prophecy; but in any case she would seem to have been suspicious of the good faith of the departing garrison. Instead of retiring to her tent she took her place at the gate, watchful, to see the enemy march forth. And her suspicion was not without reason. The allied troops, English and Burgundian, poured forth from the city gates, crestfallen, unwilling to look the way of the white witch, who might for aught they knew lay them under some dreadful spell, even in the moment of passing. But in the midst of them came a darker band, the French prisoners whom they had previously taken, who were as a sort of funded capital in their hands, each man worth so much money as a ransom, It was for this that Jeanne had prepared herself. "En nom Dieu," she cried, "they shall not be carried away." The march was stopped, the alarm given, the King unwillingly aroused once more from his slumbers. Charles must have been disturbed at the most untimely hour by the ambassadors from the town, and it mattered little to his supreme indolence and indifference what might happen to his unfortunate lieges; but he was forced to bestir himself, and even to give something from his impoverished exchequer for the ransom of the prisoners, which must have been more disagreeable still. The feelings of these men who would have been dragged away in captivity under the eyes of their victorious countrymen, but for the vigilance of the Maid, may easily be imagined.

Jeanne seems to have entered the town at once, to prepare for the reception of the King, and to take instant possession of the place, forestalling all further impediment. The people in the streets, however, received her in a very different way from those of Orleans, with trouble and alarm, staring at her as at a dangerous and malignant visitor. The Brother Richard, before mentioned, the great preacher and reformer, was the oracle of Troyes, and held the conscience of the city in his hands. When he suddenly appeared to confront her, every eye was turned upon them. But the friar himself was in no less doubt than his disciples; he approached her dubiously, crossing himself, making the sacred sign in the air, and sprinkling a shower of holy water before him to drive away the demon, if demon there was. Jeanne was not unused to support the rudest accost, and her frank voice, still assez femme, made itself heard over every clamour. "Come on, I shall not fly away," she cried, with, one hopes, a laugh of confident innocence and good-humour, in face of those significant gestures and the terrified looks of all about her. French art has been unkind to Jeanne, occupying itself very little about her till recently; but her short career is full of pictures. Here the simple page grows bright with the ancient houses and highly coloured crowd: the frightened and eager faces at every window, the white warrior in the midst, sending forth a thousand rays from the polished steel and silver of breastplate and helmet: and the brown Franciscan monk advancing amid a shower of water drops, a mysterious repetition of signs. It gives us an extraordinary epitome of the history of France at that period to turn from this scene to the wild enthusiasm of Orleans, its crowd of people thronging about her, its shouts rending the air; while Troyes was full of terror, doubt, and ill-will, though its nearest neighbour, so to speak, the next town, and so short a distance away.

A little later in the same day, the next after the surrender, Jeanne, riding with her standard by the side of the King, conducted him to the cathedral where he confirmed his previous promises and received the homage of the town. It was a beautiful sight, the chronicle tells us, to see all these magnificent people, so well dressed and well mounted; "il feroit très beau voir."

The fate of Troyes decided that of Chalons, the only other important town on the way, the gates of which were thrown open as Charles and his army, which grew and increased every day, proceeded on its road. Every promise of the Maid had been so far accomplished, both in the greater object and in the details: and now there was nothing between Charles the disinherited and almost ruined Dauphin of three months ago, trying to forget himself in the seclusion and the sports of Chinon—and the sacred ceremonial which drew with it every tradition and every assurance of an ancient and lawful throne.

Jeanne had her little adventure, personal to herself on the way. Though there were neither posts nor telegraphs in those days, there has always been a strange swift current in the air or soil which has conveyed news, in a great national crisis, from one end of the country to the other. It was not so great a distance to Domremy on the Meuse from Troyes on the Loire, and it appears that a little group of peasants, bolder than the rest, had come forth to hang about the road when the army passed and see what was so fine a sight, and perhaps to catch a glimpse of their payse, their little neighbour, the commèrewho was godmother to Gerard d'Epinal's child, the youthful gossip of his young wife—but who was now, if all tales were true, a great person, and rode by the side of the King. They went as far as Chalons to see if perhaps all this were true and not a fable; and no doubt stood astonished to see her ride by, to hear all the marvellous tales that were told of her, and to assure themselves that it was truly Jeanne upon whom, more than upon the King, every eye was bent. This small scene in the midst of so many great ones would probably have been the most interesting of all had it been told us at any length. The peasant travellers surrounded her with wistful questions, with wonder and admiration. Was she never afraid among all those risks of war, when the arrows hailed about her and the bouches de feu, the mouths of fire, bellowed and flung forth great stones and bullets upon her? "I fear nothing but treason," said the victorious Maid. She knew, though her humble visitors did not, how that base thing skulked at her heels, and infested every path. It must not be forgotten that this wonderful and victorious campaign, with all its lists of towns taken and armies discomfited, lasted six weeks only, almost every day of which was distinguished by some victory.

CHAPTER VI — THE CORONATION. JULY 17, 1429.

The road was now clear, and even the most timid of counsellors could not longer hold back the most indolent of kings. Jeanne had kept her word once more and fulfilled her own prophecy, and a force of enthusiasm and certainty, not to be put down, pressed forward the unwilling Court towards the great ceremonial of the coronation, to which all except those most chiefly concerned attached so great an importance. Charles would have hesitated still, and questioned the possibility of resistance on the part of Rheims, if that city had not sent a deputation of citizens with the keys of the town, to meet him. After this it was but a triumphal march into the sacred place, where the great cathedral dominated a swarming, busy, mediæval city. King and Archbishop had a double triumph, for the priest like the monarch had been shut out from his lawful throne, and it was only in the train of the Maid that this great ecclesiastic was able to take possession of his dignities. The King alighted with the Archbishop at the Archevêché which is close to the cathedral, an immense, old palace in which the heads of the expedition were lodged. There is a magnificent old hall still remaining in which no doubt they all assembled, scarcely able to believe that their object was accomplished and that the King of France was actually in Rheims, and all the prophecies fulfilled. The Archbishop marched into the city in the morning; Charles and his Court, and all his great seigneurs, and the body of his army, in which there were many fighting men half armed, and some in their rustic clothes as they had left their fields to join the King in his march—poured in in the evening, after the ecclesiastical procession, filling the town with commotion. Jeanne rode beside the King, her banner in her hand. It was July, the vigil of the Madeleine, and every church poured forth its crowd to witness the entry, and the populace, half troubled, half glad, gazed its eyes out upon the white warrior at the side of the King. Her father and uncle were there to meet her at the old inn in the Place, which still proudly preserves the record of the peasant guests: two astonished rustics, no doubt, were thrust forth from some window to watch that incredible sight—Jacques who would rather have drowned his daughter with his own hands, than have seen her thus launched among men, gazing still aghast at the resplendent figure of the chevalière at the head of the procession. This was very different from what he had thought of when his village respectability was tortured by the idea of his girl among the troopers, yet probably the rigid peasant had never changed his mind.

We are told by M. Blaze de Bury of an ancient custom which we do not find stated elsewhere. A platform was erected, he tells us, outside the choir of the cathedral to which the King was led the evening before the coronation, surrounded by his peers, who showed him to the assembled people with a traditional proclamation: "Here is your King whom we, peers of France, crown as King and sovereign lord. And if there is a soul here which has any objection to make, let him speak and we will answer him. And to-morrow he shall be consecrated by the grace of the Holy Spirit if you have nothing to say against it." The people replied by cries of "Noël, Noël!" It is not to be supposed that the veto of the people of Rheims would have been effectual had they opposed: but the scene is wonderfully picturesque. No doubt Jeanne too was there, watching over her King, as she seems to have done, like a mother over her child, at this crisis of his affairs.

That night there was little sleep in Rheims, for everything had to be prepared in haste, the decorations of the cathedral, the provisions for the ceremonial. Many of the necessary articles were at Saint Denis in the hands of the English, and the treasury of the cathedral had to be ransacked to find the fitting vessels. Fortunately it was rich, more rich probably than it is now, when the commonplace silver of the beginning of this century has replaced the ancient vials. Through the short summer night everyone was at work in these preparations; and by the dawn of day visitors began to flow into the city, great personages and small, to attend the great ceremonial and to pay their homage. The greatest of all was the Duke of Lorraine, he who had consulted Jeanne about his health, husband of the heiress of that rich principality, and son of Queen Yolande who was no doubt with the Court. All France seemed to pour into the famous town, where so important an act was about to be accomplished, with money and wine flowing on all hands, and the enthusiasm growing along with the popular excitement and profit. Even great London is stirred to its limits, many miles off from the centre of proceedings, by such a great event; how much more the little mediæval city, in which every one might hope to see something of the pageant, as one shining group after another, with armour blazing in the sun, and sleek horses caracoling, arrived at the great gates of the Archevêché: and lesser parties scarcely less interesting poured in in need of lodging, of equipment and provisions; while every housewife searched her stores for a piece of brilliant stuff, of old silk or embroidery, to make her house shine like the rest.

Early in the morning, a wonderful procession came out of the Archbishop's house. Four splendid peers of France, in full armour with their banners, rode through the streets to the old Abbey of Saint Remy—the old church which Leo IX. consecrated, in the eleventh century, on an equally splendid occasion, and which may still be seen to-day—to fetch from its shrine, where it was strictly guarded by the monks, the Sainte Ampoule, the holy and sacred vial in which the oil of consecration had been sent to Clovis out of Heaven. These noble messengers were the "hostages" of this sacred charge, engaging themselves by an oath never to lose sight of it by night or day, till it was restored to its appointed guardians. This vow having been made, the Abbot of St. Remy, in his richest robes, appeared surrounded by his monks, carrying the treasure in his hands; and under a splendid canopy, blazing in the sunshine with cloth of gold, marched towards the cathedral under the escort of the Knights Hostages, blazing also in the flashes of their armour. This procession was met half-way, before the Church of St. Denis, by another, that of the Archbishop and his train, to whom the holy oil was solemnly confided, and carried by them to the cathedral, already filled by a dazzled and dazzling crowd.

The Maid had her occupations this July morning like the rest. We hear nothing of any interview with her father, or with Durand the good uncle who had helped her in the beginning of her career; though it was Durand who was sent for to the King and questioned as to Jeanne's life in her childhood and early youth; which we may take as proof that Jacques d'Arc still stood aloof, dour, as a Scotch peasant father might have been, suspicious of his daughter's intimacy with all these fine people, and in no way cured of his objections to the publicity which is little less than shame to such rugged folk. And there were his two sons who would take him about, and with whom probably in their easier commonplace he was more at home than with Jeanne. What the Maid had to do on the morning of the coronation day was something very different from any home talk with her relations. She who felt herself commissioned not only to lead the armies of France, but to deal with her princes and take part in her councils, occupied the morning in dictating a letter to the Duke of Burgundy. She had summoned the English by letter three times repeated, to withdraw peaceably from the possessions which by God's will were French. It was with still better reason that she summoned Philip of Burgundy to renounce his feud with his cousin, and thus to heal the breach which had torn France in two:

JHESUS, MARIA.

High and redoubtable Prince, Duke of Burgundy. Jeanne the Maid requires on the part of the King of Heaven, my most just sovereign and Lord (mon droicturier souverain seigneur), that the King of France and you make peace between yourselves, firm, strong and that will endure. Pardon each other of good heart, entirely, as loyal Christians ought to do, and if you desire to fight let it be against the Saracens. Prince of Burgundy, I pray, supplicate, and require, as humbly as may be, fight no longer against the holy kingdom of France: withdraw, at once and speedily, your people who are in any strongholds or fortresses of the said holy kingdom; and on the part of the gentle King of France, he is ready to make peace with you, having respect to his honour, and upon your life that you never will gain a battle against loyal Frenchmen and that all those who war against the said holy kingdom of France, war against the King Jesus, King of Heaven and of all the world and my just and sovereign Lord. And I pray and require with clasped hands that you fight not, nor make any battle against us, neither your friends nor your subjects; but believe always however great in number may be the men you lead against us, that you will never win, and it would be great pity for the great battle and the blood that would be shed of those who came against us. Three weeks ago I sent you a letter by a herald that you should be present at the consecration of the King, which to-day, Sunday, the seventeenth of the present month of July, is done in the city of Rheims: to which I have had no answer, nor even any news by the said herald. To God I commend you, and may He be your guard if it pleases Him, and I pray God to make good peace.

Written at the aforesaid Rheims, the seventeenth day of July, 1429.

When the letter was finished Jeanne put on her armour and prepared for the great ceremony. We are not told what part she took in it, nor is any more prominent position assigned to her than among the noble crowd of peers and generals who surrounded the altar, where her place would naturally be, upon the broad raised platform of the choir, so excellently adapted for such ceremonies. Her banner we are told was borne into the cathedral, in order, as she proudly explained afterwards, that having been foremost in the danger it should share the honour.

But we have no right to suppose that the Maid took the position of the chief actor in the pageant and stood alone by the side of Charles, as the exigencies of the pictorial art have required her to do. When, however, the ceremony was completed, and he had received on his knees the anointing which separated him as king from every other class of men, and while the lofty vaults echoed with the cries of Noël! Noël! by which the people hailed the completed ceremony, Jeanne could contain herself no longer. The object was attained for which she had laboured and struggled, and overcome every opponent. She stepped forward out of the brilliant crowd, and threw herself at the feet of the now crowned monarch, embracing his knees. "Gentle King," she cried with tears, "now is the pleasure of God fulfilled—whose will it was that I should raise the siege of Orleans and lead you to this city of Rheims to receive your consecration. Now has He shown that you are true King, and that the kingdom of France truly belongs to you alone."

Those broken words, her tears, the cry of that profound satisfaction which is almost anguish, the "Lord, now lettest thou thy servant depart in peace," which is so suitable to the lips of the old, so poignant from those of the young, pierced all hearts. It is added that she asked leave to withdraw, her work being done, and that all who saw her were filled with sympathy. It was no doubt the irresistible outburst of a heart too full; and though that fulness was all joy and triumph, yet there was in it a sense of completed work, a rending asunder and tearing away from life, the end of a wonderful and triumphant tale.

There is a considerable controversy as to the precise meaning of that outburst of emotion. Did the Maid mean that her work was over, and her divine mission fulfilled? Was this all that she believed herself to be appointed to do? or did she expect, as she sometimes said, to bouter the English out of France altogether? In the one case she ought to have relinquished her work, and in not doing so she acted without the protection of God which had hitherto made her invulnerable. In the other, her "voices," her inspiration, must have failed her, for her course of triumph went no farther. It is impossible to decide between these contending theories. She did speak in both senses, sometimes declaring that she was to take Paris, sometimes, her intention tobouter the English out of the kingdom. At the same time she betrayed a constant conviction that her office had limitations and must come to an end. "I will last but a year," she said to the King and to Alençon. The testimony of Dunois seems to be the best we can have on this point. He says in his deposition, made many years after her death: "Although Jeanne sometimes talked playfully to amuse people, of things concerning the war which were not afterwards accomplished, yet when she spoke seriously of the war, and of her own career and her vocation, she never affirmed anything but that she was sent to raise the siege of Orleans and to lead the King to Rheims to be crowned."

If this were so was she wrong in continuing her warfare, and did she place herself in the position of one who goes on her own charges, finding the mission from on high unnecessary? Or in the other case did her inspiration fail her, or were the intrigues of Charles and his Court sufficient to balk the designs of Heaven? We prefer to think that Jeanne's commission concerned only those two things which she accomplished so completely; but that in continuing the war, she acted only as a well inspired and honourable young soldier might, though no longer as the direct messenger of God. She had as much right to do so as to return to her distaff or her needle in her native village; but she became subject to all the ordinary laws of war by so doing, exposed herself to be taken or overthrown like any man-at-arms, and accepted that risk. What is certain is, that every intrigue sprang up again afresh on the evening of that brilliant and triumphant ceremonial, and that from the moment of the accomplishment of her great work the failure of the Maid began.

These intrigues had been in her way since her very first beginning, as has been seen. At Orleans, in the very field as well as in the council chamber and the presence, everything was done to balk her, and to cross her plans, but in vain; she triumphed over every contrivance against her, and broke through the plots, and overcame the plotters. But after Rheims the combination of dangers became ever greater and greater, and we may say that no merely human general would have had a chance in face of the many and bewildering influences of evil. Charles who was himself, at least at this period of his career, sufficiently indolent and unenterprising to have damped the energies of any commander, was, in addition, surrounded by advisers who had always been impatient and jealous of the interference of Jeanne, and would have cast her off as a witch, or passed her by as an impostor, had that been possible, without permitting her to strike a blow. They had now grudgingly made use of her, or rather, for this is too much to say, had permitted her action where they had no power to restrain it: but they were as little friendly, as malignant in their treatment of the Maid as ever, and more hopeful, now that so much had been done by her means, of being able to shake her off and pursue their fate in their own way.

The position of Charles crowned King of France with all the traditional pomp, master of the Orleannais, with fresh bands of supporters coming in to swell his army day by day, and Paris itself almost within his reach, was very different from that of the discredited Dauphin at Chinon, whom half the world believed to have no right to the crown which his own mother had signed away from him, and who wasted his idle days in folly to the profit of the greedy councillors who schemed and trafficked with his enemies, and to the destruction of all his hopes. The strange apparition of virginal purity, energy, and faith which had taken up and saved him against his will and all his efforts had not ceased for a moment to be hateful to La Tremouille and his party; and Charles—though he seems to have had a certain appreciation of the Maid, and even a liking for her frank and fearless character, apart from any faith in her mission—was far too ready to accept the facts of the moment, and probably to believe that, after all, his own worth and favour with Heaven had a great deal to do with this dazzling triumph and success: certainly he was not the man to make any stand for his deliverer. But that she was an auxiliary too important to be sent away was reluctantly apparent to them all. To keep her as a sort of tame angel about the Court in order to be produced when she was wanted, to put heart into the soldiers and frighten the English as she certainly had the gift of doing, no doubt appeared to all as a thing desirable enough. And they dared not let her go "because of the people," nor, may we believe, would Alençon, Dunois, La Hire, and the rest have tolerated thus the abandonment of their comrade. To dismiss her even at her own word would have been impossible, and it is hard to believe that Jeanne, after that extraordinary brief career as a triumphant general and leader, could have gone back to her father's cottage of the village, though she thought she would fain have done so. If we are to believe that she felt her mission to be fulfilled, she was yet mistress of her fate to serve France and the King as seemed best.

And we have no evidence that her "voices" forsook her, or discouraged her. They seem to have changed a little in their burden, they began to mingle a sadder tone in their intimations. It began to be breathed into her mind though not immediately, that something was to happen to her, some disaster not explained, yet that God was to be with her. It seems to me that all the circumstances are compatible with a change in Jeanne's consciousness, from the moment of the coronation. It might have been a grander thing had she retired there and then, her work being accomplished as she declared it to be; but it would not have been human. She was still a power, if no longer the direct messenger from Heaven; a general, with much skill and natural aptitude if not the Sent of God; and the ardour of a military career had got into her veins. No doubt she was much more good for that, now, than for sitting by the side of Isabeau d'Arc at Domremy, and working even into a piece of embroidery for the altar, her remembrances and visions of camp and siege and the intoxication of victory. She remained, conscious that she was no longer exactly as of old, to fight not only against the English, but with intimate enemies, far more bitter, whom now she knew, against the ordinary fortune of war, and against that which is a thousand times worse, the hatred and envy, the cruel carelessness, and the malignant schemes of her own countrymen for whom she had fought.

This, so far as we can judge, appears to be the position of Jeanne in the second portion of her career; perhaps only dimly apprehended and at moments, by herself; not much thought of probably by those around her, the wisest of whom had always been sceptical of her divine commission; while the populace never saw any change in her, and believed that at one time as well as at another the Maid was the Maid, and had victory at her command. And no doubt that influence would have endured for some time at least, and her dauntless rush against every obstacle would have carried success with it, had she been able to carry out her plans, and fly forth upon Paris as she had done upon Orleans, carrying on the campaign swiftly, promptly, without pause or uncertainty. Bedford himself said that Paris "would fall at a blow," if she came on. It had been hard enough, however, to do that, as we have seen, when she was the only hope of France and had the fire of the divine enthusiasm in her veins; but it was still more hard now to mould a young King elated with triumph, beginning to feel the crown safe upon his head, and to feel that if there was still much to gain, there was now a great deal to be lost. The position was complicated and made more difficult for Jeanne by every advantage she had gained.

In the meantime the secret negotiations, which were always being carried on under the surface, had come to this point, that Charles had made a private treaty with Philip of Burgundy by which that prince pledged himself to give up Paris into the King's hands within fifteen days. This agreement furnished a sufficient pretext for the delay in marching against Paris, delay which was Charles's invariable method, and which but for Jeanne's hardihood and determination, had all but crushed the expedition to Rheims itself. It was never with any will of his or of his adviser, La Tremouille, that any stronghold was assailed. He would fain have passed by Troyes, as the reader will remember, he would fain have delayed going to Rheims; in each case he had been forced to move by the impetuosity of the Maid. But a treaty which touched the honour of the King was a different matter. Philip of Burgundy, with whom it was made, seems to have held the key of the position. He was called to Paris by Bedford on one side to defend the city against its lawful King; he had pledged himself on the other to Charles to give it up. He had in his hands, though it is uncertain whether he ever read it, that missive of the sorceress, the letter of Jeanne which I have quoted, calling upon him on the part of God to make peace. What was he to do? There were reasons drawing him to both sides. He was the enemy of Charles on account of the murder of his father, and therefore had every interest in keeping Paris from him; he was angry with the English on account of the marriage of the Duke of Gloucester with Jacqueline of Brabant, which interfered with his own rights and safety in Flanders, and therefore might have served himself by giving up the capital to the King. As for the appeal of Jeanne, what was the letter of that mad creature to a prince and statesman? The progress of affairs was arrested by this double problem. Jeanne had been the prominent, the only important figure in the history of France for some months past. Now that shining figure was jostled aside, and the ordinary laws of life, with all the counter changes of negotiation, the ineffectual comings and goings, the meaner half-seen persons, the fierce contending personal interests—in which there was no love of either God or man, or any elevated notion of patriotism—came again into play.

Jeanne would seem to have already foreseen and felt this change even before she left Rheims; there is a new tone of sadness in some of her recorded words; or if not of sadness, at least of consciousness that an end was approaching to all these triumphs and splendours. The following tale is told in various different versions, as occurring with different people; but the account I give is taken from the lips of Dunois himself, a very competent witness. As the King, after his coronation, wended his way through the country, receiving submission and joyous welcome from every village and little town, it happened that while passing through the town of La Ferté, Jeanne rode between the Archbishop of Rheims and Dunois. The Archbishop had never been friendly to the Maid, and now it was clear, watched her with that half satirical, half amused look of the wise man, curious and cynical in presence of the incomprehensible, observing her ways and very ready to catch her tripping and to entangle her if possible in her own words. The people thronged the way, full of enthusiasm, acclaiming the King and shouting their joyful exclamations of "Noël!" though it does not appear that any part of their devotion was addressed to Jeanne herself. "Oh, the good people," she cried with tears in her eyes, "how joyful they are to see their noble King! And how happy should I be to end my days and be buried here among them!" The priest unmoved by such an exclamation from so young a mouth attempted instantly, like the Jewish doctors with our Lord, to catch her in her words and draw from her some expression that might be used against her. "Jeanne," he said, "in what place do you expect to die?" It was a direct challenge to the messenger of Heaven to take upon herself the gift of prophecy. But Jeanne in her simplicity shattered the snare which probably she did not even perceive: "When it pleases God," she said. "I know neither the place nor the time."

It was enough, however, that she should think of death and of the sweetness of it, after her work accomplished, in the very moment of her height of triumph —to show something of a new leaven working in her virgin soul.

One characteristic reward, however, Jeanne did receive. Her father and uncle were lodged at the public cost as benefactors of the kingdom, as may still be seen by the inscription on the old inn in the great Place at Rheims; and when Jacques d'Arc left the city he carried with him a patent—better than one of nobility which, however, came to the family later—of exemption for the villages of Domremy and Greux of all taxes and tributes; "an exemption maintained and confirmed up to the Revolution, in favour of the said Maid, native of that parish, in which are her relations." "In the register of the Exchequer," says M. Blaze de Bury, "at the name of the parish of Greux and Domremy, the place for the receipt is blank, with these words as explanation:à cause de la Pucelle, on account of the Maid." There could not have been a more delightful reward or one more after her own heart. It would be a graceful act of the France of to-day, which has so warmly revived the name and image of her maiden deliverer, to renew so touching a distinction to her native place.

We are told that Jeanne parted with her father and uncle with tears, longing that she might return with them and go back to her mother who would rejoice to see her again. This was no doubt quite true, though it might be equally true that she could not have gone back. Did not the father return, a little sullen, grasping the present he had himself received, not sure still that it was not disreputable to have a daughter who wore coat armour and rode by the side of the King, a position certainly not proper for maidens of humble birth? The dazzled peasants turned their backs upon her while she was thus at the height of glory, and never, so far as appears, saw her face again.

CHAPTER VII — THE SECOND PERIOD. 1429-1430.

The epic so brief, so exciting, so full of wonder had now reached its climax. Whatever we may think on the question as to whether Jeanne had now reached the limit of her commission, it is at least evident that she had reached the highest point of her triumph, and that her short day of glory and success came to an end in the great act which she had always spoken of as her chief object. She had crowned her King; she had recovered for him one of the richest of his provinces, and established a strong base for further action on his part. She had taught Frenchmen how not to fly before the English, and she had filled those stout-hearted English, who for a time had the Frenchmen in their powerful steel-clad grip, with terror and panic, and taught them how to fly in their turn. This was, from the first, what she had said she was appointed to do, and not one of her promises had been broken. Her career had been a short one, begun in April, ending in July, one brief continuous course of glory. But this triumphant career had come to its conclusion. The messenger of God had done her work; the servant must not desire to be greater than his Lord. There have been heroes in this world whose career has continued a glorious and a happy one to the end. Our hearts follow them in their noble career, but when the strain and pain are over they come into their kingdom and reap their reward the interest fails. We are glad, very glad, that they should live happy ever after, but their happiness does not attract us like their struggle.

It is different with those whose work and whose motives are not those of this world. When they step out of the brilliant lights of triumph into sorrow and suffering, all that is most human in us rises to follow the bleeding feet, our hearts swell with indignation, with sorrow and love, and that instinctive admiration for the noble and pure, which proves that our birthright too is of Heaven, however we may tarnish or even deny that highest pedigree. The chivalrous romance of that age would have made of Jeanne d'Arc the heroine of human story. She would have had a noble lover, say our young Guy de Laval, or some other generous and brilliant Seigneur of France, and after her achievements she would have laid by her sword, and clothed herself with the beautiful garments of the age, and would have grown to be a noble lady in some half regal chateau, to which her name would have given new lustre. The young reader will probably long that it should be so; he will feel it an injustice, a wrong to humanity that so generous a soul should have no reward; it will seem to him almost a personal injury that there should not be a noble chevalier at hand to snatch that devoted Maid out of the danger that threatened her, out of the horrible fate that befell her; and we can imagine a generous boy, and enthusiastic girl, ready to gnash their teeth at the terrible and dishonouring thought that it was by English hands that this noble creature was tied to the stake and perished in the flames. For the last it becomes us to repent, for it was to our everlasting shame; but not more to us than to France who condemned her, who lifted no finger to help her, who raised not even a cry, a protest, against the cruelty and wrong. But for her fate in itself let us not mourn overmuch. Had the Maid become a great and honoured lady should not we all have said as Satan says in the Book of Job: Did Jeanne serve God for nought? We should say: See what she made by it. Honour and fame and love and happiness. She did nobly, but nobly has she been rewarded.

But that is not God's way. The highest saint is born to martyrdom. To serve God for nought is the greatest distinction which He reserves for His chosen. And this was the fate to which the Maid of France was consecrated from the moment she set out upon her mission. She had the supreme glory of accomplishing that which she believed herself to be sent to do, and which I also believe she was sent to do, miraculously, by means undreamed of, and in which no one beforehand could have believed. But when that was done a higher consecration awaited her. She had to drink of the cup of which our Lord drank, and to be baptised with the baptism with which He was baptised. It was involved in every step of the progress that it should be so. And she was herself aware of it, vaguely, at heart, as soon as the object of her mission was attained. What else could have put the thought of dying into the mind of a girl of eighteen in the midst of the adoring crowd, to whom to see her, to touch her, was a benediction? When she went forth from those gates she was going to her execution, though the end was not to be yet. There was still a long struggle before her, lingering and slow, more bitter than death, the preface of discouragement, of disappointment, of failure when she had most hoped to succeed.

She was on the threshold of this second period when she rode out of Rheims all brilliant in the summer weather, her banner faded now, but glorious, her shining armour bearing signs of warfare, her end achieved—yet all the while her heart troubled, uncertain, and full of unrest. And it is impossible not to note that from this time her plans were less defined than before. Up to the coronation she had known exactly what she meant to do, and in spite of all obstructions had done it, keeping her genial humour and her patience, steering her simple way through all the intrigues of the Court, without bitterness and without fear. But now a vague mist seems to fall about the path which was so open and so clear. Paris! Yes, the best policy, the true generalship would have been to march straight upon Paris, to lose no time, to leave as little leisure as possible to the intriguers to resume their old plots. So the generals thought as well as Jeanne: but the courtiers were not of that mind. The weak and foolish notion of falling back upon what they had gained, and of contenting themselves with that, was all they thought of; and the un-French, unpatriotic temper of Paris which wanted no native king, but was content with the foreigner, gave them a certain excuse. We could not even imagine London as being ever, at any time, contented with an alien rule. But Paris evidently was so, and was ready to defend itself to the death against its lawful sovereign. Jeanne had never before been brought face to face with such a complication. It had been a straightforward struggle, each man for his own side, up to this time. But now other things had to be taken into consideration. Here was no faithful Orleans holding out eager arms to its deliverer, but a crafty, self-seeking city, deaf to patriotism, indifferent to freedom, calculating which was most to its profit—and deciding that the stranger, with Philip of Burgundy at his back, was the safer guide. This was enough of itself to make a simple mind pause in astonishment and dismay.

There is no evidence that the supernatural leaders who had shaped the course of the Maid failed her now. She still heard her "voices." She still held communion with the three saints who, she believed devoutly, came out of Heaven to aid her. The whole question of this supernatural guidance is one which is of course open to discussion. There are many in these days who do not believe in it at all, who believe in the exaltation of Jeanne's brain, in the excitement of her nerves, in some strange complication of bodily conditions, which made her believe she saw and heard what she did not really see or hear. For our part, we confess frankly that these explanations are no explanation at all so far as we are concerned; we are far more inclined to believe that the Maid spoke truth, she who never told a lie, she who fulfilled all the promises she made in the name of her guides, than that those people are right who tell us on their own authority that such interpositions of Heaven are impossible. Nobody in Jeanne's day doubted that Heaven did interpose directly in human affairs. The only question was, Was it Heaven in this instance? Was it not rather the evil one? Was it sorcery and witchcraft, or was it the agency of God? The English believed firmly that it was witchcraft; they could not imagine that it was God, the God of battles, who had always been on their side, who now took the courage out of their hearts and taught their feet to fly for the first time. It was the devil, and the Maid herself was a wicked witch. Neither one side nor the other believed that it was from Jeanne's excited nerves that these great things came. There were plenty of women with excited nerves in France, nerves much more excited than those of Jeanne, who was always reasonable at the height of her inspiration; but to none of them did it happen to mount the breach, to take the city, to drive the enemy—up to that moment invincible,—flying from the field.

But it would seem as if these celestial visitants had no longer a clear and definite message for the Maid. Their words, which she quotes, were now promises of support, vague warnings of trouble to come. "Fear not, for God will stand by you." She thought they meant that she would be delivered in safety as she had been hitherto, her wounds healing, her sacred person preserved from any profane touch. But yet such promises have always something enigmatical in them, and it might be, as proved to be the case, that they meant rather consolation and strength to endure than deliverance. For the first time the Maid was often sad; she feared nothing, but the shadow was heavy on her heart. Orleans and Rheims had been clear as daylight, her "voices" had said to her "Do this" and she had done it. Now there was no definite direction. She had to judge for herself what was best, and to walk in darkness, hoping that what she did was what she was meant to do, but with no longer any certainty. This of itself was a great change, and one which no doubt she felt to her heart. M. Fabre tells (alone among the biographers of Jeanne) that there were symptoms of danger to her sound and steady mind, in her words and ways during the moment of triumph. Her chaplain Pasquerel wrote a letter in her name to the Hussites, against whom the Pope was then sending crusades, in which "I, the Maid," threatened, if they were not converted, to come against them and give them the alternative of death or amendment. Quicherat says that to the Count d'Armagnac who had written to her, whether in good faith or bad, to ask which of the three then existent Popes was the real one, she is reported to have answered that she would tell him as soon as the English left her free to do so. But this is a perverted account of what she really did say, and M. Fabre seems to be, like the rest of us, a little confused in his dates: and the documents themselves on which he builds are not of unquestioned authority. These, however, would be but small speck upon the sunshine of her perfect humility and sobriety; if indeed they are to be depended upon as authentic at all.

The day of Jeanne, her time of glory and success, was but a short one—Orleans was delivered on the 8th of May, the coronation of Charles took place on the 17th of July; before the earliest of these dates she had spent nearly two months in an anxious yet hopeful struggle of preparation, before she was permitted to enter upon her career. The time of her discouragement was longer. It was ten months from the day when she rode out of Rheims, the 25th of July, 1429, till the 23d of May, 1430, when she was taken. She had said after the deliverance of Orleans that she had but a year in which to accomplish her work, and at a later period, Easter, 1430, her "voices" told her that "before the St. Jean" she would be in the power of her enemies. Both these statements came true. She rose quickly but fell more slowly, struggling along upon the downward course, unable to carry out what she would, hampered on every hand, and not apparently followed with the same fervour as of old. It is true that the principal cause of all seems to have been the schemes of the Court and the indolence of Charles; but all these hindrances had existed before, and the King and his treacherous advisers had been unwillingly dragged every mile of the way, though every step made had been to Charles's advantage. But now though the course is still one of victory the Maid no longer seems to be either the chief cause or the immediate leader. Perhaps this may be partly due to the fact that little fighting was necessary, town after town yielding to the King, which reduced the part of Jeanne to that of a spectator; but there is a change of atmosphere and tone which seems to point to something more fundamental than this. The historians are very unwilling to acknowledge, except Michelet who does so without hesitation, that she had herself fixed the term of her commission as ending at Rheims; it is certain that she said many things which bear this meaning, and every fact of her after career seems to us to prove it: but it is also true that her conviction wavered, and other sayings indicate a different belief or hope. She did no wrong in following the profession of arms in which she had made so glorious a beginning; she had many gifts and aptitudes for it of which she was not herself at first aware: but she was no longer the Envoy of God. Enough had been done to arouse the old spirit of France, to break the spell of the English supremacy; it was right and fitting that France should do the rest for herself. Perhaps Jeanne was not herself very clear on this point, and after her first statement of it, became less assured. It is not necessary that the servant should know the designs of the master. It did not after all affect her. Her business was to serve God to the best of her power, not to take the management out of His hands.

The army went forth joyously upon its way, directing itself towards Paris. There was a pilgrimage to make, such as the Kings of France were in the habit of making after their coronation; there were pleasant incidents, the submission of a village, the faint resistance, instantly overcome, of a small town, to make the early days pleasant. Laon and Soissons both surrendered. Senlis and Beauvais received the King's envoys with joy. The independent captains of the army made little circles about, like parties of pleasure, bringing in another and another little stronghold to the allegiance of the King. When he turned aside, taking as he passed through, without as yet any serious deflection, the road rather to the Loire than to Paris, success still attended him. At Château-Thierry resistance was expected to give zest to the movement of the forces, but that too yielded at once as the others had done. The dates are very vague and it seems difficult to find any mode of reconciling them. Almost all the historians while accusing the King of foolish dilatoriness and confusion of plans give us a description of the undefended state of Paris at the moment, which a sudden stroke on the part of Charles might have carried with little difficulty, during the absence of all the chiefs from the city and the great terror of the inhabitants; but a comparison of dates shows that the Duke of Bedford reentered Paris with strong reinforcements on the very day on which Charles left Rheims three days only after his coronation, so that he scarcely seems so much to blame as appears. But the general delay, inefficiency, and hesitation existing at headquarters, naturally lead to mistakes of this kind.

The great point was that Paris itself was by no means disposed to receive the King. Strange as it seems to say so Paris was bitterly, fiercely English at that extraordinary moment, a fact which ought to be taken into account as the most important in the whole matter. There was no answering enthusiasm in the capital of France to form an auxiliary force behind its ramparts and encourage the besiegers outside. The populace perhaps might be indifferent: at the best it had no feeling on the subject; but there was no welcome awaiting the King. During the time of Bedford's absence the city felt itself to have "no lord"— ceux de Paris avoit grand peur car nul seigneur n' y avoit. It was believed that Charles would put all the inhabitants to the sword, and their desperation of feeling was rather that which leads to a wild and hopeless defence than to submission. The Duke of Bedford, governing in the name of the infant Henry VI. Of England, was their seigneur, instead of their natural sovereign. It is a fact which to us seems scarcely credible, but it was certainly true. There seems to have been no feeling even, on the subject, no general shame as of a national betrayal; nothing of the kind. Paris was English, holding by the English kings who had never lost a certain hold on France, and thinking no shame of its party. It was a hostile town, the chief of the English possessions. In the Journal du Bourgeois de Paris—who was no bourgeois but a distinguished member of that university which held the Maid and all her ways in horror—Jeanne the deliverer, the incarnation of patriotism and of France is spoken of as "a creature in the form of a woman." How extraordinary is this evidence of a state of affairs in which it is almost impossible to believe! Paris is France nowadays to many people, though no doubt this is but a superficial judgment; but in the early part of the fifteenth century, she was frankly English, not by compulsion even, but by habit and policy. Perhaps the delays, the hesitation, the terrors of Charles and his counsellors are thus rendered more excusable than by any other explanation.

In the meantime it is almost impossible to follow the wanderings of this vacillating army without a map. If the reader should trace its movements, he would see what a stumbling and devious course it took as of a man blundering in the dark. From Rheims to Soissons the way was clear; then there came a sudden move southward to Château-Thierry from which indeed there was still a straight line to Paris but which still more clearly indicated the highroad leading to the Orleannais, the faithful districts of the Loire. This retrograde movement was not made without a great outcry from the generals. Their opinion was that the King ought to press on to conquer everything while the English forces were still depressed and discouraged. In their mind this deflection towards the south was an abandonment at once of honour and safety. An unimportant check on the way, however, gave an argument to the leaders of the army, and Charles permitted himself to be dragged back. They then made their way by La Ferté-Milon, Crépy, and Daumartin, and on this road the English troops which had been led out from Paris by Bedford to intercept them came twice within fighting distance of the French army. The English, as all the French historians are eager to inform us, invariably entrenched themselves in their positions, surrounding their lines with sharp-pointed posts by which the equally invariable rush of the French could be broken. But the French on these occasions were too wise to repeat the impetuous charge which had ruined them at Crécy and Agincourt, and the consequence was that the two forces remained within sight of each other, with a few skirmishes going on at the flanks, but without any serious encounter.

It will be more satisfactory, however, to copy the following itineraire of Charles's movements from the Chronicle of Perceval de Cagny who was a member of the household of the Duc d'Alençon, and probably present, certainly at all events bound to have the best and most correct information. He informs us that the King left Rheims on Thursday the 21st of July, and dined, supped, and lay at the Abbey of St. Nanuol that night, where were brought to him the keys of the city of Laon. He then set out on le voyage à venir devant Paris.

"And on Saturday the 23d of the same month the King dined, supped and lay at Soissons, and was there received the most honourably that the churchmen, burghers and other people of the town were capable of: for they had all great fear because of the destruction of the town which had been taken by the Burgundians and made to rebel against the King.

"Friday the 29th day of July the King and his company were all day before Château-Thierry in order of battle, hoping that the Duke of Bedford would appear to fight. The place surrendered at the hour of vespers, and the King lodged there till Monday the first of August. On that day the King lay at Monmirail in Brie.

"Tuesday the 2d of August he passed the night in the town of Provins, and had the best possible reception there, and remained till the Friday following, the 5th August. Sunday the 7th the King lay at the town of Coulommièrs in Brie. Wednesday the 10th he lay at La Ferté- Milon, Thursday at Crespy in Valois—Friday at Laigny-le-Sec. The following Saturday the 13th the King held the field near Dammartin-en-Gouelle, for the whole day looking out for the English: but they came not.

"On Sunday the 14th August the Maid, the Duc d'Alençon, the Count de Vendosme, the Marshals and other captains accompanied by six or seven thousand combatants were at the hour of vespers lodged in the fields near Montépilloy, nearly two leagues from the town of Senlis—The Duke of Bedford and other English captains with between eight and ten thousand English lying half a league from Senlis between our people and the said city on a little stream, in a village called Notre Dame de la Victoire. That evening our people skirmished with the English near to their camp and in this skirmish were people taken on each side, and of the English Captain d'Orbec and ten or twelve others, and people wounded on both sides: when night fell each retired to their own quarters."

The same writer records an appeal in the true tone of chivalry addressed to the English by Jeanne and Alençon desiring them to come out from their entrenchments and fight: and promising to withdraw to a sufficient distance to permit the enemy to place himself in the open field. The French troops had first "put themselves in the best state of conscience that could possibly be, hearing mass at an early hour and then to horse." But the English would not come out. Jeanne, with her standard in her hand rode up to the English entrenchments, and some one says (not de Cagny) struck the posts with her banner, challenging the force within to come out and fight; while they on their side waved at the French in defiance, a standard copied from that of Jeanne, on which was depicted a distaff and spindle. But neither host approached any nearer. Finally, Charles made his way to Compiègne.

At Château-Thierry there was concluded an arrangement with Philip of Burgundy for a truce of fifteen days, before the end of which time the Duke undertook to deliver Paris peaceably to the French. That this was simply to gain time and that no idea of giving up Paris had ever been entertained is evident; perhaps Charles was not even deceived. He, no more than Philip, had any desire to encounter the dangers of such a siege. But he was able at least to silence the clamours of the army and the representations of the persistent Maid by this truce. To wait for fifteen days and receive the prize without a blow struck, would not that be best? The counsellors of the King held thus a strong position, though the delay made the hearts of the warriors sick.

The figure of Jeanne appears during these marchings and counter-marchings like that of any other general, pursuing a skilful but not unusual plan of campaign. That she did well and bravely there can be no doubt, and there is a characteristic touch which we recognise, in the fact that she and all of her company "put themselves in the best state of conscience that could be," before they took to horse; but the skirmishes and repulses are such as Alençon himself might have made. "She made much diligence," the same chronicler tells us, "to reduce and place many towns in the obedience of the King," but so did many others with like success. We hear no more her vigorous knock at the door of the council chamber if the discussion there was too long or the proceedings too secret. Her appearances are those of a general among many other generals, no longer with any special certainty in her movements as of a person inspired. We are reminded of a story told of a previous period, after the fight at Patay, when blazing forth in the indignation of her youthful purity at the sight of one of the camp followers, a degraded woman with some soldiers, she struck the wanton with the flat of her sword, driving her forth from the camp, where was no longer that chastened army of awed and reverent soldiers making their confession on the eve of every battle, whom she had led to Orleans. The sword she used on this occasion, was, it is said, the miraculous sword which had been found under the high altar of St. Catharine at Fierbois; but at the touch of the unclean the maiden brand broke in two. If this was an allegory to show that the work of that weapon was over, and the common sword of the soldier enough for the warfare that remained, it could not be more clearly realised than in the history of this campaign. The only touch of our real Maid in her own distinct person comes to us in a letter written in a field on that same wavering road to Paris, dated as early as the 5th of August and addressed to the good people of Rheims, some of whom had evidently written to her to ask what was the meaning of the delay, and whether she had given up the cause of the country. There is a terse determination in its brief, indignant sentences which is a relief to the reader weary of the wavering and purposeless campaign:

"Dear and good friends, good and loyal Frenchmen of the town of Rheims. Jeanne, the Maid, sends you news of her. It is true that the King has made a truce of fifteen days with the Duke of Burgundy, who promises to render peaceably the city of Paris in that time. Do not, however, be surprised if I enter there sooner, for I like not truces so made, and know not whether I will keep them, but if I keep them, it will be only because of the honour of the King."

While Jeanne and her army thus played with the unmoving English, advancing and retiring, attempting every means of drawing them out, the enemy took advantage of one of these seeming withdrawals to march out of their camp suddenly and return to Paris, which all this time had been lying comparatively defenceless, had the French made their attack sooner. At the same time Charles moved on to Compiègne where he gave himself up to fresh intrigues with Philip of Burgundy, this time for a truce to last till Christmas. The Maid was grievously troubled by this step, moult marrie, and by the new period of delay and negotiation on which the Court had entered. Paris was not given up, nor was there any appearance that it ever would be, and to all the generals as well as to the Maid it was very evident that this was the next step to be taken. Some of the leaders wearied with inaction had pushed on to Normandy where four great fortresses—greatest of all the immense and mysterious stronghold on the high cliffs of the Seine, that imposing Château Gaillard which Richard Coeur-de-lion had built, the ruins of which, white and mystic, still dominate, like some Titanic ghost, above the course of the river—had yielded to them. So great was the danger of Normandy, the most securely English of all French provinces, that Bedford had again been drawn out of Paris to defend it. Here then was another opportunity to seize the capital. But Charles could not be induced to move. He found many ways of amusing himself at Compiègne, and the new treaty was being hatched with Burgundy which gave an excuse for doing nothing. The pause which wearied them all out, both captains and soldiers, at last became more than flesh and blood could bear.

Jeanne once more was driven to take the initiative. Already on one occasion she had forced the hand of the lingering Court, and resumed the campaign of her own accord, an impatient movement which had been perfectly successful. No doubt again the army itself was becoming demoralised, and showing symptoms of falling to pieces. One day she sent for Alençon in haste during the absence of the ambassadors at Arras. "Beau duc," she cried, "prepare your troops and the other captains. En mon Dieu, par mon martin, I will see Paris nearer than I have yet seen it." She had seen the towers from afar as she wandered over the country in Charles's lingering train. Her sudden resolution struck like fire upon the impatient band. They set out at once, Alençon and the Maid at the head of their division of the army, and all rejoiced to get to horse again, to push their way through every obstacle. They started on the 23d August, nearly a month after the departure from Rheims, a month entirely lost, though full of events, lost without remedy so far as Paris was concerned. At Senlis they made a pause, perhaps to await the King, who, it was hoped, would have been constrained to follow; then carrying with them all the forces that could be spared from that town, they spurred on to St. Denis where they arrived on the 27th: St. Denis, the other sacred town of France, the place of the tomb, as Rheims was the place of the crown.

The royalty of France was Jeanne's passion. I do not say the King, which might be capable of malinterpretation, but the kings, the monarchy, the anointed of the Lord, by whom France was represented, embodied and made into a living thing. She had loved Rheims, its associations, its triumphs, the rejoicing of its citizens. These had been the accompaniments of her own highest victory. She came to St. Denis in a different mood, her heart hot with disappointment and the thwarting of all her plans. From whatever cause it might spring, it was clear that she was no longer buoyed up by that certainty which only a little while before had carried her through every danger and over every obstacle. But to have reached St. Denis at least was something. It was a place doubly sacred, consecrated to that royal House for which she would so willingly have given her life. And at last she was within sight of Paris, the greatest prize of all. Up to this time she had known in actual warfare nothing but victory. If her heart for the first time wavered and feared, there was still no certain reason that, de par Dieu, she might not win the day again.

At St. Denis there was once more a cruel delay. Nearly a fortnight passed and there was no news of the King. The Maid employed the time in skirmishes and reconnoissances, but does not seem to have ventured on an attack without the sanction of Charles, whom Alençon, finally, going back on two several occasions, succeeded in setting in motion. Charles had remained at Compiègne to carry out his treaty with Burgundy, and the last thing he desired was this attack; but when he could resist no longer he moved on reluctantly to St. Denis, where his arrival was hailed with great delight. This was not until the 5th of September, and the army, wrought up to a high pitch of excitement and expectation, was eager for the fight. "There was no one of whatever condition, who did not say, 'She will lead the King into Paris, if he will let her,'" says the chronicler.

In the meantime the authorities in Paris were at work, strengthening its fortifications, frightening the populace with threats of the vengeance of Charles, persuading every citizen of the danger of submission.

The Bourgeois tells us that letters came from "les Arminoz," that is, the party of the King, sealed with the seal of the Duc d'Alençon, and addressed to the heads of the city guilds and municipality inviting their co-operation as Frenchmen. "But," adds the Parisian, "it was easy to see through their meaning, and an answer was returned that they need not throw away their paper as no attention was paid to it." There is no sign at all that any national feeling existed to respond to such an appeal. Paris—its courts of law, Parliaments (salaried by Bedford), University, Church—every department, was English in the first place, Burgundian in the second, dependent on English support and money. There was no French party existing. The Maid was to them an evil sorceress, a creature in the form of a woman, exercising the blackest arts. Perhaps there was even a breath of consciousness in the air that Charles himself had no desire for the fall of the city. He had left the Parisians full time to make every preparation, he had held back as long as was possible. His favour was all on the side of his enemies; for his own forces and their leaders, and especially for the Maid, he had nothing but discouragement, distrust, and auguries of evil.

Nevertheless, these oppositions came to an end, and Jeanne, though less ready and eager for the assault, found herself under the walls of Paris at last.

CHAPTER VIII — DEFEAT AND DISCOURAGEMENT. AUTUMN, 1429.

It was on the 7th September that Jeanne and her immediate followers reached the village of La Chapelle, where they encamped for the night. The next day was the day of the Nativity of the Blessed Virgin, a great festival of the Church. It could scarcely be a matter of choice on the part of so devout a Catholic as Jeanne to take this day of all others, when every church bell was tinkling forth a summons to the faithful, for the day of assault. In all probability she was not now acting on her own impulse but on that of the other generals and nobles. Had she refused, might it not have been alleged against her that after all her impatience it was she who was the cause of delay? The forces with Jeanne were not very large, a great proportion of the army remaining with Charles no one seems to know where, either at St. Denis or at some intermediate spot, possibly to form a reserve force which could be brought up when wanted. The best informed historian only knows that Charles was not with the active force. But Alençon was at the head of the troops, along with many other names well known to us, La Hire, and young Guy de Laval, and Xantrailles, all mighty men of valour and the devoted friends of Jeanne. There is a something, a mist, an incertitude in the beginning of the assault which was unlike the previous achievements of Jeanne, a certain want of precaution or knowledge of the difficulties which does not reflect honour upon the generals with her. Absolutely new to warfare as she was before Orleans she had ridden out at once on her arrival there to inspect the fortifications of the besiegers. But probably the continual skirmishing of which we are told made this impossible here, so that, though the Maid studied the situation of the town in order to choose the best point for attack, it was only when already engaged that the army discovered a double ditch round the walls, the inner one of which was full of water. By sheer impetuosity the French took the gate of St. Honoré and its "boulevard" or tower, driving its defenders back into the city: but their further progress was arrested by that discovery. It was on this occasion that Jeanne is supposed to have seized from a Burgundian in the mêlée, a sword, of which she boasted afterwards that it was a good sword capable of good blows, though we have no certain record that in all her battles she ever gave one blow, or shed blood at all.

It would seem to have been only after the taking of this gate that the discovery was made as to the two deep ditches, one dry, the other filled with water. Jeanne, whose place had always been with her standard at the immediate foot of the wall, from whence to direct and cheer on her soldiers, pressed forward to this point of peril, descending into the first fosse, and climbing up again on the second, the dos d'ane, which separated them, where she stood in the midst of a rain of arrows, fully exposed to all the enraged crowd of archers and gunners on the ramparts above, testing with her lance the depth of the water. We seem in the story to see her all alone or with her standard-bearer only by her side making this investigation; but that of course is only a pictorial suggestion, though it might for a moment be the fact. She remained there, however, from two in the afternoon till night, when she was forced away. The struggle must have raged around while she stood on the dark edge of the ditch probing the muddy water to see where it could best be crossed, shouting directions to her men in that voice assez femme, which penetrated the noise of battle, and summoning the active and desperate enemy overhead. "Renty! Renty!" she cried as she had done at Orleans—"surrender to the King of France!"

We hear nothing now of the white armour; it must have been dimmed and worn by much fighting, and the banner torn and glorious with the chances of the war; but it still waved over her head, and she still stood fast, on the ridge between the two ditches, shouting her summons, cheering the men, a spot of light still, amid all the steely glimmering of the mail-coats and the dark downpour of that iron rain. Half a hundred war cries rending the air, shrieks from the walls of "Witch, Devil, Ribaude," and names still more insulting to her purity, could not silence that treble shout, the most wonderful, surely, that ever ran through such an infernal clamour, so prodigious, the chronicler says, that it was a marvel to hear it. De par Dieu, Rendez vous, rendez vous, au roy de France. If as we believe she never struck a blow, the aspect of that wonderful figure becomes more extraordinary still. While the boldest of her companions struggled across to fling themselves and what beams and ladders they could drag with them against the wall, she stood without even such shelter as close proximity to it might have given, cheering them on, exposed to every shot.

The fight was desperate, and though there was no marked success on the part of the besiegers, yet there seems to have been nothing to discourage them, as the fight raged on. Few were wounded, notwithstanding the noise of the cannons and culverins, "by the grace of God and the good luck of the Maid." But towards the evening Jeanne herself suddenly swayed and fell, an arrow having pierced her thigh; she seems, however, to have struggled to her feet again, undismayed, when a still greater misfortune befell: her standard-bearer was hit, first in the foot, and then, as he raised his visor to pull the arrow from the wound, between his eyes, falling dead at her feet. What happened to the banner, we are not told; Jeanne most likely herself caught it as it fell. But at this stroke, more dreadful than her own wound, her strength failed her, and she crept behind a bush or heap of stones, where she lay, refusing to quit the place. Some say she managed to slide into the dry ditch where there was a little shelter, but resisted all attempts to carry her away, and some add that while she lay there she employed herself in a vain attempt to throw faggots into the ditch to make it passable. It is said that she kept calling out to them to persevere, to go on and Paris would be won. She had promised, they say, to sleep that night within the conquered city; but this promise comes to us with no seal of authority. Jeanne knew that it had taken her eight days to free Orleans, and she could scarcely have promised so sudden a success in the more formidable achievement. But she was at least determined in her conviction that perseverance only was needed. She must have lain for hours on the slope of the outer moat, urging on the troops with such force as her dauntless voice could give, repeating again and again that the place could be taken if they but held on. But when night came Alençon and some other of the captains overcame her resistance, and there being clearly no further possibility for the moment, succeeded in setting her upon her horse, and conveyed her back to the camp. While they rode with her, supporting her on her charger, she did nothing but repeat "Quel dommage!" Oh, what a misfortune, that the siege of Paris should fail, all for want of constancy and courage. "If they had but gone on till morning," she cried, "the inhabitants would have known." It is evident from this that she must have expected a rising within, and could not yet believe that no such thing was to be looked for. "Par mon martin, the place would have been taken," she said in the hearing one cannot but feel of the chronicler, who reports so often those homely words.

Thus Jeanne was led back after the first day's attack. Her wound was not serious, and she had been repulsed during one of the day's fighting at Orleans without losing courage. But something had changed her spirit as well as the spirit of the army she led. There is a curious glimpse given us into her camp at this point, which indeed comes to us through the observation of an enemy, yet seems to have in it an unmistakable gleam of truth. It comes from one of the parties which had been granted a safe-conduct to carry away the dead of the English and Burgundian side. They tell us, among other circumstances,—such as that the French burnt their dead, a manifest falsehood, but admirably calculated to make them a horror to their neighbours,—that many in the ranks cursed the Maid who had promised that they should without any doubt sleep that night in Paris and plunder the wealthy city. The men with their safe-conduct creeping among the dead, to recover those bodies which had fallen on their own side, and furtively to count the fallen on the other—who were delighted to bring a report that the Maid was no longer the fountain of strength and blessing, but secretly cursed by her own forces—are sinister figures groping their way through the darkness of the September night.

Next morning, however, her wound being slight, Jeanne was up early and in conference with Alençon, begging him to sound his trumpets and set forth once more. "I shall not budge from here, till Paris is taken," she said. No doubt her spirit was up, and a determination to recover lost ground strong in her mind. While the commanders consulted together, there came a band of joyful augury into the camp, the Seigneur of Montmorency with sixty gentlemen, who had left the party of Burgundy in order to take service under the banner of the Maid. No doubt this important and welcome addition to their number exhilarated the entire camp, in the commotion of the reveillé, while each man looked to his weapons, wiping off from breastplate and helmet the heavy dew of the September morning, greeting the new friends and brothers-in-arms who had come in, and arranging, with a better knowledge of the ground than that of yesterday, the mode of attack. Jeanne would not confess that she felt her wound, in her eagerness to begin the assault a second time. And all were in good spirits, the disappointment of the night having blown away, and the determination to do or die being stronger than ever. Were the men-at-arms perhaps less amenable? Were they whispering to each other that Jeanne had promised them Paris yesterday, and for the first time had not kept her word? It would almost require such a fact as this to explain what follows. For as they began to set out, the whole field in movement, there was suddenly seen approaching another party of cavaliers—perhaps another reinforcement like that of Montmorency? This new band, however, consisted but of two gentlemen and their immediate attendants, the Duc de Bar and the Comte de Clermont, always a bird of evil omen, riding hot from St. Denis with orders from the King. These orders were abrupt and peremptory—to turn back. Jeanne and her companions were struck dumb for the moment. To turn back, and Paris at their feet! There must have burst forth a storm of remonstrance and appeal. We cannot tell how long the indignant parley lasted; the historians do not enlarge upon the disastrous incident. But at last the generals yielded to the orders of the King—Jeanne humiliated, miserable, and almost in despair. We cannot but feel that on no former occasion would she have given way so completely; she would have rushed to the King's presence, overwhelmed him with impetuous prayers, extorted somehow the permission to go on. But Charles was safe at seven miles' distance, and his envoys were imperious and peremptory, like men able to enforce obedience if it were not given. She obeyed at last, recovering courage a little in the hope of being able to persuade Charles to change his mind, and sanction another assault on Paris from the other side, by means of a bridge over the Seine towards St. Denis, which Alençon had constructed. Next morning it appears that without even asking that permission a portion of the army set out very early for this bridge: but the King had divined their project, and when they reached the river side the first thing they saw was their bridge in ruins. It had been treacherously destroyed in the night, not by their enemies, but by their King.

It is natural that the French historians should exhaust themselves in explanation of this fatal change of policy. Quicherat, who was the first to bring to light all the most important records of this period of history, lays the entire blame upon La Tremoïlle, the chief adviser of Charles. But that Charles himself was at heart equally guilty no one can doubt. He was a man who proved himself in the end of his career to possess both sense and energy, though tardily developed. It was to him that Jeanne had given that private sign of the truth of her mission, by which he was overawed and convinced in the first moment of their intercourse. Within the few months which had elapsed since she appeared at Chinon every thing that was wonderful had been done for him by her means. He was then a fugitive pretender, not even very certain of his own claim, driven into a corner of his lawful dominions, and fully prepared to abandon even that small standing ground, to fly into Spain or Scotland, and give up the attempt to hold his place as King of France. Now he was the consecrated King, with the holy oil upon his brows, and the crown of his ancestors on his head, accepted and proclaimed, all France stirring to her old allegiance, new conquests falling into his hands every day, and the richest portion of his kingdom secure under his sway. To check thus peremptorily the career of the deliverer who had done so much for him, degrading her from her place, throwing more than doubt upon her inspiration, falsifying by force the promises which she had made—promises which had never failed before,—was a worse and deeper sin on the part of a young man, by right of his kingly office the very head of knighthood and every chivalrous undertaking, than it could be on the part of an old and subtle diplomatist who had never believed in such wild measures, and all through had clogged the steps and endeavoured to neutralise the mission of the warrior Maid. It is very clear, however, that between them it was the King and his chamberlain who made this assault upon Paris so evident and complete a failure. One day's repulse was nothing in a siege. There had been one great repulse and several lesser ones at Orleans. Jeanne, even though weakened by her wound, had sprung up that morning full of confidence and courage. In no way was the failure to be laid to her charge.

But this could never, perhaps, have been explained to the whole body of the army, who had believed her word without a doubt and taken her success for granted. If they had been wavering before, which seems possible—for they must have been, to a considerable extent, new levies, the campaigners of the Loire having accomplished their period of feudal service,—this sudden downfall must have strengthened every doubt and damped every enthusiasm. The Maid of whom such wonderful tales had been told, she who had been the angel of triumph, the irresistible, before whom the English fled, and the very walls fell down—was she after all only a sorceress, as the others called her, a creature whose incantations had failed after the flash of momentary success? Such impressions are too apt to come like clouds over every popular enthusiasm, quenching the light and chilling the heart.

Jeanne was thus dragged back to St. Denis against her will and every instinct of her being, and there ensued three days of passionate debate and discussion. For a moment it appeared as if she would have thrown off the bonds of loyal obedience and pursued her mission at all hazards. Her "voices," if they had previously given her uncertain sound, promising only the support and succour of God, but no success, now spoke more plainly and urged the continuance of the siege; and the Maid was torn in pieces between the requirements of her celestial guardians and the force of authority around her. If she had broken out into open rebellion who would have followed her? She had never yet done so; when the King was against her she had pleaded or forced an agreement, and received or snatched a consent from the malevolent chamberlain, as at Jargeau and Troyes. Never yet had she set herself in public opposition to the will of her sovereign. She had submitted to all kinds of tests and trials rather than this. And to have lain half a day wounded outside Paris and to stand there pleading her cause with her wound still unhealed were not likely things to strengthen her powers of resistance. "The Voices bade me remain at St. Denis," she said afterwards at her trial, "and I desired to remain; but the seigneurs took me away in spite of myself. If I had not been wounded I should never have left." Added to the force of these circumstances, it was no doubt apparent to all that to resume operations after that forced retreat, and the betrayal it gave of divided counsels, would be less hopeful than ever. These arguments even convinced the bold La Hire, who for his part, being no better than a Free Lance, could move hither and thither as he would; and thus the first defeat of the Maid, a disaster involving all the misfortunes that followed in its train, was accomplished.

Jeanne's last act in St. Denis was one to which perhaps the modern reader gives undue significance, but which certainly must have had a certain melancholy meaning. Before she left, dragged almost a captive in the train of the King, we are told that she laid on the altar of the cathedral the armour she had worn on that evil day before Paris. It was not an unusual act for a warrior to do this on his return from the wars. And if she had been about to renounce her mission it would have been easily comprehensible. But no such thought was in her mind. Was it a movement of despair, was it with some womanish fancy that the arms in which she had suffered defeat should not be borne again?—or was it done in some gleam of higher revelation made to her that defeat, too, was a part of victory, and that not without that bitterness of failure could the fame of the soldier of Christ be perfected? I have remarked already that we hear no more of the white armour, inlaid with silver and dazzling like a mirror, in which she had begun her career; perhaps it was the remains of that panoply of triumph which she laid out before the altar of the patron saint of France, all dim now with hard work and the shadow of defeat. It must have marked a renunciation of one kind or another, the sacrifice of some hope. She was no longer Jeanne the invincible, the triumphant, whose very look made the enemy tremble and flee, and gave double force to every Frenchman's arm. Was she then and there abdicating, becoming to her own consciousness Jeanne the champion only, honest and true, but no longer the inspired Maid, the Envoy of God? To these questions we can give no answer; but the act is pathetic, and fills the mind with suggestions. She who had carried every force triumphantly with her, and quenched every opposition, bitter and determined though that had been, was now a thrall to be dragged almost by force in an unworthy train. It is evident that she felt the humiliation to the bottom of her heart. It is not for human nature to have the triumph alone: the humiliation, the overthrow, the chill and tragic shadow must follow. Jeanne had entered into that cloud when she offered the armour, that had been like a star in front of the battle, at the shrine of St. Denis. Hers was now to be a sadder, a humbler, perhaps a still nobler part.

It is enough to trace the further movements of the King to perceive how at every step the iron must have entered deeper and deeper into the heart of the Maid. He made his arrangements for the government of each of the towns which had acknowledged him: Beauvais, Compiègne, Senlis, and the rest. He appointed commissioners for the due regulation of the truce with Philip of Burgundy. And then the retreating army took its march southward towards the mild and wealthy country, all fertility and quiet, where a recreant prince might feel himself safe and amuse himself at his leisure—by Lagny, by Provins, by Bercy-sur Seine, where he had been checked before in his retreat and almost forced to the march on Paris—by Sens, and Montargis: until at last on the 29th of September, no doubt diminished by the withdrawal of many a local troop and knight whose service was over, the forces arrived at Gien, whence they had set forth at the end of June for a series of victories. It is to be supposed that the King was well enough satisfied with the conquests accomplished in three months. And, indeed, in ordinary circumstances they would have formed a triumphant list. Charles must have felt himself free to play after the work which he had not done; and to leave his good fortune and the able negotiators, who hoped to get Paris and other good things from Philip of Burgundy without paying anything for them, to do the rest.

We can imagine nothing more dreadful for the Maid than the months that followed. The Court was not ungrateful to her; she received the warmest welcome from the Queen; she had a maison arranged for her like the household of a noble chief, with the addition of women and maidens of rank to her existing staff, and everything which could serve to show that she was one whom the King delighted to honour. And Charles would have her apparelled gloriously like the king's daughter in the psalm. "He gave her a mantle of cloth of gold, open at both sides, to wear over her armour," and apparently did his best to make her, if not a noble lady, yet into the semblance of a noble young chevalière, one the glories of his Court, with all the distinction of her achievements and all the complacences of a carpet knight. It was said afterwards, in the absence of any graver possibility of accusation, that she liked her fine clothes. The tears rise to the eyes at such a suggestion. She was so natural that let us hope she did, the martyr Maid whose torture had already begun. If that mantle of gold gave her a moment of pleasure, it is something to be thankful for in the midst of the dismal shadows that were already closing round her. They were ready to give her any shining mantle, any beautiful dress, even a title and a noble name if she would; but what the King and his counsellors were determined on, was, that she should no more have the fame of individual triumph, or do anything save under their orders.

Alençon, the gentle duke, with whom she had taken so much trouble, and who had grown into a true and noble comrade, made one effort to free his friend and leader. He planned an expedition into Normandy, where, with the help of Jeanne, he hoped to inflict upon the English a loss so tremendous, the destruction of their base of operations, that they would be compelled to abandon the centre of France altogether, and leave the way open to Paris and to the recovery of the entire kingdom; but the King, or La Tremoïlle, as the historians prefer to say, would not permit Jeanne to accompany him, and this hope came to nothing. Alençon disbanded his troops, everything in the form of an army was broken up—the short period of feudal service making this inevitable, unless new levies were made—and no forces were left under arms except those bands which formed the body-guard of the King. Nevertheless, there was plenty of work to be done still, and the breaking up of the French forces encouraged many a little garrison of English partisans, which would have yielded naturally and easily to a strong national party.

In the midst of the winter, however, it seemed appropriate to the Court to launch forth an expedition against some of the unsubdued towns, perhaps on account of the mortal languishment of Jeanne herself, perhaps for some other reason of its own. The first necessity was to collect the necessary forces, and for this reason Jeanne came to Bourges, where she was lodged in one of the great houses of the city, that of Raynard de Bouligny, conseiller de roi, and his wife, Marguerite, one of the Queen's ladies. She was there for three weeks collecting her men, and the noble gentlewoman, who was her hostess, was afterwards in the Rehabilitation trial, one of the witnesses to the purity of her life.

From this lady and others we have a clear enough view of what the Maid was in this second chapter of her history. She spent her time in the most intimate intercourse with Madam Marguerite, sharing even her room, so that nothing could be more complete than the knowledge of her hostess of every detail of her young guest's life. And wonderful as was the difference between the peasant maiden of Domremy and the most famous woman in France, the life of Jeanne, the Deliverer of her country, is as the life of Jeanne, the cottage sempstress,—as simple, as devout, and as pure. She loved to go to church for the early matins, but as it was not fit that she should go out alone at that hour, she besought Madame Marguerite to go with her. In the evening she went to the nearest church, and there with all her old childish love for the church bells, she had them rung for half an hour, calling together the poor, the beggars who haunt every Catholic church, the poor friars and bedesmen, the penniless and forlorn from all the neighbourhood. This custom would, no doubt, soon become known, and not only her poor pensioners, but the general crowd would gather to gaze at the Maid as well as to join in her prayers. It was her great pleasure to sing a hymn to the Virgin, probably one of the litanies which the unlearned worshipper loves, with its choruses and constant repetitions, in company with all those untutored voices, in the dimness of the church, while the twilight sank into night, and the twinkling stars of candles on the altar made a radiance in the middle of the gloom. When she had money to give she divided it, according to the liberal custom of her time, among her poor fellow-worshippers. These evening services were her recreation. The days were full of business, of enrolling soldiers, and regulating the "lances," groups of retainers, headed by their lord, who came to perform their feudal service.

The ladies of the town who had the advantage of knowing Madame Marguerite did not fail to avail themselves of this privilege, and thronged to visit her wonderful guest. They brought her their sacred medals and rosaries to bless, and asked her a hundred questions. Was she afraid of being wounded; or was she assured that she would not be wounded? "No more than others," she said; and she put away their religious ornaments with a smile, bidding Madame Marguerite touch them, or the visitors themselves, which would be just as good as if she did it. She would seem to have been always smiling, friendly, checking with a laugh the adulation of her visitors, many of whom wore medals with her own effigy (if only one had been saved for us!) as there were many banners made after the pattern of hers. But cheerful as she was, a prevailing tone of sadness now appears to run through her life. On several occasions she spoke to her confessor and chaplain, who attended her everywhere, of her death. "If it should be my fate to die soon, tell the King our master on my part to build chapels where prayer may be made to the Most High for the salvation of the souls of those who shall die in the wars for the defence of the kingdom." This was the one thing she seemed anxious for, and it returned again and again to her mind. Her thoughts indeed were heavy enough. Her larger enterprises had been cruelly put a stop to: her companions-in-arms had been dispersed: she had been separated from her lieutenant Alençon, and from all the friends between whom and herself great mutual confidence had sprung up. Even the commission which had at last been put in her hands was a trifling one and led to nothing, bringing the King no nearer to any satisfactory end: and the troops were under command of a new captain whom she scarcely knew, d'Albert, who was the son-in-law of La Tremoïlle, and probably little inclined to be a friend to Jeanne. In these circumstances there was little of an exhilarating or promising kind.

Nevertheless as an episode, few things had happened to Jeanne more memorable than the siege of St. Pierre-le-Moutier. The first assault upon the town was unsuccessful; the retreat had sounded and the troops were streaming back from the point of attack, when Jean d'Aulon, the faithful friend and brave gentleman who was at the head of the Maid's military household, being himself wounded in the heel and unable to stand or walk, saw the Maid almost alone before the stronghold, four or five men only with her. He dragged himself up as well as he could upon his horse, and hastened towards her, calling out to her to ask what she did there, and why she did not retire with the rest. She answered him, taking off her helmet to speak, that she would leave only when the place was taken—and went on shouting for faggots and beams to make a bridge across the ditch. It is to be supposed that seeing she paid no attention, nor budged a step from that dangerous point, this brave man, wounded though he was, must have made an effort to rally the retiring besiegers: but Jeanne seems to have taken no notice of her desertion nor ever to have paused in her shout for planks and gabions. "All to the bridge," she shouted, "aux fagots et aux claies tout le monde! every one to the bridge." "Jeanne, withdraw, withdraw! You are alone," some one said to her. Bareheaded, her countenance all aglow, the Maid replied: "I have still with me fifty thousand of my men." Were those the men whom the prophet's servant saw when his eyes were opened and he beheld the innumerable company of angels that surrounded his master? But Jeanne, rapt in the trance and ecstasy of battle, gave no explanation. "To work, to work!" her clear voice went on, ringing over the startled head of the good knight who knew war, but not any rapture like this. History itself, awe-stricken, would almost have us believe that alone with her own hand the Maid took the city, so entirely does every figure disappear but that one, and the perplexed and terrified spectator vainly urging her to give up so desperate an attempt. But no doubt the shouts of a voice so strange to every such scene, the vox infantile, the amazing and clear voice, silvery and womanly, assez femme, and the efforts of d'Aulon to bring back the retreating troops were successful, and Jeanne once more, triumphantly kept her word. The place was strongly fortified, well provisioned, and full of people. Therefore the whole narrative is little less than miraculous, though very little is said of it. Had they but persevered, as she had said, a few hours longer before Paris, who could tell that the same result might not have been obtained?

She was not successful, however, with La Charité, which after a siege of a month's duration still held out, and had to be abandoned. These long operations of regular warfare were not in Jeanne's way; and her coadjutor in command, it must be remembered, was in this case commissioned by her chief enemy. We are told that she was left without supplies, and in the depths of winter, in cold and rain and snow, with every movement hampered, and the ineffective government ever ready to send orders of retreat, or to cause bewildering and confusing delays by the want of every munition of war. Finally, at all events, the French forces withdrew, and again an unsuccessful enterprise was added to the record of the once victorious Maid. That she went on continually promising victory as in her early times, is probably the mere rumour spread by her detractors who were now so many, for there is no real evidence that she did so. Everything rather points to discouragement, uncertainty, and to a silent rage against the coercion which she could not overcome.

CHAPTER IX — COMPIÈGNE. 1430.

By this time France was once more all in flames: the English and Burgundians had entered and then abandoned Paris—Duke Philip cynically leaving that city, which he had promised to give up to Charles, to its own protection, in order to look after his more pressing personal concerns: while Bedford spread fire and flame about the adjacent country, retaking with much slaughter many of the towns which had opened their gates to the King. Thus while Charles gave no attention to anything beyond the Loire, and kept his chief champion there, as it were, on the leash, permitting no return to the most important field of operations, almost all that had been gained was again lost upon the banks of the Seine. This was the state of affairs when Jeanne returned humbled and sad from the abandoned siege of La Charité. Her enemy's counsels had triumphed all round and this was the result. Individual fightings of no particular account and under no efficient organisation were taking place day by day; here a town stood out heroically, there another yielded to the foreign arms; the population were thrown back into universal misery, the spring fields trampled under foot, the villages burned, every evil of war in full operation, invasion aggravated by faction, the English always aided by one side of France against the other, and neither peace nor security anywhere.

This was the aspect of affairs on one side. On the other appeared a still less satisfactory scene. Charles amusing himself, his counsellors, La Tremoïlle, and the Archbishop of Rheims carrying on fictitious negotiations with Burgundy and playing with the Maid who was in their power, sending her out to make a show and cast a spell, then dragging her back at the end of their shameful chain: while the Court, the King and Queen, and all their flattering attendants gilded that chain and tried to make her forget by fine clothes and caresses, at once her mission and her despair. They were not ungrateful, no: let us do them justice, for they might well have added this to the number of their sins: mantles of cloth of gold, patents of nobility were at her command, had these been what she wanted. The only personal wrong they did to Jeanne was to set up against her a sort of opposition, another enchantress and visionary who had "voices" and apparitions too, and who was admitted to all the councils and gave her advice in contradiction of the Maid, a certain Catherine de la Rochelle, who was ready to say anything that was put into her mouth, but who had done nothing to prove any mission for France or from God. We have little light however upon the state of affairs in those castles, which one after another were the abode of the Court during this disastrous winter. They were safe enough on the other side of the Loire in the fat country where the vines still flourished and the young corn grew. Now and then a band of armed men was sent forth to succour a fighting town in the suffering and struggling Île-de-France, always under the conflicting orders of those intrigants and courtiers: but within the Court, all was gay; "never man," as rough La Hire had said on an earlier occasion, "lost his kingdom more gaily or with better grace" than did Charles. Where was La Hire? Where was Dunois?—there is no appearance of these champions anywhere. Alençon had returned to his province. Only La Tremoïlle and the Archbishop holding all the strings in their hands, upsetting all military plans, disgusting every chief, met and talked and carried on their busy intrigues, and played their Sibyl—Sibylle de carrefour, says one of the historians indignantly—against the Maid, who, all discouraged and downcast, fretted by caresses, sick of inactivity, dragged out the uneasy days in an uncongenial world; but Jeanne has left no record of the sensations with which she saw these days pass, eating her heart out, gazing over that rapid river, on the other side of which all the devils were unchained and every result of her brief revolution was being lost.

At length however the impatience and despair were more than she could bear; the Court was then at Sully and the spring had begun with its longer days and more passable roads. Without a word to anyone the Maid left the castle. The war had rolled towards these princely walls, as near as Melun, which was threatened by the English. A little band of intimate servants and associates, her two brothers, and a few faithful followers, were with her. So far as we know she never saw Charles or his courtiers again. They arrived at Melun in time to witness and to take part in the repulse of the English, and it was here that a communication was make to Jeanne by her saints of which afterwards there was frequent mention. Little had been said of them during her dark time of inaction, and their tone was no longer as of old. It was on the side of the moat of Melun where probably she was superintending some necessary work to strengthen the fortifications or to put them in better order for defence, that this message reached her. The "Voices" which so often had urged her to victory and engaged the faith of heaven for her success, had now a word to say, secret and personal to herself. It was that she should be taken prisoner; and the date was fixed, before the St. Jean. It was the middle of April when this communication was made and the Feast of St. Jean, as everybody knows, is in the end of June; two months only to work in, to strike another blow for France. The "Voices" bade her not to fear, that God would sustain her. But it would be impossible not to be startled by such a sudden intimation in the midst of her reviving plans. The Maid made one terrified prayer, that God would let her die when she was taken, not subject her to long imprisonment; her heart prophetically sprang to a sudden consciousness of the most likely, most terrible end that lay before her, for she had been often enough threatened with the stake and the fire to know what to expect. But the saintly voices made no reply. They bade her be strong and of good courage: is not that the all-sustaining, all-delusive message for every martyr? It was the will of God, and His support and sustaining power, which we often take to mean deliverance, but which is not always so—were promised. She asked where this terrible thing was to happen, but received no reply. Natural and simple as she was, she confessed afterwards that had she known she was to be taken on any certain day, she would not have gone out to meet the catastrophe unless she had been forced by evident duty to do so. But this was not revealed to her. "Before the St. Jean!" It must almost have seemed a guarantee that until that time or near it she was safe. She would seem to have said nothing immediately of this vision to sadden those about her.

In the meantime, however, there were other adventures in store for her. From Melun to Lagny was no long journey, but it was through a country full of enemies in which she must have been subject to attack at every corner of every road or field. And she had not been long in the latter place which is said to have had a garrison of Scots, when news came of the passing of a band of Burgundians, a troop of raiders indeed, ravaging the country, taking advantage of the war to rob and lay waste churches, villages, and the growing fields wherever they passed. The troops was led by Franquet d'Arras, a famous "pillard," robber of God and man. Jeanne set out to encounter this bandit with a party of some four hundred men, and various noble companions, among whom, however, we find no name familiar in her previous career, a certain Hugh Kennedy, a Scot, who is to be met with in various records of fighting, being one of the most notable among them. Franquet's band fought vigorously but were cut to pieces, and the leader was taken prisoner. When this man was brought back to Lagny, a prisoner to be ransomed, and whom Jeanne desired to exchange for one of her own side, the law laid claim to him as a criminal. He was a prisoner of war: what was it the Maid's duty to do? The question is hotly debated by the historians and it was brought against her at her trial. He was a murderer, a robber, the scourge of the country—especially to the poor whom Jeanne protected and cared for everywhere, was he pitiless and cruel. She gave him up to justice, and he was tried, condemned, and beheaded. If it was wrong from a military point of view, it was her only error, and shows how little there was with which to reproach her.

In Lagny other things passed of a more private nature. Every day and all day long her "voices" repeated their message in her ears. "Before the St. Jean." She repeated it to some of her closest comrades but left herself no time to dwell upon it. Still worse than the giving up of Franquet was the supposed resuscitation of a child, born dead, which its parents implored her to pray for that it might live again to be baptised. She explained the story to her judges afterwards. It was the habit of the time, nay, we believe continues to this day in some primitive places, to lay the dead infant on the altar in such a case, in hope of a miracle. "It is true," said Jeanne, "that the maidens of the town were all assembled in the church praying God to restore life that it might be baptised. It is also true that I went and prayed with them. The child opened its eyes, yawned three or four times, was christened and died. This is all I know." The miracle is not one that will find much credit nowadays. But the devout custom was at least simple and intelligible enough, though it afforded an excellent occasion to attribute witchcraft to the one among those maidens who was not of Lagny but of God.

From Lagny Jeanne went on to various other places in danger, or which wanted encouragement and help. She made two or three hurried visits to Compiègne, which was threatened by both parties of the enemy; at one time raising the siege of Choicy, near Compiègne, in company with the Archbishop of Rheims, a strange brother in arms. On another of her visits to Compiègne there is said to have occurred an incident which, if true, reveals to us with very sad reality the trouble that overshadowed the Maid. She had gone to early mass in the Church of St. Jacques, and communicated, as was her custom. It must have been near Easter—perhaps the occasion of the first communion of some of the children who are so often referred to, among whom she loved to worship. She had retired behind a pillar on which she leaned as she stood, and a number of people, among whom were many children, drew near after the service to gaze at her. Jeanne's heart was full, and she had no one near to whom she could open it and relieve her soul. As she stood against the pillar her trouble burst forth. "Dear friends and children," she said, "I have to tell you that I have been sold and betrayed, and will soon be given up to death. I beg of you to pray for me; for soon I shall no longer have any power to serve the King and the kingdom." These words were told to the writer who records them, in the year 1498, by two very old men who had heard them, being children at the time. The scene was one to dwell in a child's recollection, and, if true, it throws a melancholy light upon the thoughts that filled the mind of Jeanne, though her actions may have seemed as energetic and her impulses as strong as in her best days.

At last the news came speeding through the country that Compiègne was being invested on all sides. It had been the headquarters of Charles and had received him with acclamations, and therefore the alarm of the townsfolk for the retribution awaiting them, should they fall into the hands of the enemy, was great; it was besides a very important position. Jeanne was at Crespy en Valois when this news reached her. She set out immediately (May 22, 1430) to carry aid to the garrison: "F'irai voir mes bons amis de Compiègne," she said. The words are on the base of her statue which now stands in the Place of that town. Something of her early impetuosity was in this impulse, and no apparent dread of any fatality. She rode all night at the head of her party, and arrived before the dawn, a May morning, the 23d, still a month from the fatal "St. Jean." Though the prophecy was always in her ears, she must have felt that whole month still before her, with a sensation of almost greater safety because the dangerous moment was fixed. The town received her with joy, and no doubt the satisfaction and relief which hailed her and her reinforcements gave additional fervour to the Maid, and drove out of her mind for a moment the fatal knowledge which oppressed it. There is some difficulty in understanding the events of this day, but the lucid narrative of Quicherat, which we shall now quote, gives a very vivid picture of it. Jeanne had timed her arrival so early in the morning, probably with the intention of keeping the adversaries in their camps unaware of so important an addition to the garrison, in order that she might surprise them by the sortie she had determined upon; but no doubt the news had leaked forth somehow, if through no other means, by the sudden ringing of the bells and sounds of joy from the city. She paid her usual visits to the churches, and noted and made all her arrangements for the sortie with her usual care, occupying the long summer day in these preparations. And it was not till five o'clock in the evening that everything was complete, and she sallied forth. We hear nothing of the state of the town, or of any suspicion existing at the time as to the governor Flavy who was afterwards believed by some to be the man who sold and betrayed her. It is a question debated warmly like all these questions. He was a man of bad reputation, but there is no evidence that he was a traitor. The incidents are all natural enough, and seem to indicate clearly the mere fortune of war upon which no man can calculate. We add from Quicherat the description of the field and what took place there:

"Compiègne is situated on the left bank of the Oise. On the other side extends a great meadow, nearly a mile broad, at the end of which the rising ground of Picardy rises suddenly like a wall, shutting in the horizon. The meadow is so low and so subject to floods that it is crossed by an ancient foot of the low hills. Three village churches mark the extent of the landscape visible from the walls of Compiègne; Margny (sometimes spelt Marigny) at the end of the road; Clairoix three quarters of a league higher up, at the confluence of the two rivers, the Aronde and the Oise, close to the spot where another tributary, the Aisne, also flows into the Oise; and Venette a mile and a half lower down. The Burgundians had one camp at Margny, another at Clairoix; the headquarters of the English were at Venette. As for the inhabitants of

Compiègne, their first defence facing the enemy was one of those redoubts or towers which the chronicles of the fifteenth century called a boulevard. It was placed at the end of the bridge and commanded the road.

"The plan of the Maid was to make a sortie towards the evening, to attack Margny and afterwards Clairoix, and then at the opening of the Aronde valley to meet the Duke of Burgundy and his forces who were lodged there, and who would naturally come to the aid of his other troops when attacked. She took no thought for the English, having already carefully arranged with Flavy how they should be prevented from cutting off her retreat. The governor provided against any chance of this by arming the boulevard strongly with archers to drive off any advancing force, and also by keeping ready on the Oise a number of covered boats to receive the foot-soldiers in case of a retrograde movement.

"The action began well: the garrison of Margny yielded in the twinkling of an eye. That of Clairoix rushing to the support of their brothers in arms was repulsed, then in its turn repulsed the French; and three times this alternative of advance and retreat took place on the flat ground of the meadow without serious injury to either party. This gave time to the English to take part in the fray; though thanks to the precautions of Flavy all they could do was to swell the ranks of the Burgundians. But unfortunately the rear of the Maid's army was struck with the possibility that a diversion might be attempted from behind, and their retreat cut off. A panic seized them; they broke their ranks, turned back and fled, some to the boats, some to the barrier of the boulevard. The English witnessing this flight rushed after them, secure now on the side of Compiègne, where the archers no longer ventured to shoot lest they should kill the fugitives instead of the enemies. They (the English) thus got possession of the raised road, and pushed on so hotly after the fugitives that their horses' heads touched the backs of the crowd. It thus became necessary for the safety of the town to close the gates until the barrier of the boulevard should be set up again."

These disastrous accidents had taken place while Jeanne, charging in front with her companions and body-guard, remained quite unaware of any misfortune. She would hear no call to retreat, even when her companions were roused to the dangers of their position. "Forward, they are ours!" was all her cry. As at St. Pierre-le-Moutier she was ready to defeat the Burgundian army alone. At length the others perceiving something of what had happened seized her bridle and forced her to retire. She was of herself too remarkable a figure to be concealed amid the group of armed men who rode with her, encircling her, defending the rear of the flying party. Over her armour she wore a crimson tunic, or according to some authorities a short cloak, of gorgeous material embroidered with gold, and though by this time the twilight must have afforded a partial shelter, yet the knowledge that she was there gave keenness to every eye. Behind, the scattered Burgundians had rallied and begun to pursue, while the armour and spears of the English glittered in front between the little party and the barrier which was blocked by a terrified crowd of fugitives. Even then a party of horsemen might have cut their way through; but at the moment when Jeanne and her followers drew near, the barrier was sharply closed and the wild, confused, and fighting crowd, treading each other down, struggling for life, were forced back upon the English lances. Thus the retreating band riding hard along the raised road, in order and unbroken, found the path suddenly barred by the forces of the enemy, the fugitives of their own army, and the closed gates of the town.

An attempt was then made by the Maid and her companions to turn towards the western gate where there still might have been a chance of safety; but by this time the smaller figure among all those steel-clad men, and the waving mantle, must have been distinguished through the dusk and the dust. There was a wild rush of combat and confusion, and in a moment she was surrounded, seized, her horse and her person, notwithstanding all resistance. With cries of "Rendez vous," and many an evil name, fierce faces and threatening weapons closed round her. One of her assailants—a Burgundian knight, a Picard archer, the accounts differ—caught her by her mantle and dragged her from her horse; no Englishman let us be thankful, though no doubt all were equally eager and ready. Into the midst of that shouting mass of men, in the blinding cloud of dust, in the darkening of the night, the Maid of France disappeared for one terrible moment, and was lost to view. And then, and not till then, came a clamour of bells into the night, and all the steeples of Compiègne trembled with the call to arms, a sally to save the deliverer. Was it treachery? Was it only a perception, too late, of the danger? There are not wanting voices to say that a prompt sally might have saved Jeanne, and that it was quite within the power of the Governor and city had they chosen. Who can answer so dreadful a suggestion? it is too much shame to human nature to believe it. Perhaps within Compiègne as without, they were too slow to perceive the supreme moment, too much overwhelmed to snatch any chance of rescue till it was too late.

Happily we have no light upon the tumult around the prisoner, the ugly triumph, the shouts and exultation of the captors who had seized the sorceress at last; nor upon the thoughts of Jeanne, with her threatened doom fulfilled and unknown horrors before her, upon which imagination must have thrown the most dreadful light, however strongly her courage was sustained by the promise of succour from on high. She had not been sent upon this mission as of old. No heavenly voice had said to her "Go and deliver Compiègne." She had undertaken that warfare on her own charges with no promise to encourage her, only the certainty of being overthrown "before the St. Jean." But the St. Jean was still far off, a long month of summer days between her and that moment of fate! So far as we can see Jeanne showed no unseemly weakness in this dark hour. One account tells us that she held her sword high over her head declaring that it was given by a higher than any who could claim its surrender there. But she neither struggled nor wept. Not a word against her constancy and courage could any one, then or after, find to say. The Burgundian chronicler tells us one thing, the French another. "The Maid, easily recognised by her costume of crimson and by the standard which she carried in her hand, alone continued to defend herself," says one; but that we are sure could not have been the case as long as d'Aulon, who accompanied her, was still able to keep on his horse. "She yielded and gave her parole to Lyonnel, bâtard de Wandomme," says another; but Jeanne herself declares that she gave her faith to no one, reserving to herself the right to escape if she could. In that dark evening scene nothing is clear except the fact that the Maid was taken, to the exultation and delight of her captors and to the terror and grief of the unhappy town, vainly screaming with all its bells to arms,—and with its sons and champions by hundreds dying under the English lances and in the dark waves of the Oise.

The archer or whoever it was who secured this prize, took Jeanne back, along the bloody road with its relics of the fight, to Margny, the Burgundian camp, where the leaders crowded together to see so important a prisoner. "Thither came soon after," says Monstrelet, "the Duke of Burgundy from his camp of Coudon, and there assembled the English, the said Duke and those of the other camps in great numbers, making, one with the other, great cries and rejoicings on the taking of the Maid: whom the said Duke went to see in the lodging where she was and spoke some words to her which I cannot call to mind, though I was there present; after which the said Duke and the others withdrew for the night, leaving the Maid in the keeping of Messer John of Luxembourg"—to whom she had been immediately sold by her first captor. The same night, Philip, this noble Duke and Prince of France, wrote a letter to convey the blessed information:

"The great news of this capture should be spread everywhere and brought to the knowledge of all, that they may see the error of those who could believe and lend themselves to the pretensions of such a woman. We write this in the hope of giving you joy, comfort, and consolation, and that you may thank God our Creator. Pray that it may be His holy will to be more and more favourable to the enterprises of our royal master and to the restoration of his sway over all his good and faithful subjects."

This royal master was Henry VI. of England, the baby king, doomed already to expiate sins that were not his, by the saddest life and reign. The French historians whimsically but perhaps not unnaturally, have the air of putting down this baseness on Philip's part, and on that of his contemporaries in general, to the score of the English, which is hard measure, seeing that the treachery of a Frenchman could in no way be attributed to the other nation of which he was the natural enemy, or at least, antagonist. Very naturally the subsequent proceedings in all their horror and cruelty are equally put down to the English account, although Frenchmen took, exulted over as a prisoner, tried and condemned as an enemy of God and the Church, the spotless creature who was France incarnate, the very embodiment of her country in all that was purest and noblest. We shall see with what spontaneous zeal all France, except her own small party, set to work to accomplish this noble office.

Almost before one could draw breath the University of Paris claimed her as a proper victim for the Inquisition. Compiègne made no sally for her deliverance; Charles, no attempt to ransom her. From end to end of France not a finger was lifted for her rescue; the women wept over her, the poor people still crowded around the prisoner wherever seen, but the France of every public document, of every practical power, the living nation, when it did not utter cries of hatred, kept silence. We in England have over and over again acknowledged with shame our guilty part in her murder; but still to this day the Frenchman tries to shield his under cover of the English influence and terror. He cannot deny La Tremoïlle, nor Cauchon, nor the University, nor the learned doctors who did the deed; individually he is ready to give them all up to the everlasting fires which one cannot but hope are kept alive for some people in spite of all modern benevolences; but he skilfully turns back to the English as a moving cause of everything. Nothing can be more untrue. The English were not better than the French, but they had the excuse at least of being the enemy. France saved by a happy chance her blanches mains from the actual blood of the pure and spotless Maid; but with exultation she prepared the victim for the stake, sent her thither, played with her like a cat with a mouse and condemned her to the fire. This is not to free us from our share: but it is the height of hypocrisy to lay the blood of Jeanne, entirely to our door.

Thus Jeanne's inspiration proved itself over again in blood and tears; it had been proved already on battle-field and city wall, with loud trumpets of joy and victory. But the "voices" had spoken again, sounding another strain; not always of glory—it is not the way of God; but of prison, downfall, distress. "Be not astonished at it," they said to her; "God will be with you." From day to day they had spoken in the same strain, with no joyful commands to go forth and conquer, but the one refrain: "Before the St. Jean." Perhaps there was a certain relief in her mind at first when the blow fell and the prophecy was accomplished. All she had to do now was to suffer, not to be surprised, to trust in God that He would support her. To Jeanne, no doubt, in the confidence and inexperience of her youth, that meant that God would deliver her. And so He did; but not as she expected. The sunshine of her life was over, and now the long shadow, the bitter storm was to come.

Nothing could be more remarkable than the response of France in general to this extraordinary event. In Paris there were bonfires lighted to show their joy, the Te Deum was sung at Notre Dame. At the Court Charles and his counsellors amused themselves with another prophet, a shepherd from the hills who was to rival Jeanne's best achievements, but never did so. Only the towns which she had delivered had still a tender thought for Jeanne. At Tours the entire population appeared in the streets with bare feet, singing the Miserere in penance and affliction. Orleans and Blois made public prayers for her safety. Rheims, in which there was much independent interest in Jeanne and her truth, had to be specially soothed by a letter from the Archbishop, in which he made out with great cleverness that it was the fault of Jeanne alone that she was taken. "She did nothing but by her own will, without obeying the commandments of God," he says; "she would hear no counsel, but followed her own pleasure,"; and it is in this letter that we hear of the shepherd lad who was to replace Jeanne, and that it was his opinion or revelation that God had suffered the Maid to be taken because of her growing pride, because she loved fine clothes, and preferred her own will to any guidance. We do not know whether this contented the city of Rheims; similar reasoning however seems to have silenced France. Nobody uttered a protest, nor struck a blow; the mournful procession of Tours, where she had been first known in the outset of her career, the prayers of Orleans which she had delivered, are the only exceptions we know of. Otherwise there was lifted in France neither voice nor hand to avert her doom.

CHAPTER X — THE CAPTIVE. MAY, 1430-JAN., 1431.

We have here to remark a complete suspension of all the ordinary laws at once of chivalry and of honest warfare. Jeanne had been captured as a general at the head of her forces. She was a prisoner of war. Such a prisoner ordinarily, even in the most cruel ages, is in no bodily danger. He is worth more alive than dead—a great ransom perhaps—perhaps the very end of the warfare, and the accomplishment of everything it was intended to gain: at least he is most valuable to exchange for other important prisoners on the opposite side. It was like taking away so much personal property to kill a prisoner, an outrage deeply resented by his captor and unjustified by any law. It was true that Jeanne herself had transgressed this universal custom but a little while before, by giving up Franquet d'Arras to his prosecutors. But Franquet was beyond the courtesies of war, a noted criminal, robber, and destroyer: yet she ought not perhaps to have departed from the military laws of right and wrong while everything in the country was under the hasty arbitration of war. No one, however, so far as we know, produces this matter of Franquet as a precedent in her own case. From the first moment of her seizure there was no question of the custom and privilege of warfare. She was taken as a wild animal might have been taken, the only doubt being how to make the most signal example of her. Vengeance in the gloomy form of the Inquisition claimed her the first day. No such word as ransom was breathed from her own side, none was demanded, none was offered. Her case is at once separated from every other.

Yet the reign of chivalry was at its height, and women were supposed to be the objects of a kind of worship, every knight being sworn to succour and help them in need and trouble. There was perhaps something of the subtle jealousy of sex so constantly denied on the stronger side, but yet always existing, in the abrogation of every law of chivalry as well as of warfare, in respect to the Maid. That man is indeed of the highest strain of generosity who can bear to be beaten by a woman. And all the seething, agitated world of France had been beaten by this girl. The English and Burgundians, in the ordinary sense of the word, had been overcome in fair field, forced to fly before her; the French, her own side, had experienced an even more penetrating downfall by having the honours of victory taken from them, she alone winning the day where they had all failed. This is bitterer, perhaps, than merely to be compelled to raise a siege or to fail in a fight. The Frenchmen fought like lions, but the praise was to Jeanne who never struck a blow. Such great hearts as Dunois, such a courteous prince as Alençon, were too magnanimous to feel, or at least to resent, the grievance; they seconded her and fought under her with a nobility of mind and disinterestedness beyond praise; but it was not to be supposed that the common mass of the French captains were like these; she had wronged and shamed them by taking the glory from them, as much as she had shamed the English by making those universal victors fly before her. The burghers whom she had rescued, the poor people who were her brethren and whom she sought everywhere, might weep and cry out to Heaven, but they were powerless at such a moment. And every law that might have helped her was pushed aside.

On the 25th the news was known in Paris, and immediately there appears in the record a new adversary to Jeanne, the most bitter and implacable of all; the next day, May 26, 1430, without the loss of an hour, a letter was addressed to the Burgundian camp from the capital. Quicherat speaks of it as a letter from the Inquisitor or vicar-general of the Inquisition, written by the officials of the University; others tell us that an independent letter was sent from the University to second that of the Inquisitor. The University we may add was not a university like one of ours, or like any existing at the present day. It was an ecclesiastical corporation of the highest authority in every cause connected with the Church, while gathering law, philosophy, and literature under its wing. The first theologians, the most eminent jurists were collected there, not by any means always in alliance with the narrower tendencies and methods of the Inquisition. It is notable, however, that this great institution lost no time in claiming the prisoner, whose chief offence in its eyes was less her career as a warrior than her position as a sorceress. The actual facts of her life were of secondary importance to them. Orleans, Rheims, even her attack upon Paris were nothing in comparison with the black art which they believed to be her inspiration. The guidance of Heaven which was not the guidance of the Church was to them a claim which meant only rebellion of the direst kind. They had longed to seize her and strip her of her presumptuous pretensions from the first moment of her appearance. They could not allow a day of her overthrow to pass by without snatching at this much-desired victim.

No one perhaps will ever be able to say what it is that makes a trial for heresy and sorcery, especially in the days when fire and flame, the rack and the stake, stood at the end, so exciting and horribly attractive to the mind. Whether it is the revelations that are hoped for, of these strange commerces between earth and the unknown, into which we would all fain pry if we could, in pursuit of some better understanding than has ever yet fallen to the lot of man; whether it is the strange and dreadful pleasure of seeing a soul driven to extremity and fighting for its life through all the subtleties of thought and fierce attacks of interrogation—or the mere love of inflicting torture, misery, and death, which the Church was prevented from doing in the common way, it is impossible to tell; but there is no doubt that a thrill like the wings of vultures crowding to the prey, a sense of horrible claws and beaks and greedy eyes is in the air, whenever such a tribunal is thought of. The thrill, the stir, the eagerness among those black birds of doom is more evident than usual in the headlong haste of that demand. Sous l'influence de l'Angleterre, say the historians; the more shame for them if it was so; but they were clearly under influence wider and more infallible, the influence of that instinct, whatever it may be, which makes a trial for heresy ten thousand times more cruel, less restrained by any humanities of nature, than any other kind of trial which history records.

That is what the Inquisitor demanded after a long description of Jeanne, "called the Maid," as having "dogmatised, sown, published, and caused to be published, many and diverse errors from which have ensued great scandals against the divine honour and our holy faith." "Using the rights of our office and the authority committed to us by the Holy See of Rome we instantly command, and enjoin you in the name of the Catholic faith, and under penalty of the law: and all other Catholic persons of whatsoever condition, pre-eminence, authority, or estate, to send or to bring as prisoner before us with all speed and surety the said Jeanne, vehemently suspected of various crimes springing from heresy, that proceedings may be taken against her before us in the name of the Holy Inquisition, and with the favour and aid of the doctors and masters of the University of Paris, and other notable counsellors present there."

It was the English who put it into the heads of the Inquisitor and the University to do this, all the anxious Frenchmen cry. We can only reply again, the more shame for the French doctors and priests! But there was very little time to bring that influence to bear; and there is an eagerness and precipitation in the demand which is far more like the headlong natural rush for a much desired prize than any course of action suggested by a third party. Nor is there anything to lead us to believe that the movement was not spontaneous. It is little likely, indeed, that the Sorbonne nowadays would concern itself about any inspired maid, any more than the enlightened Oxford would do so. But the ideas of the fifteenth century were widely different, and witchcraft and heresy were the most enthralling and exciting of subjects, as they are still to whosoever believes in them, learned or unlearned, great or small.

It must be added that the entire mind of France, even of those who loved Jeanne and believed in her, must have been shaken to its depths by this catastrophe. We have no sympathy with those who compare the career of any mortal martyr with the far more mysterious agony and passion of our Lord. Yet we cannot but remember what a tremendous element the disappointment of their hopes must have been in the misery of the first disciples, the Apostles, the mother, all the spectators who had watched with wonder and faith the mission of the Messiah. Had it failed? had all the signs come to nothing, all those divine words and ways, to our minds so much more wonderful than any miracles? Was there no meaning in them? Were they mere unaccountable delusions, deceptions of the senses, inspirations perhaps of mere genius—not from God at all except in a secondary way? In the three terrible days that followed the Crucifixion the burden of a world must have lain on the minds of those who had seen every hope fail: no legions of angels appearing, no overwhelming revelation from heaven, no change in a moment out of misery into the universal kingship, the triumphant march. That was but the self-delusion of the earth which continually travesties the schemes of Heaven; yet the most terrible of all despairs is such a pause and horror of doubt lest nothing should be true.

But in the case of this little Maiden, this handmaid of the Lord, the deception might have been all natural and perhaps shared by herself. Were her first triumphs accidents merely, were her "voices" delusions, had she been given up by Heaven, of which she had called herself the servant? It was a stupor which quenched every voice—a great silence through the country, only broken by the penitential psalms at Tours. The Compiègne people, writing to Charles two days after May 23d, do not mention Jeanne at all. We need not immediately take into account the baser souls always plentiful, the envious captains and the rest who might be secretly rejoicing. The entire country, both friends and foes, had come to a dreadful pause and did not know what to think. The last circumstance of which we must remind the reader, and which was of the greatest importance, is, that it was only a small part of France that knew anything personally of Jeanne. From Tours it is a far cry to Picardy. All her triumphs had taken place in the south. The captive of Beaulieu and Beaurevoir spent the sad months of her captivity among a population which could have heard of her only by flying rumours coming from hostile quarters. From the midland of France to the sea, near to which her prison was situated, is a long way, and those northern districts were as unlike the Orleannais as if they had been in two different countries. Rouen in Normandy no more resembled Rheims, than Edinburgh resembled London: and in the fifteenth century that was saying a great deal. Nothing can be more deceptive than to think of these separate and often hostile duchies as if they bore any resemblance to the France of to-day.

The captor of Jeanne was a vassal of Jean de Luxembourg and took her as we have seen to the quarters of his master at Margny, into whose hands she thenceforward passed. She was kept in the camp three or four days and then transferred to the castle of Beaulieu, which belonged to him; and afterwards to the more important stronghold of Beaurevoir, which seems to have been his principal residence. We know very few details of her captivity. According to one chronicler, d'Aulon, her faithful friend and intendant, was with her at least in the former of those prisons, where at first she would appear to have been hopeful and in good spirits, if we may trust to the brief conversation between her and d'Aulon, which is one of the few details which reach us of that period. While he lamented over the probable fate of Compiègne she was confident. "That poor town of Compiègne that you loved so much," he said, "by this time it will be in the hands of the enemies of France." "No," said the Maid, "the places which the king of Heaven brought back to the allegiance of the gentle King Charles by me, will not be retaken by his enemies." In this case at least the prophecy came true.

And perhaps there might have been at first a certain relief in Jeanne's mind, such as often follows after a long threatened blow has fallen. She had no longer the vague tortures of suspense, and probably believed that she would be ransomed as was usual: and in this silence and seclusion her "voices" which she had not obeyed as at first, but yet which had not abandoned her, nor shown estrangement, were more near and audible than amid the noise and tumult of war. They spoke to her often, sometimes three times a day, as she afterwards said, in the unbroken quiet of her prison. And though they no longer spoke of new enterprises and victories, their words were full of consolation. But it was not long that Jeanne's young and vigorous spirit could content itself with inaction. She was no mystic; willingly giving herself over to dreams and visions is more possible to the old than to the young. Her confidence and hope for her good friends of Compiègne gave way before the continued tale of their sufferings, and the inveterate siege which was driving them to desperation. No doubt the worst news was told to Jeanne, and twice over she made a desperate attempt to escape, in hope of being able to succour them, but without any sanction, as she confesses, from her spiritual instructors. At Beaulieu the attempt was simple enough: the narrative seems to imply that the doorway, or some part of the wall of her room, had been closed with laths or planks nailed across an opening: and between these she succeeded in slipping, "as she was very slight," with the hope of locking the door to an adjoining guard-room upon the men who had charge of her, and thus getting free. But alas! The porter of the château, who had no business there, suddenly appeared in the corridor, and she was discovered and taken back to her chamber. At Beaurevoir, which was farther off, her attempt was a much more desperate one, and indicates a despair and irritation of mind which had become unbearable. At this place her own condition was much alleviated; the castle was the residence of Jean de Luxembourg's wife and aunt, ladies who visited Jeanne continually, and soon became interested and attached to her; but as the master of the house was himself in the camp before Compiègne, they had the advantage or disadvantage, as far as the prisoner was concerned, of constant news, and Jeanne's trouble for her friends grew daily.

She seems, indeed, after the assurance she had expressed at first, to have fallen into great doubt and even carried on within herself a despairing argument with her spiritual guides on this point, battling with these saintly influences as in the depths of the troubled heart many have done with the Creator Himself in similar circumstances. "How," she cried, "could God let them perish who had been so good and loyal to their King?" St. Catherine replied gently that He would Himself care for these bons amis, and even promised that "before the St. Martin" relief would come. But Jeanne had probably by this time—in her great disappointment and loneliness, and with the sense in her of so much power to help were she only free—got beyond her own control. They bade her to be patient. One of them, amid their exhortations to accept her fate cheerfully, and not to be astonished at it, seems to have conveyed to her mind the impression that she should not be delivered till she had seen the King of England. "Truly I will not see him! I would rather die than fall into the hands of the English," cried Jeanne in her petulance. The King of England is spoken of always, it is curious to note, as if he had been a great, severe ruler like his father, never as the child he really was. But Jeanne in her helplessness and impotence was impatient even with her saints. Day by day the news came in from Compiègne, all that was favourable to the Burgundians received with joy and thanksgiving by the ladies of Luxembourg, while the captive consumed her heart with vain indignation. At last Jeanne would seem to have wrought herself up to the most desperate of expedients. Whether her room was in the donjon, or whether she was allowed sufficient freedom in the house to mount to the battlements there, we are not informed—probably the latter was the case: for it was from the top of the tower that the rash girl at last flung herself down, carried away by what sudden frenzy of alarm or sting of evil tidings can never be known. Probably she had hoped that a miracle would be wrought on her behalf, and that faith was all that was wanted, as on so many other occasions. Perhaps she had heard of the negotiations to sell her to the English, which would give a keener urgency to her determination to get free; all that appears in the story, however, is her wild anxiety about Compiègne and her bons amis. How she escaped destruction no one knows. She was rescued for a more tremendous and harder fate.

The Maid was taken up as dead from the foot of the tower (the height is estimated at sixty feet); but she was not dead, nor even seriously hurt. Her frame, so slight that she had been able to slip between the bars put up to secure her, had so little solidity that the shock would seem to have been all that ailed her. She was stunned and unconscious and remained so far some time; and for three days neither ate nor drank. But though she was so humbled by the effects of the fall, "she was comforted by St. Catherine, who bade her confess and implore the mercy of God" for her rash disobedience—and repeated the promise that before Martinmas Compiègne should be relieved. Jeanne did not perhaps in her rebellion deserve this encouragement; but the heavenly ladies were kind and pitiful and did not stand upon their dignity. The wonderful thing was that Jeanne recovered perfectly from this tremendous leap.

The earthly ladies, though so completely on the other side, were scarcely less kind to the Maid. They visited her daily, carried their news to her, were very friendly and sweet: and no doubt other visitors came to make the acquaintance of a prisoner so wonderful. There was one point on which they were very urgent, and this was about her dress. It shamed and troubled them to see her in the costume of a man. Jeanne had her good reasons for that, which perhaps she did not care to tell them, fearing to shock the ears of a demoiselle of Luxembourg with the suggestion of dangers of which she knew nothing. No doubt it was true that while doing the serious work of war, as she said afterwards, it was best that she should be dressed as a man; but Jeanne had reason to know besides, that it was safer, among the rough comrades and gaolers who now surrounded her, to wear the tight-fitting and firmly fastened dress of a soldier. She answered the ladies and their remonstrances with all the grace of a courtier. Could she have done it she would rather have yielded the point to them, she said, than to any one else in France, except the Queen. The women wherever she went were always faithful to this young creature, so pure-womanly in her young angel-hood and man-hood. The poor followed to kiss her hands or her armour, the rich wooed her with tender flatteries and persuasions. There is not record in all her career of any woman who was not her friend.

For the last dreary month of that winter she was sent to the fortress of Crotoy on the Somme, for what reason we are not told, probably to be more near the English into whose hands she was about to be given up: again another shameful bargain in which the guilt lies with the Burgundians and not with the English. If Charles I. was sold as we Scots all indignantly deny, the shame of the sale was on our nation, not on England, whom nobody has ever blamed for the transaction. The sale of Jeanne was brutally frank. It was indeed a ransom which was paid to Jean of Luxembourg with a share to the first captor, the archer who had secured her; but it was simple blood-money as everybody knew. At Crotoy she had once more the solace of female society, again with much pressing upon her of their own heavy skirts and hanging sleeves. A fellow-prisoner in the dungeon of Crotoy, a priest, said mass every day and gave her the holy communion. And her mind seems to have been soothed and calmed. Compiègne was relieved; the saints had kept their word: she had that burden the less upon her soul: and over the country there were against stirrings of French valour and success. The day of the Maid was over, but it began to bear the fruit of a national quickening of vigour and life.

It was at Crotoy, in December, that she was transferred to English hands. The eager offer of the University of Paris to see her speedy condemnation had not been accepted, and perhaps the Burgundians had been willing to wait, to see if any ransom was forthcoming from France. Perhaps too, Paris, which sang the Te Deum when she was taken prisoner, began to be a little startled by its own enthusiasm and to ask itself the question what there was to be so thankful about?—a result which has happened before in the history of that impulsive city:—and Paris was too near the centre of France, where the balance seemed to be turning again in favour of the national party, to have its thoughts distracted by such a trial as was impending. It seemed better to the English leaders to conduct their prisoner to a safer place, to the depths of Normandy where they were most strong. They seem to have carried her away in the end of the year, travelling slowly along the coast, and reaching Rouen by way of Eu and Dieppe, as far away as possible from any risk of rescue. She arrived in Rouen in the beginning of the year 1431, having thus been already for nearly eight months in close custody. But there were no further ministrations of kind women for Jeanne. She was now distinctly in the hands of her enemies, those who had no sympathy or natural softening of feeling towards her.

The severities inflicted upon her in her new prison at Rouen were terrible, almost incredible. We are told that she was kept in an iron cage (like the Countess of Buchan in earlier days by Edward I.), bound hands, and feet, and throat, to a pillar, and watched incessantly by English soldiers—the latter being an abominable and hideous method of torture which was never departed from during the rest of her life. Afterwards, at the beginning of her trial she was relieved from the cage, but never from the presence and scrutiny of this fierce and hateful bodyguard. Such detestable cruelties were in the manner of the time, which does not make us the less sicken at them with burning indignation and the rage of shame. For this aggravation of her sufferings England alone was responsible. The Burgundians at their worst had not used her so. It is true that she was to them a piece of valuable property worth so much good money; which is a powerful argument everywhere. But to the English she meant no money: no one offered to ransom Jeanne on the side of her own party, for whom she had done so much. Even at Tours and Orleans, so far as appears, there was no subscription—to speak in modern terms,—no cry among the burghers to gather their crowns for her redemption—not a word, not an effort, only a barefooted procession, a mass, a Miserere, which had no issue. France stood silent to see what would come of it; and her scholars and divines swarmed towards Rouen to make sure that nothing but harm should come of it to the ignorant country lass, who had set up such pretences of knowing better than others. The King congratulated himself that he had another prophetess as good as she, and a Heaven-sent boy from the mountains who would do as well and better than Jeanne. Where was Dunois? Where was La Hire, a soldier bound by no conventions, a captain whose troop went like the wind where it listed, and whose valour was known? Where was young Guy de Laval, so ready to sell his lands that his men might be fit for service? All silent; no man drawing a sword or saying a word. It is evident that in this frightful pause of fate, Jeanne had become to France as to England, the Witch whom it was perhaps a danger to have had anything to do with, whose spells had turned the world upside down for a moment: but these spells had become ineffectual or worn out as is the nature of sorcery. No explanation, not even the well-worn and so often valid one of human baseness, could explain the terrible situation, if not this.

CHAPTER XI — THE JUDGES. 1431.

The name of Pierre Cauchon, Bishop of Beauvais, appears to us at this long distance as arising out of the infernal mists, into which, when his ministry of shame was accomplished, he disappeared again, bearing with him nothing but hatred and ill fame. Yet in his own day and to his contemporaries, he was not an inconsiderable man. He was of Rheims, a great student, and excellent scholar, the friend of many good men, highly esteemed among the ranks of the learned, a good man of business, which is not always the attribute of a scholar, and at the same time a Burgundian of pronounced sentiments, holding for his Duke, against the King. When Beauvais was summoned by Charles, after his coronation, at that moment of universal triumph when all seemed open for him to march upon Paris if he would, the city had joyfully thrown open its doors to the royal army, and in doing so had driven out its Bishop, who was hot on the other side. He would not seem to have been wanted in Paris at that moment. The "triste Bedford," as Michelet calls him, had no means of employing an ambitious priest, no dirty work for the moment to give him. It is natural to suppose that a man so admirably adapted for that employment went in search of it to the ecclesiastical court, not beloved of England, which the Cardinal Bishop of Winchester held there. Winchester was the only one of the House of Lancaster who had money to carry on the government either at home or abroad. The two priests, as the historians are always pleased to insinuate in respect to ecclesiastics, soon understood each other, and Winchester became aware that he had in Cauchon a tool ready for any shameful enterprise. It is not, however, necessary to assume so much as this, for we have not the least reason to believe that either one or the other of them had the slightest doubt on the subject of Jeanne, or as to her character. She was a pernicious witch, filling a hitherto invincible army with that savage fright which is but too well understood among men, and which produces cruel outrages as well as cowardly panic. The air of this very day, while I write, is ringing with the story of a woman burnt to death by her own family under the influence of that same horrible panic and terror. Cauchon was the countryman, almost the pays—an untranslatable expression,—of Jeanne; but he did not believe in her any more than the loftier ecclesiastics of France believed in Bernadette of Lourdes, who was of the spiritual lineage of Jeanne, nor than we should believe to-day in a similar pretender. It seems unnecessary then to think of dark plots hatched between these two dark priests against the white, angelic apparition of the Maid.

What services Cauchon had done to recommend him to the favour of Winchester we are not told, but he was so much in favour that the Cardinal had recommended him to the Pope for the vacant archbishopric of Rouen a few months before there was any immediate question of Jeanne. The appointment was opposed by the clergy of Rouen, and the Pope had not come to any decision as yet on the subject. But no doubt the ambition of Cauchon made him very eager, with such a tempting prize before him, to recommend himself to his English patron by every means in his power. And he it was who undertook the office of negotiating the ransom of Jeanne from the hands of Jean de Luxembourg. We doubt whether after all it would be just even to call this a nefarious bargain. To the careless seigneur it would probably be very much a matter of course. The ransom offered—six thousand francs—was as good as if she had been a prince. The ladies at home might be indignant, but what was their foolish fancy for a high-flown girl in comparison with these substantial crowns in his pocket; and to be free from the responsibility of guarding her would be an advantage too. And if her own party did not stir on her behalf, why should he? A most pertinent question. Cauchon, on the other hand, could assure all objectors that no summary vengeance was to be taken on the Maid. She was to be judged by the Church, and by the best men the University could provide, and if she were found innocent, no doubt would go free.

They must have been sanguine indeed who hoped for a triumphant acquittal of Jeanne; but still it may have been hoped that a trial by her countrymen would in every case be better for her than to languish in prison or to be seized perhaps by the English on some after occasion, and to perish by their hands. Let us therefore be fair to Cauchon, if possible, up to the beginning of the Procès. He was no Frenchman, but a Burgundian; his allegiance was to his Duke, not to the King of England; but his natural sovereign did so, and many, very many men of note and importance were equally base, and did not esteem it base at all. Had the inhabitants of Rheims, his native town, or of Rouen, in which his trial and downfall took place as well as Jeanne's, pronounced for the King of Prussia in the last war, and proclaimed themselves his subjects, the traitors would have been hung with infamy from their own high towers, or driven into their river headlong. But things were very different in the fifteenth century. There has never been a moment in our history when either England or Scotland has pronounced for a foreign sway. Scotland fought with desperation for centuries against the mere name of suzerainty, though of a kindred race. There have been terrible moments of forced subjugation at the point of the sword; but never any such phenomena as appeared in France, so far on in the world's history as was that brilliant and highly cultured age. Such a state of affairs is to our minds impossible to understand or almost to believe: but in the interests of justice it must be fully acknowledged and understood.

Cauchon arises accordingly, not at first with any infamy, out of the obscurity. He had been expelled and dethroned from his See, but this only for political reasons. He was ecclesiastically Bishop of Beauvais still; it was within his diocese that the Maid had taken prisoner, and there also her last acts of magic, if magic there was, had taken place. He had therefore a legal right to claim the jurisdiction, a right which no one had any interest in taking from him. If Paris was disappointed at not having so interesting a trial carried on before its courts, there was compensation in the fact that many doctors of the University were called to assist Cauchon in his examination of the Maid, and to bring her, witch, sorceress, heretic, whatever she might be, to question. These doctors were not undistinguished or unworthy men. A number of them held high office in the Church; almost all were honourably connected with the University, the source of learning in France. "With what art were they chosen!" exclaims M. Blaze de Bury. "A number of theologians, the élite of the time, had been named to represent France at the council of Bâle; of these Cauchon chose the flower." This does not seem on the face of it to be a fact against, but rather in favour of, the tribunal, which the reader naturally supposes must have been the better, the more just, for being chosen among the flower of learning in France. They were not men who could be imagined to be the tools of any Bishop. Quicherat, in his moderate and able remarks on this subject, selects for special mention three men who took a very important part in it, Guillame Érard, Nicole Midi, and Tomas de Courcelles. They were all men who held a high place in the respect of their generation. Érard was a friend of Machet, the confessor of Charles VII., who had been a member of the tribunal at Poitiers which first pronounced upon the pretensions of Jeanne; yet after the trial of the Maid Machet still describes him as a man of the highest virtue and heavenly wisdom. Nicole Midi continued to hold an honourable place in his University for many years, and was the man chosen to congratulate Charles when Paris finally became again the residence of the King. Courcelles was considered the first theologian of the age. "He was an austere and eloquent young man," says Quicherat, "of a lucid mind, though nourished on abstractions. He was the first of theologians long before he had attained the age at which he could assume the rank of doctor, and even before he had finished his studies he was considered as the successor of Gerson. He was the light of the council of Bâle. Eneas Piccolomini (Pope Pius II.) speaks with admiration of his capacity and his modesty. In him we recognise the father of the freedom of the Gallican Church. His disinterestedness is shown by the simple position with which he contented himself. He died with no higher rank than that of Dean of the Chapter of Paris."

Did this in Cæsar seem ambitious? Was this the man to be used for their vile ends by a savage English party thirsting for the blood of an innocent victim, and by the vile priest who was its tool? It does not seem so to our eyes across the long level of the centuries which clear away so many mists. And no more dreadful accusation can be brought against France than the suggestion that men like these, her best and most carefully trained, were willing to act as blood-hounds for the advantage and the pay of the invader. But there are many French historians to whom the mere fact of a black gown or at least an ecclesiastical robe, confounds every testimony, and to whom even the name of Frenchman does not make it appear possible that a priest should retain a shred of honour or of honesty. We should have said by the light of nature and probability that had every guarantee been required for the impartiality and justice of such a tribunal, they could not have been better secured than by the selection of such men to conduct its proceedings. They made a great and terrible mistake, as the wisest of men have made before now. They did much worse, they behaved to an unfortunate girl who was in their power with indescribable ferocity and cruelty; but we must hope that this was owing to the period at which they lived rather than to themselves.

It is not perhaps indeed from the wise and learned, the Stoics and Pundits of a University, that we should choose judges for the divine simplicity of those babes and sucklings out of whose mouth praise is perfected. At the same time to choose the best men is not generally the way adopted to procure a base judgement. Cauchon might have been subject to this blame had he filled the benches of his court with creatures of his own, nameless priests and dialecticians, knowing nothing but their own poor science of words. He did not do so. There were but two Englishmen in the assembly, neither of them men of any importance or influence although there must have been many English priests in the country and in the train of Winchester. There were not even any special partisans of Burgundy, though some of the assessors were Burgundian by birth. We should have said, had we known no more than this, that every precaution had been taken to give the Maid the fairest trial. But at the same time a trial which is conducted under the name of the Inquisition is always suspect. The mere fact of that terrible name seems to establish a foregone conclusion; few are the prisoners at that bar who have ever escaped. This fact is almost all that can be set against the high character of the individuals who composed the tribunal. At all events it is no argument against the English that they permitted the best men in France to be chosen as Jeanne's judges. It is the most bewildering and astonishing of historical facts that they were so, and yet came to the conclusion they did, by the means they did, and that without falling under the condemnation, or scorn, or horror of their fellow-men.

This then was the assembly which gathered in Rouen in the beginning of 1431. Quicherat will not venture to affirm even that intimidation was directly employed to effect their decision. He says that the evidence "tends to prove" that this was the case, but honestly allows that, "it is well to remark that the witnesses contradict each other." "In all that I have said," he adds, "my intention has been to prove that the judges of the Maid had in no way the appearance of partisans hotly pursuing a political vengeance; but that, on the contrary, their known weight, the consideration which most of them enjoyed, and the nature of the tribunal for which they were assembled, were all calculated to produce generally an expectation full of confidence and respect."

Meanwhile there is not a word to be said for the treatment to which Jeanne herself was subjected, she being, so far as is apparent, entirely in English custody. She had been treated with tolerable gentleness it would seem in the first part of her captivity while in the hands of Jean de Luxembourg, the Count de Ligny. The fact that the ladies of the house were for her friends must have assured this, and there is no complaint made anywhere of cruelty or even unkindness. When she arrived in Rouen she was confined in the middle chamber of the donjon, which was the best we may suppose, neither a dungeon under the soil, nor a room under the leads, but one to which there was access by a short flight of steps from the courtyard, and which was fully lighted and not out of reach or sight of life. But in this chamber was an iron cage, within which she was bound, feet, and waist and neck, from the time of her arrival until the beginning of the trial, a period of about six weeks. Five English soldiers of the lowest class watched her night and day, three in the room itself, two at the door. It is enough to think for a moment of the probable manners and morals of these troopers to imagine what torture must have been inflicted by their presence upon a young woman who had always been sensitive above all things to the laws of personal modesty and reserve. Their course jests would no doubt be unintelligible to her, which would be an alleviation; but their coarse laughter, their revolting touch, their impure looks, would be an endless incessant misery. We are told that she indignantly bestowed a hearty buffet on the cheek of a tailor who approached her too closely when it was intended to furnish her with female dress; but she was helpless to defend herself when in her irons, and had to endure as she best could—the bars of her cage let us hope, if cage there was, affording her some little protection from the horror of the continual presence of these rude attendants, with whom it was a shame to English gentlemen and knights to surround a helpless woman.

When her trial began Jeanne was released from her cage, but was still chained by one foot to a wooden beam during the day, and at night to the posts of her bed. Sometimes her guards would wake her to tell her that she had been condemned and was immediately to be led forth to execution; but that was a small matter. Attempts were also made to inflict the barest insult and outrage upon her, and on one occasion she is said to have been saved only by the Earl of Warwick, who heard her cries and went to her rescue. By night as by day she clung to her male garb, tightly fastened by the innumerable "points" of which Shakespeare so often speaks. Such were the horrible circumstances in which she awaited her public appearance before her judges. She was brought before them every day for months together, to be badgered by the keenest wits in France, coming back and back with artful questions upon every detail of every subject, to endeavour to shake her firmness or force her into self-contradiction. Imagine a cross-examination going on for months, like those—only more cruel than those—to which we sometimes see an unfortunate witness exposed in our own courts of law. There is nothing more usual than to see people break down entirely after a day or two of such a tremendous ordeal, in which their hearts and lives are turned inside out, their minds so bewildered that they know not what they are saying, and everything they have done in their lives exhibited in the worst, often in an entirely fictitious, light, to the curiosity and amusement of the world.

But all our processes are mercy in comparison with those to which French prisoners at the bar are still exposed. It is unnecessary to enter into an account of these which are so well known; but they show that even such a trial as that of Jeanne was by no means so contrary to common usage, as it would be, and always would have been in England. In England we warn the accused to utter no rash word which may be used against him; in France the first principle is to draw from him every rash word that he can be made to bring forth. This was the method employed with Jeanne. Her judges were all Churchmen and dialecticians of the subtlest wit and most dexterous faculties in France; they had all, or almost all, a strong prepossession against her. Though we cannot believe that men of such quality were suborned, there was, no doubt, enough of jealous and indignant feeling among them to make the desire of convicting Jeanne more powerful with them than the desire for pure justice. She was a true Christian, but not perhaps the soundest of Church-women. Her visions had not the sanction of any priest's approval, except indeed the official but not warm affirmation of the Council at Poitiers. She had not hastened to take the Church into her confidence nor to put herself under its protection. Though her claims had been guaranteed by the company of divines at Poitiers, she herself had always appealed to her private instructions, through her saints, rather than to the guiding of any priest. The chief ecclesiastical dignitary of her own party had just held her up to the reprobation of the people for this cause: she was too independent, so proud that she would take no advice but acted according to her own will. The more accustomed a Churchman is to experience the unbounded devotion and obedience of women, the more enraged he is against those who judge for themselves or have other guides on whom they rely. Jeanne was, beside all other sins alleged against her, a presumptuous woman: and very few of these men had any desire to acquit her. They were little accustomed to researches which were solely intended to discover the truth: their principle rather was, as it has been the principle of many, to obtain proofs that their own particular way of thinking was the right one. It is not perhaps very good even for a system of doctrine when this is the principle by which it is tested. It is more fatal still, on this principle, to judge an individual for death or for life. It will be abundantly proved, however, by all that is to follow, that in face of this tribunal, learned, able, powerful, and prejudiced, the peasant girl of nineteen stood like a rock, unmoved by all their cleverness, undaunted by their severity, seldom or never losing her head, or her temper, her modest steadfastness, or her high spirit. If they hoped to have an easy bargain of her, never were men more mistaken. Not knowing a from b, as she herself said, untrained, unaided, she was more than a match for them all.

Round about this centre of eager intelligence, curiosity, and prejudice, the cathedral and council chamber teeming with Churchmen, was a dark and silent ring of laymen and soldiers. A number of the English leaders were in Rouen, but they appear very little. Winchester, who had very lately come from England with an army, which according to some of the historians would not budge from Calais, where it had landed, "for fear of the Maid"—was the chief person in the place, but did not make any appearance at the trial, curiously enough; the Duke of Bedford we are informed was visible on one shameful occasion, but no more. But Warwick, who was the Governor of the town, appears frequently and various other lords with him. We see them in the mirror held up to us by the French historians, pressing round in an ever narrowing circle, closing up upon the tribunal in the midst, pricking the priests with perpetual sword points if they seem to loiter. They would have had everything pushed on, no delay, no possibility of escape. It is very possible that this was the case, for it is evident that the Witch was deeply obnoxious to the English, and that they were eager to have her and her endless process out of the way; but the evidence for their terror and fierce desire to expedite matters is of the feeblest. A canon of Rouen declared at the trial that he had heard it said by Maître Pierre Morice, and Nicolas l'Oyseleur, judges assessors, and by other whose names he does not recollect, "that the said English were so afraid of her that they did not dare to begin the siege of Louviers until she was dead; and that it was necessary if one would please them, to hasten the trial as much as possible and to find the means of condemning her." Very likely this was quite true: but it cannot at all be taken for proved by such evidence. Another contemporary witness allows that though some of the English pushed on her trial for hate, some were well disposed to her; the manner of Jeanne's imprisonment is the only thing which inclines the reader to believe every evil thing that is said against them.

Such were the circumstances in which Jeanne was brought to trail. The population, moved to pity and to tears as any population would have been, before the end, would seem at the beginning to have been indifferent and not to have taken much interest one way or another: the court, a hundred men and more with all their hangers-on, the cleverest men in France, one more distinguished and impeccable than the others: the stern ring of the Englishmen outside keeping an eye upon the tedious suit and all its convolutions: these all appear before us, surrounding as with bands of iron the young lonely victim in the donjon, who submitting to every indignity, and deprived of every aid, feeling that all her friends had abandoned her, yet stood steadfast and strong in her absolute simplicity and honesty. It was but two years in that same spring weather since she had left Vaucouleurs to seek the fortune of France, to offer herself to the struggle which now was coming to an end. Not a soul had Jeanne to comfort or stand by her. She had her saints who—one wonders if such a thought ever entered into her young visionary head—had lured her to her doom, and who still comforted her with enigmatical words, promises which came true in so sadly different a sense from that in which they were understood.

CHAPTER XII — BEFORE THE TRIAL. LENT, 1431.

We have not, however, sufficiently described the horror of the prison, and the treatment to which Jeanne was exposed, though the picture is already dark enough. It throws a horrible yet also a grotesque light upon the savage manners of the time to find that the chamber in which she was confined, had secret provision for an espionnage of the most base kind, openings made in the walls through which everything that took place in the room, every proceeding of the unfortunate prisoner, could be spied upon and every word heard. The idea of such a secret watch has always been attractive to the vulgar mind, and no doubt it has been believed to exist many times when there was little or no justification for such an infernal thought. From the "ear" of Dionysius, down to the Trou Judas, which early tourists on the Continent were taught to fear in every chamber door, the idea has descended to our own times. It would seem, however, to be beyond doubt that this odious means of acquiring information was in full operation during the trial of Jeanne, and various spies were permitted to peep at her, and to watch for any unadvised word she might say in her most private moments. We are told that the Duke of Bedford made use of the opportunity in a still more revolting way, and was present, a secret spectator, at the fantastic scene when Jeanne was visited by a committee of matrons who examined her person to prove or to disprove one of the hateful insinuations which were made about her. The imagination, however, refuses to conceive that a man of serious age and of high functions should have degraded himself to the level of a Peeping Tom in this way; all the French historians, nevertheless, repeat the story though on the merest hearsay evidence. And they also relate, with more apparent truth, how a double treachery was committed upon the unfortunate prisoner by stationing two secretaries at these openings, to take down her conversation with a spy who had been sent to her in the guise of a countryman of her own; and that not only Cauchon but Warwick also was present on this occasion, listening, while their plot was carried out by the vile traitor inside. The clerks, we are glad to say, are credited with a refusal to act: but Warwick did not shrink from the ignominy. The Englishmen indeed shrank from no ignominy; nor did the great French savants assembled under the presidency of the Bishop. It is necessary to grant to begin with that they were neither ignorant nor base men, yet from the beginning of the trial almost every step taken by them appears base, as well as marked, in the midst of all their subtlety and diabolical cunning, by the profoundest ignorance of human nature. The spy of whom we have spoken, L'Oyseleur (bird-snarer, a significant name), was sent, and consented to be sent, to Jeanne in her prison, as a fellow prisoner, a pays, like herself from Lorraine, to invite her confidence: but his long conversations with the Maid, which were heard behind their backs by the secretaries, elicited nothing from her that she did not say in the public examination. She had no secret devices to betray to a traitor.

She would not seem, indeed, to have suspected the man at all, not even when she saw him among her judges taking part against her. Jeanne herself suspected no falsehood, but made her confession to him, when she found that he was a priest, and trusted him fully. The bewildering and confusing fact, turning all the contrivances of her judges into foolishness, was, that she had nothing to confess that she was not ready to tell in the eye of day.

The adoption of this abominable method of eliciting secrets from the candid soul which had none, was justified, it appears, by the manner of her trial, which was after the rules of the Inquisition—by which even more than by those which regulate an ordinary French trial the guilt of the accused is a foregone conclusion for which proof is sought, not a fair investigation of facts for abstract purposes of justice. The first thing to be determined by the tribunal was the counts of the indictment against Jeanne; was she to be tried for magical arts, for sorcery and witchcraft? It is very probable that the mission of L'Oyseleur was to obtain evidence that would clear up this question by means of recalling to her the stories of her childhood, of the enchanted tree, and the Fairies' Well; from which sources, her accusers anxiously hoped to prove that she derived her inspiration. But it is very clear that no such evidence was forthcoming, and that it seemed to them hopeless to attribute sorcery to her; therefore the accusation was changed to that of heresy alone. The following mandate from the University authorising her prosecution will show what the charge was; and the reader will note that one of its darkest items is the costume, which for so many good and sufficient reasons she wore. Here is the official description of the accused:

"A woman, calling herself the Maid, leaving the dress and habit of her sex against the divine law, a thing abominable to God, clothed and armed in the habit and condition of a man, has done cruel deeds of homicide, and as is said has made the simple people believe, in order to abuse and lead them astray, that she was sent by God, and had knowledge of His divine secrets; along with several other doctrines (dogmatisations), very dangerous, prejudicial, and scandalous to our holy Catholic faith, in pursuing which abuses, and exercising hostility against us and our people, she has been taken in arms, before Compiègne, and brought as a prisoner before us."

According to French law the indictment ought to have been founded upon a preliminary examination into the previous life of the accused, which, as it does not appear in the formal accusations, it was supposed had never been made. Recent researches, however, have proved that it was made, but was not of a nature to strengthen or justify any accusation. All that the examiners could discover was that Jeanne d'Arc was a good and honest maid who left a spotless reputation behind her in her native village, and that not a suspicion of dogmatisations, nor worship of fairies, nor any other unseemly thing was associated with her name. Other things less favourable, we are told, were reported of her: the statement, for instance, made in apparent good faith by Monstrelet the Burgundian chronicler, that she had been for some time a servant in an auberge, and there had learned to ride, and to consort with men—a statement totally without foundation, which was scarcely referred to in the trial.

The skill of M. Quicherat discovered the substance of those inquiries among the many secondary papers, but they were not made use of in the formal proceedings. This also we are told, though contrary to the habit of French law, was justified by the methods of the Inquisition, which were followed throughout the trial. One breach of law and justice, however, is permitted by no code. It is expressly forbidden by French, and even by inquisitorial law, that a prisoner should be tried by his enemies—that is by judges avowedly hostile to him: an initial difficulty which it would have been impossible to get over and which had therefore to be ignored. One brave and honest man, Nicolas de Houppeville, had the courage to make this observation in one of the earliest sittings of the assembly:

"Neither the Bishop of Beauvais" (he said) "nor the other members of the tribunal ought to be judges in the matter; and it did not seem to him a good mode of procedure that those who were of the opposite party to the accused should be her judges—considering also that she had been examined already by the clergy of Poitiers, and by the Archbishop of Rheims, who was the metropolitan of the said Bishop of Beauvais."

Nicolas de Houppeville was a lawyer and had a right to be heard on such a point; but the reply of the judges was to throw him into prison, not without threats on the part of the civil authorities to carry the point further by throwing him into the Seine. This was the method by which every honest objection was silenced. That the examination at Poitiers, where the judges, as has been seen, were by no means too favourable to Jeanne, should never have been referred to by her present examiners, though there was no doubt it ought to have been one of the most important sources of the preliminary information—is also very remarkable. It was suggested indeed to Jeanne at a late period of the trial, that she might appeal to the Archbishop; but he was, as she well knew, one of her most cruel enemies.

Still more important was the breach of all justice apparent in the fact that she had no advocate, no counsel on her side, no one to speak to her and conduct her defence. It was suggested to her near the end of the proceedings that she might choose one of her judges to fill this office; but even if the proposal had been a genuine one or at all likely to be to her advantage, it was then too late to be of any use. These particulars, we believe, were enough to invalidate any process in strict law; but the name of law seems ridiculous altogether as applied to this rambling and cruel cross-examination in which was neither sense nor decorum. The reader will understand that there were no witnesses either for or against her, the answers of the accused herself forming the entire evidence.

One or two particulars may still be added to make the background at least more clear. The prison of Jeanne, as we have seen, was not left in the usual silence of such a place; the constant noise with which the English troopers filled the air, jesting, gossiping, and carrying on their noisy conversation, if nothing worse and more offensive—sometimes, as Jeanne complains, preventing her from hearing (her sole solace) the soft voices of her saintly visitors—was not her only disturbance. Her solitude was broken by curious and inquisitive visitors of various kinds. L'Oyseleur, the abominable detective, who professed to be her countryman and who beguiled her into talk of her childhood and native place, was the first of these; and it is possible that at first his presence was a pleasure to her. One other visitor of whom we hear accidentally, a citizen of Rouen, Pierre Casquel, seems to have got in private interest and with a more or less good motive and no evil meaning. He warned her to answer with prudence the questions put to her, since it was a matter of life and death. She seemed to him to be "very simple" and still to believe that she might be ransomed. Earl Warwick, the commander of the town, appears on various occasions. He probably had his headquarters in the Castle, and thus heard her cry for help in her danger, executing, let us hope, summary vengeance on her brutal assailant; but he also evidently took advantage of his power to show his interesting prisoner to his friends on occasion. And it was he who took her original captor, Jean de Luxembourg, now Comte de Ligny, by whom she had been given up, to see her, along with an English lord, sometimes named as Lord Sheffield. The Belgian who had put so many good crowns in his pocket for her ransom, thought it good taste to enter with a jesting suggestion that he had come to buy her back.

"Jeanne, I will have you ransomed if you will promise never to bear arms against us again," he said. The Maid was not deceived by this mocking suggestion. "It is well for you to jest," she said, "but I know you have no such power. I know that the English will kill me, believing, after I am dead, that they will be able to win all the kingdom of France: but if there were a hundred thousand more Goddens than there are, they shall never win the kingdom of France." The English lord drew his dagger to strike the helpless girl, all the stories say, but was prevented by Warwick. Warwick, however, we are told, though he had thus saved her twice, "recovered his barbarous instincts" as soon as he got outside, and indignantly lamented the possibility of Jeanne's escape from the stake.

Such incidents as these alone lightened or darkened her weary days in prison.

A traitor or spy, a prophet of evil shaking his head over her danger, a contemptuous party of jeering nobles; afterwards inquisitors, for ever repeating in private their tedious questions: these all visited her—but never a friend. Jeanne was not afraid of the English lord's dagger, or of the watchful eye of Warwick over her. Even when spying through a hole, if the English earl and knight, indeed permitted himself that strange indulgence, his presence and inspection must have been almost the only defence of the prisoner. Our historians all quote, with an admiration almost as misplaced as their horror of Warwick's "barbarous instincts," the vrai galant homme of an Englishman who in the midst of the trial cried out "Brave femme!" (it is difficult to translate the words, for brave means more than brave)—"why was she not English?" However we are not concerned to defend the English share of the crime. The worst feature of all is that she never seems to have been visited by any one favourable and friendly to her, except afterwards, the two or three pitying priests whose hearts were touched by her great sufferings, though they remained among her judges, and gave sentence against her. No woman seems ever to have entered that dreadful prison except those "matrons" who came officially as has been already said. The ladies de Ligny had cheered her in her first confinement, the kind women of Abbeville had not been shut out even from the gloomy fortress of Le Crotoy. But here no woman ever seems to have been permitted to enter, a fact which must either be taken to prove the hostility of the population, or the very vigorous regulations of the prison. Perhaps the barbarous watch set upon her, the soldiers ever present, may have been a reason for the absence of any female visitor. At all events it is a very distinct fact that during the whole period of her trial, five months of misery, except on the one occasion already referred to, no woman came to console the unfortunate Maid. She had never before during all her vicissitudes been without their constant ministrations.

One woman, the only one we ever hear of who was not the partisan and lover of the Maid, does, however, make herself faintly seen amid the crowd. Catherine of La Rochelle—the woman who had laid claim to saintly visitors and voices like those of Jeanne, and who had been for a time received and fêted at the Court of Charles with vile satisfaction, as making the loss of the Maid no such great thing—had by this time been dropped as useless, on the appearance of the shepherd boy quoted by the Archbishop of Rheims, and had fallen into the hands of the English: was not she too a witch, and admirably qualified to give evidence as to the other witch, for whose blood all around her were thirsting? Catherine was ready to say anything that was evil of her sister sorceress. "Take care of her," she said; "if you lose sight of her for one moment, the devil will carry her away." Perhaps this was the cause of the guard in Jeanne's room, the ceaseless scrutiny to which she was exposed. The vulgar slanderer was allowed to escape after this valuable testimony. She comes into history like a will-o'-the-wisp, one of the marsh lights that mean nothing but putrescence and decay, and then flickers out again with her false witness into the wastes of inanity. That she should have been treated so leniently and Jeanne so cruelly! say the historians. Reason good: she was nothing, came of nothing, and meant nothing. It is profane to associate Jeanne's pure and beautiful name with that of a mountebank. This is the only woman in all her generation, so far as appears to us, who was not the partisan and devoted friend of the spotless Maid.

The aspect of that old-world city of Rouen, still so old and picturesque to the visitor of to-day, though all new since that time except the churches, is curious and interesting to look back upon. It must have hummed and rustled with life through every street; not only with the English troops, and many a Burgundian man-at-arms, swaggering about, swearing big oaths and filling the air with loud voices,—but with all the polished bands of the doctors, men first in fame and learning of the famous University, and beneficed priests of all classes, canons and deans and bishops, with the countless array that followed them, the cardinal's tonsured Court in addition, standing by and taking no share in the business: but all French and English alike, occupied with one subject, talking of the trial, of the new points brought out, of the opinions of this doctor and that, of Maître Nicolas who had presumed on his lawyership to correct the bishop, and had suffered for it: of the bold canon who ventured to whisper a suggestion to the prisoner, and who ever since had had the eye of the governor upon him: of Warwick, keeping a rough shield of protection around the Maid but himself fiercely impatient of the law's delay, anxious to burn the witch and be done with her. And Jeanne herself, the one strange figure that nobody understood; was she a witch? Was she an angelic messenger? Her answers so simple, so bold, so full of the spirit and sentiment of truth, must have been reported from one to another. This is what she said; does that look like a deceiver? could the devils inspire that steadfastness, that constancy and quiet? or was it not rather the angels, the saints as she said? Never, we may be sure, had there been in Rouen a time of so much interest, such a theme for conversations, such a subject for all thoughts. The eager court sat with their tonsured heads together, keen to seize every weak point. Did you observe how she hesitated on this? Let us push that, we'll get an admission on that point to-morrow. It is impossible to believe that in such an assembly every man was a partisan, much less that each one of them was thinking of the fee of the English, the daily allowance which it was the English habit to make. That were to imagine a France, base indeed beyond the limits of human baseness. All the Norman dignitaries of the Church, all the most learned doctors of the University—no! that is too great a stretch of our faith. The greater part no doubt believed as an indisputable fact, that Jeanne was either a witch or an impostor, as we should all probably do now. And the vertigo of Inquisition gained upon them; they became day by day more exasperated with her seeming innocence, with what must have seemed to them the cunning and cleverness, impossible to her age and sex, of her replies. Who could have kept the girl so cool, so dauntless, so embarrassing in her straight-forwardness and sincerity? The saints? the saints were not dialecticians; far more likely the evil one himself, in whom the Church has always such faith. "He hath a devil and by Beelzebub casteth out devils." It was all like a play, only more exciting than any play, and going on endlessly, the excitement always getting stronger till it became the chief stimulus and occupation of life.

CHAPTER XIII — THE PUBLIC EXAMINATION. FEBRUARY, 1431.

It was in the chapel of the Castle of Rouen, on the 21st of February, that the trial of Jeanne was begun. The judges present numbered about forty, and are carefully classed as doctors in theology, abbots, canons, doctors in canonical and civil law, with the Bishop of Beauvais at their head (the archepiscopal see of Rouen being vacant, as is added: but not that my lord of Beauvais hoped for that promotion). They were assembled there in all the solemnity of their priestly and professional robes, the reporters ready with their pens, the range of dark figures forming a semicircle round the presiding Bishop, when the officer of the court led in the prisoner, clothed in her worn and war-stained tunic, like a boy, with her hair cut close as for the helmet, and her slim figure, no doubt more slim than ever, after her long imprisonment. She had asked to be allowed to hear mass before coming to the bar, but this was refused. It was a privilege which she had never failed to avail herself of in her most triumphant days. Now the chapel—the sanctuary of God contained for her no sacred sacrifice, but only those dark benches of priests amid whom she found no responsive countenance, no look of kindness.

Jeanne was addressed sternly by Cauchon, in an exhortation which it is sad to think was not in Latin, as it appears in the Procès. She was then required to take the oath on the Scriptures to speak the truth, and to answer all questions addressed to her. Jeanne had already held that conversation with L'Oyseleur in the prison which Cauchon and Warwick had listened to in secret with greedy ears, but which Manchon, the honest reporter, had refused to take down. Perhaps, therefore, the Bishop knew that the slim creature before him, half boy half girl, was not likely to be overawed by his presence or questions; but it cannot have been but a wonder to the others, all gazing at her, the first men in Normandy, the most learned in Paris, to hear her voice, assez femme, young and clear, arising in the midst of them, "I know not what things I may be asked," said Jeanne. "Perhaps you may ask me questions which I cannot answer." The assembly was startled by this beginning.

"Will you swear to answer truly all that concerns the faith, and that you know?"

"I will swear," said Jeanne, "about my father and mother and what I have done since coming to France; but concerning my revelations from God I will answer to no man, except only to Charles my King; I should not reveal them were you to cut off my head, unless by the secret counsel of my visions."

The Bishop continued not without gentleness, enjoining her to swear at least that in everything that touched the faith she would speak truth; and Jeanne kneeling down crossed her hands upon the book of the Gospel, or Missal as it is called in the report, and took the required oath, always under the condition she stated, to answer truly on everything she knew concerning the faith, except in respect to her revelations.

The examination then began with the usual formalities. She was asked her name (which she said with touching simplicity was Jeannette at home but Jeanne in France), the names of her father and mother, godfather and godmothers, the priest who baptised her, the place where she was born, etc., her age, almost nineteen; her education, consisting of the Pater Noster, Ave Maria, and Credo, which her mother had taught her.

Here she was asked, a curious interruption to the formal interrogatory, to say the Pater Noster—the reason of which sudden demand was that witches and sorcerers were supposed to be unable to repeat that prayer. As unexpected as the question was Jeanne's reply. She answered that if the Bishop would hear her in confession she would say it willingly. She had been refused all the exercises of piety, and she was speaking to a company of priests.

There is a great dignity of implied protest against this treatment in such an answer. The request was made a second time with a promise of selecting two worthy Frenchmen to hear her: but her reply was the same. She would say the prayer when she made her confession but not otherwise. She was ready it would seem in proud humility to confess to any or to all of her enemies, as one whose conscience was clear, and who had nothing to conceal.

She was then commanded not to attempt to escape from her prison, on pain of being condemned for heresy, but to this again she demurred at once. She would not accept the prohibition, but would escape if she could, so that no man could say that she had broken faith; although since her capture she had been bound in chains and her feet fastened with irons. To this, her examiner said that it was necessary so to secure her in order that she might not escape. "It is true and certain," she replied, "whatever others may wish, that to every prisoner it is lawful to escape if he can." It may be remarked, as she forcibly pointed out afterwards, that she had never given her faith, never surrendered, but had always retained her freedom of action.

The tribunal thereupon called in the captain in charge of Jeanne's prison, a gentleman called John Gris in the record, probably John Grey, along with two soldiers, Bernoit and Talbot, and enjoined them to guard her securely and not to permit her to talk with any one without the permission of the court. This was all the business done on the first day of audience.

On the 22d of February at eight o'clock in the morning, the sitting was resumed. In the meantime, however, the chapel had been found too small and too near the outer world, the proceedings being much interrupted by shouts and noises from without, and probably incommoded within by the audience which had crowded it the first day. The judges accordingly assembled in the great hall of the castle; they were forty-nine in number on the second day, the number being chiefly swelled by canons of Rouen. After some preliminary business the accused was once more introduced, and desired again to take the oath. Jeanne replied that she had done so on the previous day and that this was enough; upon which there followed a short altercation, which, however, ended by her consent to swear again that she would answer truly in all things that concerned the faith. The questioner this day was Jean Beaupère (Pulchri patris, as he is called in the Latin), a theologian, Master of Arts, Canon of Paris and of Besançon, "one of the greatest props of the University of Paris," a man holding a number of important offices, and who afterwards appeared at the Council of Bâle as the deputy of Normandy. He began by another exhortation to speak the truth, to which Jeanne replied as before that what she did say she would say truly, but that she would not answer upon all subjects. "I have done nothing but by revelation," she said.

These preliminaries on both sides having been gone through, the examination was resumed. Jeanne informed the court in answer to Beaupère's question that she had been taught by her mother to sew and did not fear to compete with any woman in Rouen in these crafts; that she had once been absent from home when her family were driven out of their village by fear of the Burgundians, and that she had then lived for about fifteen days in the house of a woman called La Rousse, at Neufchâteau; that when she was at home she was occupied in the work of the house and did not go to the fields with the sheep and other animals; that she went to confession regularly to the Curé of her own village, or when he could not hear her, to some other priest, by permission of the Curé; also that two or three times she had made her confession to the mendicant friars—this being during her stay in Neufchâteau (where presumably she was not acquainted with the clergy); and that she received the sacrament always at Easter. Asked whether she had communicated at other feasts than Easter, she said briefly that this was enough. "Go on to the rest," passez outre, she added, and the questioner seems to have been satisfied. Then came the really vital part of the matter. She proceeded—no direct question on the point being recorded, though no doubt it was made—to tell how when she was about thirteen she heard voices from God bidding her to be good and obedient. The first time she was much afraid. The voice came about the hour of noon, in summer, in her father's garden. She was fasting but had not fasted the preceding day. The voice came from the right, towards the church; and came rarely without a great light. This light came always from the side whence the voice proceeded, and was a very bright radiance. When she came into France she still continued to hear the same voices.

She was then asked how she could see the light when it was at the side; to which foolish question Jeanne gave no reply, but "turned to other matters," saying voluntarily with a soft implied reproof of the noise around her—that if she were in a wood, that is in a quiet place, she could hear the voices coming towards her. She added (going on, one could imagine, in a musing, forgetting the congregation of sinners about her) that it seemed to her a noble voice, and that she believed it came from God, and that when she had heard it three times she knew it was the voice of an angel; the voice always came quite clearly to her, and she understood it well.

She was then asked what it said to her concerning the salvation of her soul.

She said that it taught her to rule her life well, to go often to church: and told her that it was necessary that she, Jeanne, should go to France. The said Jeanne added that she would not be questioned further concerning the voice, or the manner in which it was made known to her, but that two or three times in a week it had said to her that she must go to France; but that her father knew nothing of this. The voice said to her that she should go to France, until she could endure it no longer; it said to her that she should raise the siege, which was set against the city of Orleans. It said also that she must go to Robert of Baudricourt, in the city of Vaucouleurs, who was captain of that place, and that he would give her people to go with her; to which she had answered that she was a poor girl who knew not how to ride, nor how to conduct war. She then said that she went to her uncle and told him that she wished to go with him for a little while to his house, and that she lived there for eight days; she then told her uncle that she must go to Vaucouleurs, and the said uncle took her there. Also she went on to say that when she came to the said city of Vaucouleurs, she recognised Robert of Baudricourt; though she had never seen him before she knew him by the voice that said to her which was he. She then told this Robert that it was necessary that she should go to France, but twice over he refused and repulsed her; the third time, however, he received her, and gave her certain men to go with her; the voice had told her that this would be so.

She said also that the Duke of Lorraine sent for her to come to him, and that she went under a safe conduct granted by him, and told him that she must go to France. He asked her whether he should recover from his illness; but she told him that she knew nothing of that, and she talked very little to him of her journey. She told the Duke that he ought to send his son and his people with her to take her to France, and that she would pray God to restore his health; and then she was taken back to Vaucouleurs. She said also that when she left Vaucouleurs she wore the dress of a man, without any other arms than a sword which Robert de Baudricourt had given her; and that she had with her a chevalier, a squire, and four servants, and that they slept for the first night at St. Urbain, in the abbey there. She was then asked by whose advice she wore the dress of a man, but refused to answer. Finally she said that she charged no man with giving her this advice.

She went on to say that the said Robert de Baudricourt exacted an oath from those who went with her, that they would conduct her to the end of her journey well and safely; and that he said, as she left him, "Go, and let come what will." She also said that she knew well that God loved the Duke of Orleans, concerning whom she had more revelations than about any other living man, except him whom she called her King. She added that it was necessary for her to wear male attire, and that whoever advised her to do so had given her wise counsel.

She then said that she sent a letter to the English before Orleans, in which she required them to go away, a copy of which letter had been read to her in Rouen; but there were two or three mistakes, especially in the words which called upon them to surrender to the Maid instead of to surrender to the King. (There is no indication why these two latter statements should have been introduced into the midst of her narrative of the journey; it may have been in reply to some other question interjected by another of her examiners: Passez outre, as she herself says. She immediately resumes the simple and straightforward tale.)

The said Jeanne went on to say that her further journey to him whom she called her King was without any impediment; and that when she arrived at the town of St. Catherine de Fierbois she sent news of her arrival to the town of Chasteau-Chinon where the said King was. She arrived there herself about noon and went to an inn; and after dinner went to him whom she called her King, who was in the castle. She then said that when she entered the chamber where he was, she knew him among all others, by the revelation of her "voices." She told her King that she wished to make war against the English.

She was then asked whether when she heard the "voices" in the presence of the King the light was also seen in that place. She answered as before:Passez outre: Transeatis ultra. "Go on," as we might say, "to the other questions."

She was asked if she had seen an angel hovering over her King. She answered: "Spare me; passez outre." She added afterwards, however, that before he put his hand to the work, the King had many beautiful apparitions and revelations. She was asked what these were. She answered: "I will not tell you; it is not I who should answer; send to the King and he will tell you."

She was then asked if her voices had promised her that when she came to the King he would receive her. She answered that those of her own party knew that she had been sent from God and that some had heard and recognised the voices. Further, she said that her King and various others had heard and seen the voices coming to her—Charles of Bourbon (Comte de Clermont) and two or three others with him. She then said that there was no day in which she did not hear that voice; but that she asked nothing from it except the salvation of her soul. Besides this, Jeanne confessed that the voice said she should be led to the town of St. Denis in France, where she wished to remain—that is after the attack on Paris—but that against her will the lords forced her to leave it: if she had not been wounded she would not have gone: but she was wounded in the moats of Paris: however she was healed in five days. She then said that she had made an assault, called in French escarmouche (skirmish), upon the town of Paris. She was asked if it was on a holy day, and said that she believed it was on a festival. She was then asked if she thought it well done to fight on a holy day, and answered, "Passez outre." Go on to the next question.

This is a verbatim account of one day of the trial. Most of the translations which exist give questions as well as answers: but these are but occasionally given in the original document, and Jeanne's narrative reads like a calm, continuous statement, only interrupted now and then by a question, usually a cunning attempt to startle her with a new subject, and to hurry some admission from her. The great dignity with which she makes her replies, the occasional flash of high spirit, the calm determination with which she refuses to be led into discussion of the subjects which she had from the first moment reserved, are very remarkable. We have seen her hitherto only in conflict, in the din of battle and the fatigue, yet exuberant energy, of rapid journeys. Her circumstances were now very different. She had been shut up in prison for months, for six weeks at least she had been in irons, and the air of heaven had not blown upon this daughter of the fields; her robust yet sensitive maidenhood had been exposed to a hundred offences, and to the constant society, infecting the very air about, of the rudest of men; yet so far is her spirit from being broken that she meets all those potent, grave, and reverend doctors and ecclesiastics, with the simplicity and freedom of a princess, answering frankly or holding her peace as seems good to her, afraid of nothing, keeping her self-possession, all her wits about her as we say, without panic and without presumption. The trial of Jeanne is indeed almost more miraculous than her fighting; a girl not yet nineteen, forsaken of all, without a friend! It is less wonderful that she should have developed the qualities of a general, of a gunner, every gift of war—than that in her humiliation and distress she should thus hold head against all the most subtle intellects in France, and bear, with but one moment of faltering, a continued cross-examination of three months, without losing her patience, her heart, or her courage.

The third day brought a still larger accession of judges, sixty-two of them taking their places on the benches round the Bishop in the great hall; and the day began with another and longer altercation between Cauchon and Jeanne on the subject of the oath again demanded of her. She maintained her resolution to say nothing of her voices. "We" according to the record "required of her that she should swear simply and absolutely without reservation." She would seem to have replied with impatience, "Let me speak freely:" adding "By my faith you may ask me many questions which I will not answer": then explaining, "Many things you may ask me, but I will tell you nothing truly that concerns my revelations; for you might compel me to say things which I have sworn not to say; and so I should perjure myself, which you ought not to wish." This explains several statements which she made later in respect to her introduction to the King. She repeated emphatically: "I warn you well, you who call yourselves my judges, that you take a great responsibility upon you, and that you burden me too much." She said also that it was enough to have already sworn twice. She was again asked to swear simply and absolutely, and answered, "It is enough to have sworn twice," and that all the clerks in Rouen and Paris could not condemn her unless lawfully; also that of her coming she would speak the truth but not all the truth; and that the space of eight days would not be enough to tell all.

"We the said Bishop" (continues the report) "then said to her that she should ask advice from those present whether she ought to swear or not. She replied again that of her coming she would speak truly and not otherwise, nor would it be fit that she should talk at large. We then told her that it would throw suspicion on what she said if she did not swear to speak the truth. She answered as before. We repeated that she must swear precisely and absolutely. She answered that she would say what she knew, but not all, and that she had come on the part of God, and appealed to God from whom she came. Again requested and admonished to swear on pain of every punishment that could be put on her, again answered 'Passez outre.' Finally she consented to swear that she would speak the truth in everything that concerned the trial."

Her examination was then resumed by Beaupère as before, who elicited from her that she had fasted (he seems to have wished to make out that the fasting had something to do with her visions) since noon the day before (it was Lent); and also that she had heard her voices both on that day and the day before, three times on the previous day, the first time in the morning when she was asleep, and awakened by them. Did she kneel and thank them? She thanked them, sitting up in her bed (to which she was chained, as her questioner knew) and clasping her hands. She asked them what she was to do, and they told her to answer boldly.

It may be remarked here that more frequently as the examination goes on, part of Jeanne's words are quoted in the first person, as if the reporters had been specially struck by them, while the bulk of her evidence goes on more calmly in the third person, the narrative form. After saying that she was bidden to answer boldly, she seems to have turned to the Bishop, and to have addressed him individually: "You say you are my judge; I warn you to take care what you are doing, for I am sent from God, and you are putting yourself in much peril" (magno periculo: gallice, adds the reporter, en grant dangier).

She was then asked if her voices ever changed their meaning, and answered that she had never heard two speak contrary to each other; what they had said that day was that she should speak boldly. Asked, if the voice forbade her to reply to questions asked, she replied; "I will not answer you. I have revelations touching the King which I will not tell you." Asked, if the voices forbade her to reveal these revelations, she answered, "I have not consulted them; give me fifteen days' delay and I will answer you"; but being again exhorted to reply, said: "If the voice forbade me to speak, how many times should I tell you?" Again asked, if she were forbidden to speak, answered, "I believe I am not forbidden by men"—repeating that she would not reply, and knew not how far she should reply, for it had not been revealed to her; but that she believed firmly, as firmly as the Christian faith, and that God had redeemed us from the pains of hell, that this voice came from Him.

Questioned concerning the voice, what it appeared to be when it spoke, if that of an angel, or from God Himself; or if it was the voice of a saint or of saints (feminine), answered: "The voice comes from God; and I believe that I should not tell you all I know, for I should displease these voices if I answered you; and as for this question I pray you to leave me free." Asked if she thought that to speak the truth would displease God, she answered, "What the voices say I am to tell to the King, not to you," adding that during that night they had said much to her for the good of the King, and that if she could but let him know she would willingly drink no wine up to Easter (the reader will remember that her frugal fare consisted of bread dipped in the wine and water, which is justly called eau rougie in France). Asked, if she could not induce the voices to speak to her King directly, she answered that she knew not whether her voices would consent, unless it were the will of God, and God consented to it, adding, "They might well reveal it to the King; and with that I should be content." Asked, if the voices could not communicate with the King as they did in her presence, she answered, that she did not know whether this was God's will; and added, that unless it were the will of God she would not know how to act.

Asked, if it was by the advice of her voices that she attempted to escape from her prison, she answered, "I have nothing to say to you on that point." Asked, if she always saw a light when the voices were heard, she answered: "Yes: that with the sound of the voices light came." Asked if she saw anything else coming with the voices, answered: "I do not tell you all. I am not allowed to do so, nor does my oath touch that; the voices are good and noble, but neither of that will I answer." She was then asked to give in writing the points on which she would not reply. Then she was asked if her voices had eyes and ears, and answered, "You shall not have this either," adding, that it was a saying among children that men were sometimes hanged for speaking the truth.

She was then asked if she knew herself to be in the grace of God. She replied: "If I am not so, may God put me in His grace; if I am, may God keep me in it. I should be the most miserable in the world if I were not in the grace of God." She said besides, that if she were in a state of sin she did not believe her voices would come to her, and she wished that everyone could understand them as she did, adding, that she was about thirteen when they came to her first.

She was then asked, whether in her childhood she had played with the other children in the fields, and various other particulars about Domremy, whether there were any Burgundians there? to which Jeanne answered boldly that there was one, and that she wished his head might be cut off, adding piously, "that is, if it pleased God"; she was also asked whether she had fought along with the other children against the children of the neighbouring Burgundian village of Maxy (Maxey sur Meuse): why she hated the Burgundians, and many questions of this kind, with a close examination about a certain tree near the village of Domremy, which some called the Tree of the good Ladies, and others, the Fairies' Tree; and also about a well there, the Fairies' Well, of which poor patients were said to drink and get well. Jeanne (no doubt relieved by the simple character of these questions) made answer freely and without hesitation, in no way denying that she had danced and sung with the other children, and made garlands for the image of the Blessed Marie of Domremy; but she did not remember whether she had ever done so after attaining years of discretion, and certainly she had never seen a fairy, nor worked any spell by their means. At the end, after having thus been put off her guard, she was suddenly asked about her dress (a capital point in the eyes of her judges): whether she wished to have a woman's dress. Probably she was, as they hoped, tired, and expecting no such question, for she answered quickly yet with instant recovery: "Bring me one to go home in and I will accept it; otherwise no. I prefer this, since it pleases God that I should wear it." The recollection of Domremy and of the pleasant fields, must have carried her back to the days when the little Jeanne was like the rest in her short, full petticoats of crimson stuff, free of any danger: what could be better to go home in? but she immediately remembered the obvious and excellent reasons she had for wearing another costume now. So ended the third day.

In the meantime there had been, we are told, various interruptions during the examination; perhaps it was then that Nicolas de Houppeville protested against Bishop Cauchon as a partisan and a Burgundian, and therefore incapable by law of judging a member of the opposite party: and had been rudely silenced, and afterwards punished, as we have already heard. Another kind of opposition less bold had begun to be remarked, which was that one of the persons present, by word and sign, whispering suggestions to her, or warning her with his eyes, was helping the unfortunate prisoner in her defence. Probably this did little good, "for she was often troubled and hurried in her answers," we are told; but it was a sign of good-will, at least. When Frère Isambard, who was the person in question, speaks at a later period he tells us that "the questions put to Jeanne were too difficult, subtle, and dangerous, so that the great clerks and learned men who were present scarcely would have known how to answer them, and that many in the assembly murmured at them." Perhaps the good Frère Isambard might have spared himself the trouble; for Jeanne, however she may have suffered, was probably more able to hold her own than many of those great clerks, and did so with unfailing courage and spirit. One of the other judges, Jean Fabry, a bishop, declared afterwards that "her answers were so good, that for three weeks he believed that they were inspired." Manchon, the reporter, he who had refused to take down the private conversation of Jeanne in her prison with the vile traitor, L'Oyseleur, makes his voice heard also to the effect that "Monseigneur of Beauvais would have had everything written as pleased him, and when there was anything that displeased him he forbade the secretaries to report it as being of no importance for the trial." On another day a humbler witness still, Massieu, one of the officers of the court, who had the charge of taking Jeanne daily from her prison to the hall, and back again, met in the courtyard an Englishman, who seems to have been a singing man or lay clerk "of the King's chapel in England," probably attached to Winchester's ecclesiastical retinue. This man asked him: "What do you think of her answers? Will she be burned? What will happen?" "Up to this time," said Massieu, "I have heard nothing from her that was not honourable and good. She seems to me a good woman, but how it will all end God only knows!"

No doubt conversations of this kind were being carried on all over Rouen. Would she be burned? What would happen? Could any one stand and answer like that hour after hour and day by day, inspired only by the devil? There was no popular enthusiasm for her even now. How should there have been in that partisan province, more English than French? But a chill doubt began to steal into many minds whether she was so bad as had been thought, whether indeed she might not after all be something quite different from what she had been thought? Nature had begun to work in the agitated place, and even in that black-robed, eager assembly. If there was a vile L'Oyseleur trying to get her confidence in private, and so betray her, there was also a kind Frère Isambard, privately plucking at her sleeve, imploring her to be cautious, whispering an answer probably not half so wise as her own natural reply, yet warming her heart with the suggestion of a friend at hand.

On the fourth day, Jeanne was again required to swear, and replied as before, that so far as concerned the trial she would answer truly, but not all she knew. "You ought to be satisfied: I have sworn sufficiently," she said; and with this her judges seem to have been content. Beaupère then resumed his questions, but first asked her, perhaps with a momentary gleam of compassion and a sudden consciousness of the pallor and weariness of the young prisoner, how she did. She answered, one can imagine with what tone of indignant disdain: "You see how I am: I am as well as I can be." He then cross-examined her closely as to what voices she had heard since her last appearance in court, but drew from her only the same answer, "The voice tells me to answer boldly," and that she would tell them as much as she was permitted by God to tell them, but concerning her revelations for the King of France she would say nothing except by permission of her voices.

She was then asked what kind of voices they were which she heard, were they voices of angels, or of saints (sancti aut sanctæ, male or female saints) or from God Himself? She answered that the voices were those of St. Catherine and St. Margaret, whose heads were crowned with beautiful crowns, very rich and precious. "So much as this God allows me to say. If you doubt send to Poitiers, where I was questioned before." (It may perhaps be permissible to suppose that the kind whisperer at her elbow might have suggested the repeated references to Poitiers that follow, but which are not to be found before: though it was most natural she should refer to this place where she was examined at the beginning of her mission.) Asked how she knew which of these two saints, she answered that she could quite distinguish one from the other by the manner of their salutation; that she had been led and guided by them for seven years, and that she knew them because they had named themselves to her. She was then asked how they were dressed? and answered: "I cannot tell you; I am not permitted to reveal this; if you do not believe me send to Poitiers." She said also that at her coming into France she had revealed these things, but could not now. She was asked what was the age of her saints, but replied that she was not permitted to tell. Asked, if both saints spoke at once or one after the other, she replied: "I have not permission to tell you: but I always consult them both together." Asked, which had appeared to her first, and answered: "I do not know which it was; I did know, but have forgotten. It is written in the register of Poitiers."

"She then said she had much comfort from St. Michael. Again, asked, which had come first, she replied that it was St. Michael. Asked, if a long time had passed since she first heard the voice of St. Michael, answered: "I do not name to you the voice of St. Michael; but his conversation was of great comfort to me." Asked, again, what voice came first to her when she was thirteen, answered, that it was St. Michael whom she saw before her eyes, and that he was not alone, but accompanied by many angels of Heaven. She said also that she would not have come into France but by the command of God. Asked, if she saw St. Michael and the angels really, with her ordinary senses, she answered: "I saw them with my bodily eyes as I see you, and when they left me I wept, desiring much that they would take me with them." Asked, what was the form in which he appeared, she replied: "I cannot answer you; I am not permitted." Asked, what St. Michael said to her the first time, she cried, "You shall have no answer to-day." Then went on to say that her voices told her to reply boldly. Afterwards she said that she had told her King once all that had been revealed to her; said also that she was not permitted to say here what St. Michael had said; but that it would be better to send for a copy of the books which were at Poitiers than to question her on this subject. Asked, what sign she had that these were revelations of God, and that it was really St. Catherine and St. Margaret with whom she talked, she answered: "It is enough that I tell you they were St. Catherine and St. Margaret: believe me or not as you will."

Asked how she distinguished the points on which she was allowed to speak from the others, she answered, that on some points she had asked permission to speak, and not on others, adding, that she would rather have been torn by wild horses than to have come to France, unless by the license of God. Asked how it was that she put on a man's dress, she answered, that dress appeared to her a small matter, that she did not adopt that dress by the counsel of any man, and that she neither put on a dress nor did anything, but according as God, or the angels, commanded her to do so. Asked, if she knew whether such a command to assume the dress of a man was lawful, she answered: "All that I did, I did by the precepts of our Lord; and if I were bidden to wear another dress I would do so, because it was at the bidding of God." Asked, if she had done it by the orders of Robert de Baudricourt, answered "No." Asked, if she thought that she had done well in assuming a man's dress, answered, that as all she did was by the command of the Lord, she believed that she had done well, and expected a good guarantee and good succour. Asked, if in this particular case of assuming the dress of a man she thought she had done well, answered, that nothing in the world had made her do it, but the command of God.

She was then asked whether light always accompanied the voices when they came to her, she answered, with an evident reference to her first interview with Charles, that there were many lights on every side as was fit. "It is not only to you that light comes" (or you have not all the light to yourself,—a curious phrase). Asked, if there was an angel over the head of the King when she saw him for the first time, she answered: "By the Blessed Mary, if there were, I know not, I saw none." Asked, if there was light, she answered: "There were about three hundred soldiers, and fifty of them held torches, without counting any spiritual light. And rarely do I have the revelations without light." Asked, if her King had faith in what she said, she answered, that he had good signs, and also by his clergy. Asked, what revelations her King had, she answered: "You shall have nothing from me this year." Then added that for three weeks she was cross-examined by the clergy, both in the town of Chinon and at Poitiers, and that her King had signs concerning her, before he believed in her. And the clergy of his party had found nothing in her, in respect to her faith, that was not good. Asked, whether she gone to the church of St. Catherine of Fierbois, answered: "yes," and that she had there heard three masses in one day, and from thence went to Chinon; she added that she had sent a letter thence to the King, in which it was contained that she sent this to know if she might come to the town in which the King was; for that she had travelled a hundred and fifty leagues to come to him and to bring him help, for she knew much good concerning him. And she thought it was contained in this letter that she should recognise the King among all the rest.

She said besides, that she had a sword which was given to her at Vaucouleurs; she said also that, being in Tours or at Chinon, she sent for a sword which was in the church of St. Catherine of Fierbois behind the altar, and that when it was found it was rusty. Asked, how she knew about this sword, she answered, that it was rusty because of being in the ground, and there were five crosses on it, and that she knew this sword by her voices, and not by any man's report. She wrote to the ecclesiastics of the place where it was and asked them for this sword, and they sent it to her. It was found not much below the ground behind the altar; she was not sure if it was before or behind the altar, but wrote that it was behind the altar. And when it was found the clergy cleaned it and rubbed off the rust, which came off easily; and it was an armourer of Tours who went to fetch it. The clergy made a scabbard for it before sending it to the said Jeanne, and they of Tours made another, so that it had two scabbards, one of crimson velvet and one of cloth of gold. And she herself procured another of strong leather. She said also that when she was captured she had not that sword. Said also that she continued to wear the said sword until she left St. Denis after the assault on Paris. Asked, what benediction she made, or if she made any on this sword, she answered, that she made no benediction, nor knew how to make one, but that she loved the sword because it had come to her from the Church of the blessed Catherine whom she loved much. Asked, if she had placed it on the altar at the village of Coulenges, Les Vineuses, or elsewhere, placing it there that it might bring good luck, she answered, that she knew nothing of this. Asked, if she did not pray that the sword might have good fortune: "It is good to know that I wish all my armour (harnesseum meum; gallice, mon harnois) to be very fortunate." Asked, where she had left the sword, answered, that she had deposited a sword and armour at St. Denis, but it was not this sword. She added that she had it in Lagny: but that she afterwards wore the sword which had been taken from a Burgundian, which was a good sword for war and gave good strokes (gallice, de bonnes bouffes and de bons torchons). Said also that to tell where she left it had nothing to do with the trial, and she would answer nothing.

She said also that her brothers had everything that belonged to her, her horses, swords, and everything, and that she believed they were worth in all about 12,000 francs. She was also asked whether when she was at Orleans she had a standard, and what colour it was; answered, that she had a standard, the field of which was sown with lilies, and on it was a figure of the world with angels on each side. It was white, and made of a stuff called boucassin, upon which was written the name Jhesus Maria, so that all might see, and it was fringed with silk. Asked, if the name Jhesus Maria was written above or below or at the side, she answered, "At the side." Asked, if she loved her sword or standard best, she answered, that she loved her standard best. Asked, why she had that picture on the standard, she answered: "I have sufficiently told you that I did nothing but by the command of God." She added that she herself carried her standard when in battle that she might not hurt anyone, and said that she had never killed any man.

Asked, how many men her King gave her when she began her work, answered, from ten to twelve thousand men, and that she attacked first the bastile of St. Loup at Orleans, and afterwards that of the bridge. Asked, from which bastile it was that her men were driven back, she answered, that she did not remember; adding, that she had been sure that she could raise the siege at Orleans, for it had been so revealed to her; and that she told this to her King before it occurred. Asked, whether, when she made assault, she told her men that all the arrows, stones, cannon-balls, etc., would be intercepted by her, she answered no—that more than a hundred were wounded: that what she had said to her people was that they should have no doubts, for they should certainly raise the siege of Orleans. She said also that in attacking the bastile of the bridge she herself was wounded by an arrow in the neck, and was much comforted by St. Catherine, and was healed in fifteen days; but that she never gave up riding and working all that time. Asked, if she knew that she would be wounded, she answered, that she knew it well and had told her King, but that, notwithstanding, she went about her business. It was revealed to her by the voices of her two saints, the blessed Catherine and the blessed Margaret. She said besides, that she was the first to place a scaling ladder on the bastile of the bridge, and as she raised it she was struck in the neck.

She was then asked why she did not treat with the Captain of Jargeau; she answered that the lords of her party had replied to the English, who had asked for a truce of fifteen days, that they could not have it, but that they might retire, they and their horses at once; she had said for her part that if they retired in their doublets and tunics their lives should be spared, otherwise the city would be taken by storm. Asked, if she had consulted with her counsel, that is with her voices, whether the truce should be granted or not, she answered, that she did not remember.

It will be remarked, as the slow examination goes on day after day, that Jeanne, becoming at moments impatient, sometimes gives a rough answer, and at other times plays a little with her questioner as if in contempt. "By the Blessed Mary, I know not!" is evidently an outburst of impatience at the exhausting, exasperating folly of some of these questions, and this will be further visible in future sittings. It seems very likely that the reference to Poitiers, which was an excellent suggestion, commending itself to her invariable good sense, came from the kind priest who tried to serve her as he best could; but there are other answers a little incoherent, which look as if Frère Isambard, if it were he, had confused her in her own response without conveying anything better to her mind, especially on the occasions when she refuses to reply, and then does so, abandoning her ground at once. Her patience and steadiness are quite extraordinary however even in the less self-collected moments. Thus end the proceedings of the fourth day.

The fifth day began with the usual dispute about the oath, Jeanne still retaining her reservation with the greatest firmness. She seems, however, at the end, to have repeated her oath to answer everything that had to do with the trial —"And as much as I say I will say as if I were before the Pope of Rome." These words must have given the Magister Beaupère an admirable occasion for introducing one of the things charged against her for which there was actual proof—her letter to the Comte d'Armagnac in respect to the Pope. He seized upon it evidently with eagerness, and asked her which she held to be the true Pope. To this she answered quietly, "Are there two?"—the most confusing reply.

She was asked if she had received letters from the Comte d'Armagnac, asking to know which of the three existing Popes he ought to obey; she answered that she had his letter, and had replied to it, saying among other things that when she was in Paris and at rest she would answer him; and added that she was on the point of mounting her horse when she gave that reply. The copy of the letter and the reply being read to her she was asked if that was what she had said; to which she replied that she had answered his letter in part, not in full. Asked, if she knew the counsels of the King of Kings so as to be able to say which the count should obey, she answered, that she knew nothing. Asked, if she was in doubt as to which the count ought to obey, she replied that she knew not which to bid him obey; but that she, the said Jeanne, held and believed that we ought to obey our Pope who was in Rome; that as for what he asked, that she should tell him which God desired him to obey, she had said she knew nothing; but she sent much to him which was not put in writing. And as for herself she believed in the Lord Pope of Rome. Asked, whether in respect to the three pontiffs she had received counsel, she answered, that she had neither written nor made to be written anything about the three pontiffs. And this she swore on her oath. Asked, if she were in the habit of putting on her letters the name Jhesus Maria with a cross, answered, that she did so sometimes but not always, and that sometimes she put a cross to shew that these letters were not to be taken seriously (as likely to fall into the enemy's hands).

Some questions were then put to her about her letters to the Duke of Bedford and to the English King, and copies were read to her to which she objected on some small points, but mistakenly it would seem, as that she had summoned them to surrender to the King, while the scribe had put "surrender to the Maid." She said, however, that they were her letters, and that she held by them. She added that before seven years the English would lose more than they had lost at Orleans, and that their cause would be lost in France; she said also that the said English should have greater disasters than they had yet had in France, and that God would give greater victories to France. Asked, how she knew this, she replied: "I know it by the revelations made to me, and that it will happen in seven years, and I might well be angry that it is deferred so long." Asked, when this would happen, she said that she knew neither the day nor the hour.

She was tormented a little further as to the dates, whether this would happen before the St. Jean, or before the St. Martin in winter, but made no answer except that before the St. Martin in winter they should see many things, and it might be that the English should fail; as a matter of fact Paris opened its gates to Charles VII. within the seven years specified, so that Jeanne's prophecy may be held to have been fulfilled.

We then come once more to a long and profitless interrogatory upon her saints, in which the crowd of judges forgot their dignity and overwhelmed her with a flood of often very foolish, and sometimes worse than foolish questions.

Asked, how she knew the future, she answered that she knew it by St. Catherine and St. Margaret; asked, if St. Gabriel was with St. Michael when he came to her, she answered, that she could not remember. Asked, if she saw them always in the same dress, answered yes, and they were crowned very richly. Of their other garments she could not speak; she knew nothing of their tunics. Asked, how she knew whether they were men or women, answered, that she knew well by their voices which revealed them to her; and that she knew nothing save by revelation and the precepts of God. Asked, what appearances she saw, she answered, that she saw faces. Asked, if these saints had hair, she answered, "It is good to know." Asked, if there was anything between their crowns and their hair, answered, no. Asked, if their hair was long and hanging down, answered, "I know nothing about it." She also said that their voices were beautiful sweet, and humble, and that she understood them well. Asked, how they could speak when they had no bodies, she answered, "I refer it to God." She repeated that the voices were beautiful, humble, and sweet, and that they could speak French. Asked, if St. Margaret did not speak English, answered: "How could she speak English when she was not on the English side?"

This would seem to infer that the St. Margaret referred to was not the legendary St. Margaret of the dragon, but St. Margaret of Scotland, well known in France from the long connection between those two countries, and a popular mediæval saint. She would naturally have spoken English, being a Saxon, but also quite naturally would have been against the English, as a Scottish queen; but of these refinements it is very unlikely that Jeanne knew anything, and her prompt and somewhat sharp reply evidently cut the inquiry short. The next question was, did they wear gold rings in their ears or elsewhere, these crowned saints; to which she answered a little contemptuously, "I know nothing about it." She was then asked if she herself had rings: on which "turning to us the aforesaid Bishop, she said, 'You have one of mine; give it back to me.' She then said that the Burgundians had her other ring, and asked of us if we had the ring to shew it to her. Asked, who gave her this ring, answered, her father or her mother, and that the name Jhesus Maria was written upon it, but that she knew not who put it there, nor even whether there was a stone in the ring; it was given to her in the village of Domremy. She added that her brother gave her another ring which we had, and said that she desired that it might be given to the Church."

A sudden change was now made in the cross-examination according to the methods of that operation, throwing her back without warning upon the village superstitions of Domremy, the magic tree and fountain. Many of the questions which follow are so trivial and are so evidently instinct with evil meaning, that it seems a wrong to Beaupère to impute the whole of the interrogatory to him; other questions were evidently interposed by the excited assembly.

Asked, if St. Catherine and St. Margaret talked with her under the tree of which mention had been made above, she answered, "I know nothing about it." Asked, if the saints were seen at the fountain near the tree, answered yes, that she had heard them there; but what her saints promised to her, there or elsewhere, she answered, that nothing was promised except by permission from God. Asked, what promises were made to her, she answered, "This has nothing at all to do with your trial," but added, that among other things they said to her that her King should be restored to his kingdom, and that his adversaries should be destroyed. She said also that they promised to take her, the said Jeanne, to Paradise, as she had asked them to do. Asked, if she had any other promises, she said there was one promise that had nothing to do with the trial, but that in three months she would tell them what that other promise was. Asked, if the voices told her she would be set free from her prison in three months, she answered: "This does not concern your trial; nor do I know when I shall be set free." And she added that those who wished to send her out of this world might well go before her. Asked, if her council did not tell her when she should be set free from her present prison, answered: "Ask me this in three months' time; I can promise you as much as that"—but added: "You may ask those present, on their oaths, if this has anything to do with the trial."

Startled by this suggestion, the judges seem to have held a hurried consultation among themselves to see whether these matters did really touch the trial; the result apparently decided them to return again to the question of the local superstitions of Domremy, the only point on which there seemed a chance of breaking down the extraordinarily just and steadfast intelligence of the girl who stood before them. After this pause she resumed, apparently not in answer to any question.

"I have well told you that there were things you should not know, and some time I must needs be set free. But I must have permission if I speak; therefore I will ask to have delay in this." Asked, if her voices forbade her to speak the truth, she said: "Do you expect me to tell you things that concern the King of France? There is a great deal here that has nothing to do with the trial." She said also that she knew that her King should enjoy the kingdom of France, as well as she knew that they were there before her in judgment. She added that she would have been dead but for the revelations which comforted her daily. She was then asked what she had done with her mandragora (mandrake)? she answered that she had no mandragora, nor had ever had. She had heard say that near her village there was one, but had never seen it. She had heard say that it was a dangerous thing, and that it was wicked to keep it; but knew nothing of its use. Asked, in what place this mandrake was, and what she had heard of it? she said that she had heard that it grew under the tree of which mention has been made, but did not know the place; she said also that she had heard that above the mandragora was a hazel tree. Asked, what she heard was done with the mandragora, answered, that she had heard that it brought money, but did not believe it; and added that her voices had never told her anything about it.

Asked, what was the appearance of St. Michael when she saw him first, she answered, that she saw no crown, and knew nothing of his dress. Asked, if he was naked, she answered, "Do you think God has nothing to clothe him with?" Asked, if he had hair, she answered, "Why should it have been cut?" She said further that she had not seen the blessed Michael since she left the castle of Crotoy, nor did she see him often. At last she said that she knew not whether he had hair or not. Asked, whether he carried scales, she answered, "I know nothing of it," but added that she had much joy in seeing him, and she knew when she saw him that she was not in a state of sin. She also said that St. Catherine and St. Margaret often made her confess to them, and said that if she had been in a state of sin it was without knowing it. She was then asked whether, when she confessed, she believed herself to be in a state of mortal sin; she answered, that she knew not whether she had been in that state, but did not believe she had done the works of sin. "It would not have pleased God," she said, "that I should have been so; nor would it have pleased Him that I should have done the works of sin by which my soul should have been burdened."

She was then asked what sign she gave to the King that she came to him from God; she answered: "I have told you always that nothing should draw this from me. Ask me no more." Asked, if she had not sworn to reveal what was asked of her touching the trial, answered, "I have told you that I will tell you nothing that was for our King; and of this which belongs to him I will not speak." Asked, if she knew the sign which she gave to the King, she answered: "You shall know nothing from me." When it was said to her that this did concern the trial, she answered, "Of that which I have promised to keep secret I shall tell you nothing"; and further she said, "I promised in that place and I could not tell you without perjuring myself." Asked, to whom she promised? answered, that she had promised to Saints Catherine and Margaret, and this was shown to the King. She also said she had promised it to these two saints, because they had required it of her. And the same Jeanne had done this at their request. "Too many people would have asked me concerning it, if I had not promised to the aforesaid saints." She was then asked, when she showed this sign to the King if there were others with him; she answered, that to her there was no one near him, even though many people might have been present. (As a matter of fact the sign was given to Charles when he talked with the Maid apart in a recess, the great hall being full of the Court and followers; so that this was strictly true.) Asked further, if she saw a crown over the head of her King when she showed him this sign, but replied: "I cannot answer you without perjury." Asked further if her King had a crown when he was at Rheims, answered, that in her opinion her King had a crown which he found at Rheims, but a very fine one was afterwards brought for him. He did this to hasten matters, at the desire of the city of Rheims; but if he had been more certain, he could have had a crown a thousand times richer. (All this is very obscure.)

Asked, if she had seen this crown, she answered: "I could not tell you without perjury, but I heard that it was a very rich one." It was then determined to conclude for this day.

On the sixth day there was again the same questions about the oath, ending in the usual way. And the cross-examination was at once continued.

She was asked if she would say whether St. Michael had wings, and what bodies and members had St. Catherine and St. Margaret; and she answered, "I have told you what I know, and will make no other reply"; she said, moreover, that when she saw St. Michael and St. Catherine and St. Margaret, she knew at once that they were saints of Paradise. Asked, if she saw anything more than their faces, she answered: "I have told you all I know of them: and I would rather have had my head taken off than tell you all I know." She then said that in whatever concerned the trial she would speak freely. Asked, if she believed that St. Michael and St. Gabriel had natural heads, she answered: "I saw them with my eyes and I believe that they are, as firmly as I believe that God is." Asked, if she believed that God made them in the form in which she saw them, she answered, "Yes." Asked, if she believed that God had created them in the same form from the beginning, answered: "You shall have no more for the present, except what I have already said."

This subject was then dropped, and the examiner made another leap forward to a different part of her life. "Did you know by revelation that you should break prison?" he said. To this Jeanne answered indignantly: "This has nothing to do with your trial. Would you have me speak against myself?"

Again questioned what her "voices" had said to her in respect to her attempts at escape, she again answered: "This has nothing to do with the trial; I go back to the trial. If all your questions were about that, I should tell you all." She said besides, on her faith, that she knew neither the day nor the hour when she should escape. She was then asked what the voices said to her generally, and answered: "In truth, they tell me I shall be freed, but neither the day nor the hour; and that I ought to speak boldly, and with a glad countenance." She was then asked whether, when first she saw her King, he asked her whether it was by revelation that she had assumed the dress of a man? she replied: "I have answered this. I cannot recollect whether he asked me. But it is written in the book at Poitiers." Asked, whether the doctors who examined her there, some for a month, some for three weeks, had asked her about her change of dress; she answered: "I don't remember; but I know they asked me when I assumed the dress of a man, and I told them it was in the town of Vaucouleurs." Asked, whether these doctors had inquired whether it was her voices which had made her take that dress, answered, "I don't remember." Asked if her Queen wished her to change her dress when she first saw her, answered, "I don't remember."

Asked if her King, Queen, and all of her party did not ask her to lay aside the dress of a man, she answered, "This has nothing to do with the trial." Asked, if the same was not requested of her in the castle of Beaurevoir, she answered: "It is true. And I replied that I could not lay it aside without the permission of God." She said further that the demoiselle of Luxembourg (aunt of Jeanne's captor, and a very old woman) and the lady of Beaurevoir offered her a woman's dress, or stuff to make one, and begged her to wear it; but she replied that she had not yet the permission of our Lord, and that it was not yet time. Asked, if M. Jean de Pressy and others at Arras had offered her a woman's dress, she answered, "He and others have often asked it of me." Asked, if she thought she would have done wrong in putting on a woman's dress, she answered, that it was better to obey her sovereign Lord, that is, God; she said also that if she had done it, she would rather have done it at the request of these two ladies than of any other in France, except her Queen. Asked, if, when God revealed to her that she should change her dress, it was by the voice of St. Michael, St. Catherine, or St. Margaret, she answered, "You shall hear no more about it." Asked, when the King first employed her, and her standard was made, whether the men-at-arms and others who took part in the war did not have flags imitated from hers? she answered, "It is well to know that the lords retained their own arms"; she also added that her brothers-in-arms made such pennons as pleased them. Asked, how these were made, if they were of linen or cloth, answered, that they were of white satin, some of them with lilies; that she had but two or three lances in her own company—but that in the rest of the army some carried pennons like hers, but only to distinguish them from others. Asked, if the banners were often renewed, answered: "I know not; when the staff was broken it was renewed." Asked, if she had not said that the pennons copied from hers were fortunate, answered, that she had said, "Go in boldly among the English"; and that she had done the same herself. Asked, if she said that they should have good luck if they bore the banners well, answered, that she had told them what would happen, and what should still happen. Asked, if she had caused holy water to be sprinkled on the pennons when they were new, she answered, "That has nothing to do with the trial"; but added that if she did so sprinkle them she was not instructed to answer that question now. Asked, if the others put Jhesus Maria upon their pennons, she answered: "By my faith, I know nothing about it." Asked, if she had ever carried or caused to be carried in a procession round a church or altar the linen of which the pennons were made, answered no, that she had never seen anything of the kind done.

Asked, when she was before Jargeau, what it was that she wore behind her helmet, and if she had not something round it, she answered: "By my faith, there was nothing." Asked, if she knew a certain Brother Richard, she answered: "I never saw him till I was before Troyes." Asked, what cheer

Brother Richard made to her, answered, that she thought the people of Troyes had sent him to her, doubting whether she had come on the part of God, and that as he approached her he made the sign of the cross, and sprinkled holy water; she said to him: "Come on boldly; I shall not fly away." Asked, if she had seen, or had caused to be made, any images or pictures of herself, she answered, that at Arras she had seen a picture in the hands of a Scot, where she was represented fully armed, kneeling on one knee, and presenting a letter to the King; but that she had never caused any image or picture of herself to be made. Asked concerning a table in the house of her host, upon which were painted three women, with Justice, Peace, Union inscribed beneath, answered, that she knew nothing of it. Asked, if she knew that those of her party caused masses and prayers to be made in her honour, she answered, that she knew not; and if they did so, it was not by any command of hers; but that if they did so, her opinion was that they did no wrong. Asked, if those of her party firmly believed that she was sent from God, she answered: "I know not whether they believed it; but even if they did not believe it, I am none the less sent on the part of God." Asked, whether she thought that to believe that she was sent from god was a worthy faith, she answered, that if they believed that she was sent from God they were not mistaken. Asked, if she knew what her party meant by kissing her feet and hands and her garments, answered, that many people did it, but that her hands were kissed as little as she could help it. The poor people, however, came to her of their own free will, because she never oppressed them, but protected them as far as was in her power. Asked, what reverence the people of Troyes made to her, she answered, "None at all," and added that she believed Brother Richard came into Troyes with her army, but that she had not seen him coming in. Asked, if he had not preached at the gates when she came, answered, that she scarcely paused there at all, and knew nothing of any sermon. Asked, how long she was at Rheims, and answered, four or five days. Asked, whether she baptised (stood godmother to) children there, she answered: To one at Troyes, but did not remember any at Rheims or at Château-Thierry; but there were two at St. Denis; and willingly she called the boys "Charles," in honour of her King, and the girls "Jeanne," according to what their mothers wished. Asked, if the good women of the town did not touch with their rings the rings she wore, she answered, that many women touched her hands and her rings; but she did not know why they did it. Asked, what she did with the gloves in which her King was consecrated, she answered that "Gloves were distributed to the knights and nobles that came there"; and there was one who lost his; but she did not say that she would find it for him. Also she said that her standard was in the church at Rheims, and she believed near the altar, and she herself had carried it for a short time, but did not know whether Brother Richard had held it.

She was then asked if she communicated and went to confession often while moving about the country, and if she received the sacrament in her male costume; to which she answered "yes, but without her arms"; she was then questioned about a horse belonging to the Bishop of Senlis, which had not suited her, a matter completely without importance. The inference intended was that it was taken from him without being paid for; but there was no evidence that the Maid knew anything about it. We then come to the incident of Lagny.

She was asked how old the child was which she saw at Lagny, and answered, three days; it had been brought to Lagny to the Church of Nôtre Dame, and she was told that all the maids in Lagny were before our Lady praying for it, and she also wished to go and pray God and our Lady that its life might come back; and she went, and prayed with the rest. And finally life appeared; it yawned three times, and was baptised and buried in consecrated ground. It had given no sign of life for three days and was black as her coat, but when it yawned its colour began to come back. She was there with the other maids on her knees before our Lady to make her prayer.

The reader must understand that this was no special appeal to Jeanne's miraculous power, but a custom of that intense and tender charity with which the Church of Rome corrects her dogmatism upon questions of salvation. A child unbaptised could not be buried in consecrated ground, and was subject to all the sorrows of the unredeemed; but who could doubt that the priest would be easily persuaded by some wavering of the tapers on the altar upon the little dead face, some flicker of his own compassionate eyelids, that sufficient life had come back to permit the holy rite to be administered? The whole little scene is affecting in the extreme, the young creatures all kneeling, fervently appealing to the Maiden-mother, the priest ready to take instant advantage of any possible flicker, the Maid of France, no conspicuous figure, but weeping and praying among the rest. There was no thought here of the raising of the dead—the prayer was for breath enough only to allow of the holy observance, the blessed water, the last possibility of human love and effort.

Jeanne was then questioned concerning Catherine of La Rochelle, the supposed prophetess, who had been played against her by La Tremouille and his follows, and narrated how she had watched two nights to see the mysterious lady clothed in cloth of gold who was said to appear to Catherine, but had not seen her, and that she had advised the woman to return to her husband and children. Catherine's mission was to go through the "good towns" with heralds and trumpets to call upon those who had money or treasure of any kind to give it to the King, and she professed to have a supernatural knowledge where such money was hidden. (No doubt La Tremouille must have thought that to get money, which was so scarce, in such a simple way, was worth trying at least. But Jeanne's opinion was that it was folly, and that there was nothing in it; an opinion fully verified. Catherine's advice had been that Jeanne should go to the Duke of Burgundy to make peace; but Jeanne had answered that no peace could be made save at the end of the lance.)

She was then asked about the siege of La Charité; she answered, that she had made an assault: but had not sprinkled holy water, or caused it to be sprinkled. Asked, why she did not enter the city as she had the command of God to do so, she replied: "Who told you that I was commanded to enter?" Asked, if she had not had the advice of her voices, she answered, that she had desired to go into France (meaning towards Paris), but the generals had told her that it was better to go first to La Charité. She was then asked if she had been long in the tower of Beaurevoir; answered, that she was there about four months, and that when she heard the English come she was angry and much troubled. Her voices forbade her several times to attempt to escape; but at last, in the doubt she had of the English she threw herself down, commending herself to God and to our Lady, and was much hurt. But after she had done this the voice of St. Catherine said to her not to be afraid, that she should be healed, and that Compiègne would be relieved.

Also she said that she prayed always for the relief of Compiègne with her council. Asked, what she said after she had thrown herself down, she answered, that some said that she was dead; and as soon as the Burgundians saw that she was not dead, they told her that she had thrown herself down. Asked, if she had said that she would rather die than fall into the hands of the English, she answered, that she would much rather have rendered her soul to God than have fallen into the hands of the English. Asked, if she was not in a great rage, and if she did not blaspheme the name of God, she answered, that she never said evil of any saint, and that it was not her custom to swear. Asked respecting Soissons, when the captain had surrendered the town, whether she had not cursed God, and said that if she had gotten hold of the captain, she would have cut him into four pieces; she answered, that she never swore by any saint, and that those who said so had not understood her.

At this point the public trial of Jeanne came to a sudden end. Either the feeling produced in the town, and even among the judges, by her undeviating, simple, and dignified testimony had begun to be more than her persecutors had calculated upon; or else they hoped to make shorter work with her when deprived of the free air of publicity, the sight no doubt of some sympathetic faces, and the consciousness of being still able to vindicate her cause and to maintain her faith before men. Two or three fierce Inquisitors within her cell, and the Bishop, that man without heart or pity at their head, might still tear admissions from her weariness, which a certain sympathetic atmosphere in a large auditory, swept by waves of natural feeling, would strengthen her to keep back. The Bishop made a proclamation that in order not to vex and tire his learned associates he would have the minutes of the previous sittings reduced into form, and submitted to them for judgment, while he himself carried on apart what further interrogatory was necessary. We are told that he was warned by a counsellor of the town that secret examinations without witnesses or advocate on the prisoner's side, were illegal; but Monseigneur de Beauvais was well aware that anything would be legal which effected his purpose, and that once Jeanne was disposed of, the legality or illegality of the proceedings would be of small importance. I have thought it right to give to the best of my power a literal translation of these examinations, notwithstanding their great length; as, except in one book, now out of print and very difficult to procure, no such detailed translation, so far as I am aware, exists; and it seems to me that, even at the risk of fatiguing the reader (always capable of skipping at his pleasure), it is better to unfold the complete scene with all its tedium and badgering, which brings out by every touch the extraordinary self-command, valour, and sense of this wonderful Maid, the youngest, perhaps, and most ignorant of the assembly, yet meeting all with a modest and unabashed countenance, true, pure, and natural,—a far greater miracle in her simplicity and noble steadfastness than even in the wonders she had done.

CHAPTER XIV —THE EXAMINATION IN PRISON. LENT, 1431.

It must not be forgotten, in the history of this strange trial, that the prisoner was brought from the other side of France expressly that she might be among a people who were not of her own party, and who had no natural sympathies with her, but a hereditary connection with England, which engaged all its partialities on that side. For this purpose it was that the venue, the town expected the coming of the Witch, and all the dark revelations that might be extracted from her, her spells, and the details of that contract with the devil which was so entrancing to the popular imagination, with excitement and eagerness. Such a Cause Célèbre had never taken place among them before; and everybody no doubt looked forward to the pleasure of seeing it proved that it was not by the will of Heaven, but by some monstrous combination of black arts, that such an extraordinary result as the defeat of the invincible English soldiers had been brought about. The litigious and logical Normans no doubt looked forward to it as to the most interesting entertainment, ending in the complete vindication of their own side and the exposure of the nefarious arms used by their adversaries.

But when the proceedings had been opened, and in place of some dark-browed and termagant sorceress, with the mark of every evil passion in her face, there appeared before the spectators crowding into every available corner, the slim, youthful figure—was it boy or girl?—the serene and luminous countenance of the Maid, the flower of youth raising its whiteness and innocence in the midst of all those black-robed, subtle Doctors, it is impossible but that the very first glance must have given a shock and thrill of amazement and doubt to what may be called the lay spectators, those who had no especial bias more than common report, and whose credit or interest were not involved in bringing this unlikely criminal to condemnation. "A girl! Like our own Jeanne at home," might many a father have said, dismayed and confounded. She had, they all say, those eyes of innocence which it is so impossible not to believe, and that virginal voice, assez femme, which a sentimental Frenchman insists upon as belonging only to the spotless. At all events she had the bearing of honesty, purity, and truth. She was not afraid though all the powers of hell—or was it only of the Church and the Law?—were arrayed against her: no guilty mystery to be discovered, was in her countenance. But it must have been plain to the keen and not too charitable Normans that such semblances are not always to be trusted, and that the devil himself even, on occasion, can take upon himself the appearance of an angel of light; so that after the first shock of wonder they no doubt settled themselves to listen, believing that soon they would have their imaginations fed with tales of horror, and would discover the hoofs and the horns and unveil with triumph the lurking demon. The French historians never take into consideration the fact that it was the belief of Rouen and Normandy, as well as of any similar town or province in England, that the child Henry VI. was lawful king, and that whatever was on the other side was a hateful adversary, to be brought to such disaster and shame as was possible, without mercy and without delay.

But after a few days of the examination which we have just reported, public opinion was greatly staggered, and knew not how to turn. Gradually the conviction must have been forced upon every mind which had any candour left, that Jeanne, at that dreadful bar, with the stake in sight, and all the learning of Paris—the entire power of one great national and half of another, all England and half France against—(many more than half France, for the other part had abandoned her cause),—showed nothing of the demon, but all —if not of the angel, yet of the Maid, the emblem of perfection to that rude world, though often so barbarously handled. It might almost be said of the age, notwithstanding its immorality and rampant viciousness, that in its eyes a true virgin could do no harm. And hers was one if ever such a thing existed on earth. The talk in the streets began to take a very different tone. Massieu the clerical sheriff's officer saw nothing in her answers that was not good and right. Out of the midst of the crowd of listeners would burst an occasional cry of "Well said!" An Englishman, even a knight, overcome by his feelings, cried out: "Why was not she English, this brave girl!" All these were ominous sounds. Still more ominous was the utterance of Maître Jean Lohier, a lawyer of Rouen, who declared loudly that the trial was not a legal trial for the reasons which follow:

"In the first place because it was not in the form of an ordinary trial; secondly, because it was not held in a public court, and those present had not full and complete freedom to say what was their full and unbiassed opinion; thirdly, because there was question of the honour of the King of France of whose party Jeanne was, without calling him, or any one for him; fourthly, because neither libel nor articles were produced, and this woman who was only an uninstructed girl, had no advocate to answer for her before so many Masters and Doctors, on such grave matters, and especially those which touched upon the revelations of which she spoke; therefore it seemed to him that the trial was worth nothing. For these things Monseigneur de Beauvais was very indignant against the said Maître Lohier, saying: 'Here is Lohier who is going to make a fine fuss about our trial; he calumniates us all, and tells the world it is of no good. If one were to go by him, one would have to begin everything over again, and all that has been done would be of no use.' Monseigneur de Beauvais said besides: 'It is easy to see on which foot he halts (de quel pied il cloche). By St. John, we shall do nothing of the kind; we shall go on with our trial as we have begun it.'"

A day or two later Manchon, the Clerk of the Court (he who refused to take down Jeanne's conversation with her Judas), met this same lawyer Lohier at church, and asked him, as no doubt every man asked every other whom he met, how did he think the trial was going? to which Lohier answered: "You see the manner in which they proceed; they will take her, if they can, in her words —that is to say, the assertions in which she says I know for certain, things that concern her apparitions. If she would say, 'It seems to me' instead of 'I know for certain,' I do not see how any man could condemn her. It appears that they proceed against her rather from hate than from any other cause, and for this reason I shall not remain here. I will have nothing to do with it." This I think shows very clearly that Lohier, like the bulk of the population, by no means thought at first that it was "from hate" that the trial proceeded, but honestly believed that he had been called to try Jeanne as a professor of the black arts; and that he had discovered from her own testimony that she was not so, and that the motive of the trial was entirely a different one from that of justice; one in fact with which an honest man could have nothing to do.

It is very significant also that the number of judges present in court on the sixth day, the last of the public examination, was only thirty-eight, as against the sixty-two of the second day, which seems to prove that a general disgust and alarm was growing in the minds of those most closely concerned. Warwick and the soldiers, impatient of all such business, striding in noisily from time to time to give a careless glance at the proceedings, might not stay long enough to share the impression—or might, who can say? Their business was to get this pestilent woman, even if by chance she might be an innocent fanatic, cleared off the face of the earth and out of their way.

After the sixth day, however, it would seem that the Bishop and his tools had taken fright at the progress of public opinion. Before dismissing the court on that occasion, Cauchon made an address to the disturbed and anxious judges, informing them that he would not tire them out with prolonged sittings, but that a few specially chosen assistants would now examine into what further details were necessary. In the meantime all would be put in writing; so that they might think it over and deliberate within themselves, so as to be able each to make a report either to himself, the Bishop, or to some one deputed by him. The assessors, thus thrown out of work, were however forbidden to leave Rouen without the Bishop's permission—probably because of the threat of Lohier. Repeated meetings were held in Cauchon's house to arrange the details of the proceedings to follow; and during this time it was perhaps hoped that any excitement outside would quiet down. The Bishop himself had in the meantime other work in hand. He had to receive certain important visitors, one of them the man who held the appointment of Chancellor of France on the English side, and who was well acquainted with the mind of his masters. We have no information whatever whether Cauchon ever himself wavered, or allowed the possibility of acquitting Jeanne to enter his mind; but he must have seen that it was of the last necessity to know what would satisfy the English chiefs. No doubt he was confirmed and strengthened in the conviction that by hook or by crook her condemnation must be accomplished, by the conversation of these illustrious visitors. To save Jeanne was impossible he must have been told. No English soldier would strike a blow while she lived. England itself, the whole country, trembled at her name. Till she was got rid of nothing could be done.

There was of course great exaggeration in all this, for the English had fought desperately enough in her presence except on the one occasion of Patay, notwithstanding all the early prestige of Jeanne. But at all events it was made perfectly clear that the foregoing conclusion must be carried out, and that Jeanne must die: and, not only so, but she must die with opprobrium and disgrace as a witch, which almost everybody out of Rouen now believed her to be. The public examination which lasted six days was concluded on the third of March, 1430. On the following days, the fourth, fifth, sixth, seventh, eighth, and ninth of March, meetings were held, as we have said, in the Bishop's house to consider what it would be well to do next, at one of which a select company of Inquisitors was chosen to carry on the examination in private. These were Jean de la Fontaine, a lawyer learned in canon law; Jean Beaupère, already her interrogator; Nicolas Midi, a Doctor in Theology; Pierre Morice, Canon of Rouen and Ambassador from the English King to the Council of

Bâle; Thomas de Courcelles, the learned and excellent young Doctor already described; Nicolas l'Oyseleur, the traitor, also already sufficiently referred to; and Manchon, the honest Clerk of the court: the names of Gerard Feuillet, also a distinguished man, and Jean Fecardo, an advocate, are likewise also mentioned. They seem to have served in their turn, three or four at a time. This private session began on the 10th of March, a week after the conclusion of the public trial, and was held in the prison chamber inhabited by the Maid.

We shall not attempt to follow literally those private examinations, which would take a great deal more space than we have at our command, and would be fatiguing to the reader from the constant and prolonged repetitions; we shall therefore quote only such parts as are new or so greatly enlarged from Jeanne's original statements as to seem so. At the first day's examination in her prison she was questioned about Compiègne and her various proceedings before reaching that place. She was asked, for one thing, if her voices had bidden her make the sally in which she was taken; to which she answered that had she known the time she was to be taken she would not have gone out, unless upon the express command of the saints. She was then asked about her standard, her arms, and her horses, and replied that she had no coat-of-arms, but her brothers had, who also had all her money, from ten to twelve thousand francs, which was "no great treasure to make war upon," besides five chargers, and about seven other horses, all from the King. The examiners then came to their principal object, and having lulled her mind with these trifles, turned suddenly to a subject on which they still hoped she might commit herself, the sign which had proved her good faith to the King. It is scarcely possible to avoid the feeling, grave as all the circumstances were, that a littlemalice, a glance of mischievous pleasure, kindled in Jeanne's eye. She had refused to enter into further explanations again and again. She had warned them that she would give them no true light on the subjects that concerned the King. Now she would seem to have had sudden recourse to the mystification that is dear to youth, to have tossed her young head and said: "Have then your own way"; and forthwith proceeded to romance, according to the indications given her of what was wanted, without thought of preserving any appearance of reality. Most probably indeed, her air and tone would make it apparent to her persistent questioners how complete a fable, or at least parable, it was.

Asked, what sign she gave to the King, she replied that it was a beautiful and honourable sign, very creditable and very good, and rich above all. Asked, if it still lasted; answered, "It would be good to know; it will last a thousand years and more if well guarded," adding that it was in the treasure of the King. Asked, if it was of gold or silver or of precious stones, or in the form of a crown; answered: "I will tell you nothing more; but no man could devise a thing so rich as this sign; but the sign that is necessary for you is that God should deliver me out of your hands, and that is what He will do." She also said that when she had to go to the King it was said by her voices: "Go boldly; and when you are before the King he will have a sign which will make him receive and believe in you." Asked, what reverence she made when the sign came to the King, and if it came from God; answered, that she had thanked God for having delivered her from the priests of her own party who had argued against her, and that she had knelt down several times; she also said that an angel from God, and not from another, brought the sign to the King; and she had thanked the Lord many times; she added that the priests ceased to argue against when they had seen that sign. Asked, if the clergy of her party (de par delà) saw the above sign; answered yes, that her King if he were satisfied; and he answered yes. And afterwards she went to a little chapel close by, and heard them say that after she was gone more than three hundred people saw the said sign. She said besides that for love of her, and that they should give up questioning her, God permitted those of her party to see the sign. Asked, if the King and she made reverence to the angel when he brought the sign; answered yes, for herself, that she knelt down and took off her hood.

What Jeanne meant by this strange romance can only, I think be explained by this hypothesis. She was "dazed and bewildered," say some of the historians, evidently not knowing how to interpret so strange an interruption to her narrative; but there is no other sign of bewilderment; her mind was always clear and her intelligence complete. Granting that the whole story was boldly ironical, its object is very apparent. Honour forbade her to betray the King's secret, and she had expressly said she would not do so. But her story seems to say—since you will insist that there was a sign, though I have told you I could give you no information, have it your own way; you shall have a sign and one of the very best; it delivered me from the priests of my own party (de par delà). Jeanne was no milk-sop; she was bold enough to send a winged shaft to the confusion of the priests of the other side who had tormented her in the same way. One can imagine a lurking smile at the corner of her mouth. Let them take it since they would have it. And we may well believe there was that in her eye, and in the details heaped up so lightly to form the miraculous tale, which left little doubt in the minds of the questioners, of the spirit in which she spoke: though to us who only read the record the effect is of a more bewildering kind.

Two days after, on Monday, the 12th of March, the Inquisitors began by several additional questions concerning the angel who brought the sign to the King; was it the same whom she first saw, or another? She answered that it was the same, and no other was wanted. Asked, if this angel had not deceived her since she had been taken prisoner; answered, that SHE BELIEVED SINCE IT SO PLEASED OUR LORD THAT IT WAS BEST THAT SHE SHOULD BE TAKEN. Asked, if the angel had not failed her; answered, "How could he have failed me, when he comforts me every day?" This comfort is what she understands to come through St. Catherine and St. Margaret. Asked, whether she called them, or they came without being called, she answered, that they often came without being called, and if they did not come soon enough, she asked our Saviour to send them. Asked, if St. Denis had ever appeared to her; answered, not that she knew. Asked, if when she promised to our Lord to remain a virgin she spoke to Him; answered, that it ought to be enough to speak to those who were sent by Him that is to say, St. Catherine and St. Margaret. Asked, what induced her to summon a man to Toul, in respect to marriage; answered, "I did not summon him; it was he who summoned me"; and that on that occasion she had sworn before the judge to speak the truth, which was that she had not made him any promise. She also said that the first time she had heard the voices she made a vow of virginity so long as it pleased God, being then about the age of thirteen.

It was the object of the judges by these questions to prove that, according to a fable which had obtained some credit, Jeanne during her visit to La Rousse, the village inn-keeper at Neufchâteau, had acted as servant in the house and tarnished her good fame—so that her betrothed had refused to marry her: and that he had been brought before the Bishop's court at Toul for his breach of promise, as we should say. Exactly the reverse was the case, as the reader will remember.

Jeanne was further asked, if she had spoken of her visions to her curé or to any ecclesiastic: and answered no, but only to Robert de Baudricourt and to her King; but added that she was not bidden by her voices to conceal them, but feared to reveal them lest the Burgundians should hear of them and prevent her going. And especially she had much doubt of her father, lest he should hinder her from going. Asked, if she thought she did well to go away without the permission of her father and mother, when it is certain we ought to honour our father and mother; answered, that in every other thing she had fully obeyed him, except in respect to her departure; but she had written to them, and they had pardoned her. Asked, if when she left her father and mother she did not think it was a sin; answered, that her voices were quite willing that she should tell them, if it were not for the pain it would have given them; but as for herself, she would not have told them for any consideration; also that her voices left her to do as she pleased, to tell or not.

Having gone so far the reverend fathers went to dinner, and Jeanne we hope had her piece of bread and her eau rougie. In the afternoon these indefatigable questioners returned, and the first few questions throw a fuller light on the troubled cottage at Domremy, out of which this wonderful maiden came like a being of another kind.

She was questioned as to the dreams of her father; and answered, that while she was still at home her mother told her several times that her father said he had dreamt that Jeanne his daughter had gone away with the troopers, that her father and mother took great care of her and held her in great subjection: and she obeyed them in every point except that of her affair at Toul in respect to marriage. She also said that her mother had told her what her father had said to her brothers: "If I could think that the thing would happen of which I have dreamed, I wish she might be drowned first; and if you would not do it, I would drown her with my own hands"; and that he nearly lost his senses when she went to Vaucouleurs.

How profound is this little village tragedy! The suspicious, stern, and unhopeful peasant, never sure even that the most transparent and pure may not be capable of infamy, distracted with that horror of personal degradation which is involved in family disgrace, cruel in the intensity of his pride and fear of shame! He has been revealed to us in many lands, always one of the most impressive of human pictures, with no trust of love in him but an overwhelming faith in every vicious possibility. If there is no evidence to prove that, even at the moment when Jeanne was supreme, when he was induced to go to Rheims to see the coronation, Jacques d'Arc was still dark, unresponsive, never more sure than any of the Inquisitors that his daughter was not a witch, or worse, a shameless creature linked to the captains and the splendid personages about her by very different ties from those which appeared—there is at least not a word to prove that he had changed his mind. She does not add anything to soften the description here given. The sudden appearance of this dark remorseless figure, looking on from his village, who probably in all Domremy—when Domremy got to hear the news—would be the only person who would in his desperation almost applaud that stake and devouring flame, is too startling for words.

The end of this day's examination was remarkable also for a sudden light upon the method she had intended to adopt in respect to the Duke of Orleans, then in prison in England, whom it was one of her most cherished hopes to deliver.

Asked, how she meant to rescue the Duc d'Orléans: she answered, that by that time she hoped to have taken English prisoners enough to exchange for him: and if she had not taken enough she should have crossed the sea, in power, to search for him in England. Asked, if St. Catherine and St. Margaret had told her absolutely and without condition that she should take enough prisoners to exchange for the Duc d'Orléans, who was in England, or otherwise, that she should cross the sea to fetch him and bring him back within three years; she answered yes: and that she had told the King and had begged him to permit her to make prisoners. She said further that if she had lasted three years without hindrance, she should have delivered him. Otherwise she said she had not thought of so long a time as three years, although it should have been more than one; but she did not at present recollect exactly.

There is a curious story existing, though we do not remember whence it comes and there is not a scrap of evidence for it, which suggests a rumour that Jeanne was not the child of the d'Arc family at all, but in fact an abandoned and illegitimate child of the Queen, Isabel of Bavaria, and that her real father was the murdered Duc d'Orléans. This suggestion might explain the ease with which she fell into the way of Courts, a sort of air à la Princesse which certainly was about her, and her especial devotion to Orleans, both to the city and the duke. A shadow of a supposed child of our own Queen Mary has also appeared in history, quite without warrant or likelihood. It is a little conventional and well worn even in the way of romance, yet there are certain fanciful suggestions in the thought.

After the above, Jeanne was again questioned and at great length upon the sign given to the King, upon the angel who brought it, the manner of his coming and going, the persons who saw him, those who saw the crown bestowed upon the King, and so on, in the most minute detail. That the purpose of the sign was that "they should give up arguing and so let her proceed on her mission," she repeated again and again; but here is a curious additional note.

She was asked how the King and the people with him were convinced that it was an angel; and answered, that the King knew it by the instruction of the ecclesiastics who were there, and also by the sign of the crown. Asked, how the ecclesiastics (gens d'église) knew it was an angel she answered, "By their knowledge (science), and because they were priests."

Was this the keenest irony, or was it the wandering of a weary mind? We cannot tell; but if the latter, it was the only occasion on which Jeanne's mind wandered; and there was method and meaning in the strange tale.

She was further questioned whether it was by the advice of her voices that she attacked La Charité, and afterwards Paris, her two points of failure; the purpose of her examiners clearly being to convince her that those voices had deceived her. To both questions she answered no. To Paris she went at the request of gentlemen who wished to make a skirmish, or assault of arms (vaillance d'armes); but she intended to go farther, and to pass the moats; that is, to force the fighting and make the skirmish into a serious assault; the same was the case before La Charité. She was asked whether she had no revelation concerning Pont l'Evêque, and said that since it was revealed to her at Melun that she should be taken, she had had more recourse to the will of the captains than to her own; but she did not tell them that it was revealed to her that she should be taken. Asked, if she thought it was well done to attack Paris on the day of the Nativity of our Lady, which was a festival of the Church; she answered, that it was always well to keep the festivals of our Lady: and in her conscience it seemed to her that it was and always would be a good thing to keep the feasts of our Lady, from one end to the other.

In the afternoon the examiners returned to the attempt at escape or suicide—they seemed to have preferred the latter explanation—made at Beaurevoir; and as Jeanne expresses herself with more freedom as to her personal motives in these prison examinations and opens her heart more freely, there is much here which we give in full.

She was asked first what was the cause of her leap from the tower of Beaurevoir. She answered that she had heard that all the people of Compiègne, down to the age of seven, were to be put to the sword, and that she would rather die than live after such a destruction of good people; this was one of the reasons; the other was that she knew that she was sold to the English and that she would rather die than fall into the hands of the English, her enemies. Asked, if she made that leap by the command of her voices; answered, that St. Catherine said to her almost every day that she was not to leap, for that God would help her, and also the people of Compiègne: and she, Jeanne, said to St. Catherine that since God intended to help the people of Compiègne she would fain be there. And St. Catherine said: "You must take it in good part, but you will not be delivered till you have seen the King of the English." And she, Jeanne, answered: "Truly I do not wish to see him. I would rather die than fall into the hands of the English." Asked, if she had said to St. Catherine and St. Margaret, "Will God leave the good people of Compiègne to die so cruelly?" answered, that she did not say "so cruelly," but said it in this way: "Will God leave these good people of Compiègne to die, who have been and are so loyal to their lord?" She added that after she fell there were two or three days that she would not eat; and that she was so hurt by the leap that she could not eat; but all the time she was comforted by St. Catherine, who told her to confess and ask pardon of God for that act, and that without doubt the people of Compiègne would have succour before Martinmas. And then she took pains to recover and began to eat, and shortly was healed.

Asked, whether, when she threw herself down, she wished to kill herself, she answered no; but that in throwing herself down she commended herself to God, and hoped by means of that leap to escape and to avoid being delivered to the English. Asked, if, when she recovered the power of speech, she had denied and blasphemed God and the saints, as had been reported; answered, that she remembered nothing of the kind, and that, as far as she knew, she had never denied and blasphemed God and His saints there nor anywhere else, and did not confess that she had done so, having no recollection of it. Asked, if she would like to see the information taken on the spot, answered: "I refer myself to God, and not another, and to a good confession." Asked, if her voices ever desired delay for their replies; answered, that St. Catherine always answered her at once, but sometimes she, Jeanne, could not hear because of the tumult round her (turbacion des personnes) and the noise of her guards; but that when she asked anything of St. Catherine, sometimes she, and sometimes St.

Margaret asked of our Lord, and then by the command of our Lord an answer was given to her. Asked, if, when they came, there was always light accompanying them, and if she did not see that light when she heard the voice in the castle without knowing whether it was in her chamber or not: answered, that there was never a day that they did not come into the castle, and that they never came without light: and that time she heard the voice, but did not remember whether she saw the light, or whether she saw St. Catherine. Also she said she had asked from her voices three things: one, her release: the other, that God would help the French, and keep the town faithful: and the other the salvation of her soul. Afterwards she asked that she might have a copy of these questions and her answers if she were to be taken to Paris, that she may give them to the people in Paris, and say to them, "This is how I was questioned in Rouen, and here are my replies," that she might not be exhausted by so many questions.

Asked, what she meant when she said that Monseigneur de Beauvais put himself in danger by bringing her to trial, and why Monseigneur de Beauvais more than others, she answered, that this was and is what she said to Monseigneur de Beauvais: "You say that you are my judge. I know not whether you are so; but take care that you judge well, or you will put yourself in great danger. I warn you, so that if our Lord should chastise you for it, I may have done my duty in warning you." Asked, what was that danger? she answered, that St. Catherine had said that she should have succour, but that she knew not whether this meant that she would be delivered from prison, or that, when she was before the tribunal, there might come trouble by which she should be delivered; she thought, however, it would be the one or the other. And all the more that her voices told her that she would be delivered by a great victory; and afterwards they said to her: "Take everything cheerfully, do not be disturbed by this martyrdom: thou shalt thence come at last to the kingdom of Heaven." And this the voices said simply and absolutely—that is to say, without fail; she explained that she called It martyrdom because of all the pain and adversity that she had suffered in prison; and she knew not whether she might have still more to suffer, but waited upon our Lord. She was then asked whether, since her voices had said that she should go to Paradise, she felt assured that she should be saved and not damned in hell; she answered, that she believed firmly what her voices said about her being saved, as firmly as if she were so already. And when it was said to her that this answer was of great weight, she answered that she herself held it as a great treasure.

We have said that Jeanne's answers to the Inquisitors in prison had a more familiar form than in the public examination; which seem to prove that they were not unkind to her, further, at least, than by the persistence and tediousness of their questions. The Bishop for one thing was seldom present; the sittings were frequently presided over by the Deputy Inquisitor, who had made great efforts to be free of the business altogether, and had but very recently been forced into it; so that we may at least imagine, as he was so reluctant, that he did what he could to soften the proceedings. Jean de la Fontaine, too, was a milder man than her former questioners, and in so small an assembly she could not be disturbed and interrupted by Frère Isambard's well-meant signs and whispers. She speaks at length and with a self-disclosure which seems to have little that was painful in it, like one matured into a kind of age by long weariness and trouble, who regards the panorama of her life passing before her with almost a pensive pleasure. And it is clear that Jeanne's ear, still so young and keen, notwithstanding that attitude of mind, was still intent upon sounds from without, and that Jeanne's heart still expected a sudden assault, a great victory for France, which should open her prison doors —or even a rising in the very judgment hall to deliver her. How could they keep still outside, Dunois, Alençon, La Hire, the mighty men of valour, while they knew that she was being racked and tortured within? She who could not bear to be out of the conflict to serve her friends at Compiègne, even when succour from on high had been promised, how was it possible that these gallant knights could live and let her die, their gentle comrade, their dauntless leader? In those long hours, amid the noise of the guards within and the garrison around, how she must have thought, over and over again, where were they? when were they coming? how often imagined that a louder clang of arms than usual, a rush of hasty feet, meant that they were here!

But honour and love kept Jeanne's lips closed. Not a word did she say that could discredit King, or party, or friends; not a reproach to those who had abandoned her. She still looked for the great victory in which Monseigneur, if he did not take care, might run the risk of being roughly handled, or of a sudden tumult in his own very court that would pitch him form his guilty seat. It was but the fourteenth of March still, and there were six weary weeks to come. She did not know the hour or the day, but yet she believed that this great deliverance was on its way.

And there was a great deliverance to come: but not of this kind. The voices of God—how can we deny it?—are often, though in a loftier sense, like those fantastic voices that keep the word of promise to the ear but break it to the heart. They promised her a great victory: and she had it, and also the fullest deliverance: but only by the stake and the fire, which were not less dreadful to Jeanne than to any other girl of her age. They did not speak to deceive her, but she was deceived; they kept their promise, but not as she understood it. "These all died in faith, not having received the promises, but having seen them afar off, and were persuaded of them, and embraced them." Jeanne too was persuaded of them, but was not to receive them—except in the other way.

On the afternoon of the same day (it was still Lent, and Jeanne fasted, whatever our priests may have done), she was again closely questioned on the subject, this time, of Franquet d'Arras, who, as has been above narrated, was taken by her in the course of some indiscriminate fighting in the north. She was asked if it was not mortal sin to take a man as prisoner of war and then give him up to be executed. There was evidently no perception of similarities in the minds of the judges, for this was precisely what had been done in the case of Jeanne herself; but even she does not seem to have been struck by the fact. Their object, apparently, was by proving that she was in a state of sin, to prove also that her voices were of no authority, as being unable to discover so simple a principle as this.

When they spoke to her of "one named Franquet d'Arras, who was executed at Lagny," she answered that she consented to his death, as he deserved it, for he had confessed to being a murderer, a thief, and a traitor. She said that his trial lasted fifteen days, the Bailli de Senlis and the law officers of Lagny being the judges; and she added that she had wished to have Franquet, to exchange him for a man of Paris, Seigneur de Lours (corrected, innkeeper at the sign of l'Ours); but when she heard that this man was dead, and when the Bailli told her that she would go very much against justice if she set Franquet free, she said to the Bailli: "Since my man is dead whom I wished to deliver, do with this one whatever justice demands." Asked, if she took the money or allowed it to be taken by him who had taken Franquet, she answered, that she was not a money changer or a treasurer of France, to deal with money.

She was then reminded that having assaulted Paris on a holy day, having taken the horse of Monseigneur de Senlis, having thrown herself down from the tower of Beaurevoir, having consented to the death of Franquet d'Arras, and being still dressed in the costume of a man, did she not think that she must be in a state of mortal sin? She answered to the first question about Paris: "I do not think I was guilty of mortal sin, and if I have sinned it is to God that I would make it known, and in confession to God by the priest." To the second question, concerning the horse of Senlis, she answered, that she believed firmly that there was not mortal sin in this, seeing it was valued, and the Bishop had due notice of it, and at all events it was sent back to the Seigneur de la Trémouille to give it back to Monseigneur de Senlis. The said horse was of no use to her; and, on the other hand, she did not wish to keep it because she heard that the Bishop was displeased that his horse should have been taken. And as for the tower of Beaurevoir: "I did it not to destroy myself, but in the hope of saving myself and of going to the aid of the good people who were in need." But after having done it, she had confessed her sin, and asked pardon of our Lord, and had pardon of Him. And she allowed that it was not right to have made that leap, but that she did wrong.

The next day an important question was introduced, the only one as yet which

Jeanne does not seem to have been able to answer with understanding. On points of fact or in respect to her visions she was always quite clear, but questions concerning the Church were beyond her knowledge. It is only indeed after some time has elapsed that we perceive why such a question was introduced.

After admonitions made to her she was required, if she had done anything contrary to the faith, to submit herself to the decision of the Church. She replied, that her answers had all been heard and seen by clerks, and that they could say whether there was anything in them against the faith: and that if they would point out to her where any error was, afterwards she would tell them what was said by her counsellors. At all events if there was anything against the faith which our Lord had commanded, she would not sustain it, and would be very sorry to go against that. Here it was shown to her that there was a Church militant and a Church triumphant, and she was asked if she knew the difference between them. She was also required to put herself under the jurisdiction of the Church, in respect to what she had done, whether it was good or evil, but replied, "I will answer no more on this point for the present."

Having thrown in this tentative question which she did not understand, they returned to the question of her dress, which holds such an important place in the entire interrogatory. If she were allowed to hear mass as she wished, having been all this time deprived of religious ordinances, did not she think it would be more honest and befitting that she should go in the dress of a woman? To this she replied vaguely, that she would much rather go to mass in the dress of a woman than to retain her male costume and not to hear mass; and that if she were certified that she should hear mass, she would be there in a woman's dress. "I certify you that you shall hear mass," the examiner replied, "but you must be dressed as a woman." "What would you say," she answered as with a momentary doubt, "if I had sworn to my King never to change?" but she added: "Anyhow I answer for it. Find me a dress, long, touching the ground, without a train, and give it to me to go to mass; but I will return to my present dress when I come back." She was then asked why she would not have all the parts of a female dress to go to mass in; she said, "I will take counsel upon that, and answer you," and begged again for the honour of God and our Lady that she might be allowed to hear mass in this good town. Afterwards she was again recommended to assume the whole dress of a woman and gave a conditional assent: "Get me a dress like that of a young bourgeoise, that is to say, a long houppelande; I will wear that and a woman's hood to go to mass." After having promised, however, she made an appeal to them to leave her free, and to think no more of her garb, but to allow her to hear mass without changing it. This would seem to have been refused, and all at once without warning the jurisdiction of the Church was suddenly introduced again.

She was asked, whether in all she did and said she would submit herself to the Church, and replied: "All my deeds and works are in the hands of God, and I depend only on Him; and I certify that I desire to do nothing and say nothing against the Christian faith; and if I have done or said anything in the body that was against the Christian faith which our Lord has established, I should not defend it but cast it forth from me." Asked again, if she would not submit to the laws of the Church she replied: "I can answer no more to-day on this point; but on Saturday send the clerk to me, if you do not come, and I will answer by the grace of God, and it can be put in writing."

A great many questions followed as to her visions, but chiefly what had been asked before. One thing only we may note, since it was one of the special sayings all her own, which fell from the lips of Jeanne, during this private and almost sympathetic examination. After being questioned closely as to how she knew her first visitor to be St. Michael, etc., she was asked, how she would have known had he been "l'Anemy" himself (a Norman must surely have used this word), taking the form of an angel: and finally, what doctrine he taught her?

She answered; above all things he said that she was to be a good child and that God would help her: and among other things that she was to go to the succour of the King of France. But the greater part of what the angel taught her, she continued, was already in their book; and THE ANGEL SHOWED HER THE GREAT PITY THERE WAS OF THE KINGDOM OF FRANCE.

The pity of it! That which has always gone most to the tender heart: a country torn in pieces, brother fighting against brother, the invader seated at the native hearth, and blood and fire making the smiling land a desert: "la pitie qui estoit au royaume de France."

Did the Inquisitor break down here? Could no one go on? or was it mere human incompetence to feel the divine touch? Some one broke into a foolish question about the height of the angel, and the sitting was hurriedly concluded. Monseigneur might well be on his mettle; that very pity, was it not stealing into the souls of his private committee deputed for so different a use?

Next day the questions about St. Michael's personal appearance were resumed, as a little feint we can only suppose, for the great question of the Church was again immediately introduced; but in the meantime Jeanne had described her visitor in terms which it is pleasant to dwell on. "He was in the form of a très vrai prud' homme." The term is difficult to translate, as is the Galantuomo of Italy. The "King-Honest Man," we used to say in English in the days of his late Majesty Victor Emmanuel of Italy; but that is not all that is meant—un vrai prud' homme, a man good, honest, brave, the best man, is more like it. The girl's honest imagination thought of no paraphernalia of wings or shining plumes. It was not the theatrical angel, not even the angel of art whom she saw

—whom it would have been so easy to invent, nay to take quite truthfully from the first painted window, radiating colour and brightness through the dim, low-roofed church. But even with such material handy, Jeanne was not led into the conventional. She knew nothing about wings or emblematic scales. He was in the form of a brave and gentle man. She knew not anything greater, nor would she be seduced into fable however sacred. Then once more the true assault began.

She was asked, if she would submit all her sayings and doings, good or evil, to the judgment of our Holy Mother, the Church. She replied, that as for the Church, she loved it and would sustain it with all her might for our Christian faith; and that it was not she whom they ought to disturb and hinder from going to church or from hearing mass. As to the good things she had done, and that had happened, she must refer all to the King of Heaven, who had sent her to Charles, King of France; and it should be seen that the French would soon gain a great advantage which God would send them, so great that all the kingdom of France would be shaken. And this, she said, that when it came to pass, they might remember that she had said it. She was again asked, if she would submit to the jurisdiction of the Church, and answered, "I refer everything to our Lord who sent me, to our Lady, and to the blessed Saints of Paradise"; and added her opinion was that our Lord and the Church meant the same thing, and that difficulties should not be made concerning this, when there was no difficulty, and they were both one. She was then told that there was the Church triumphant, in which are God, the saints, the angels, and all saved souls. The Church militant is our Holy Father the Pope, vicar of God on earth, the cardinals, the prelates of the Church, and the clergy and all good Christians and Catholics, which Church properly assembled cannot err, but is guided by the Holy Spirit. And this being the case she was asked if she would refer her cause to the Church militant thus explained to her. She replied that she had come to the King of France on the part of God, on the part of the Virgin Mary, the blessed Saints of Paradise, and the Church victorious in Heaven, and at their commandment; and to that Church she submitted all her good deeds, and all that she had done and might do. And if they asked her whether she would submit to the Church militant, answered, that she would now answer no more than this.

Here again the argument strayed back to the futile subject of dress, always at hand to be taken up again, one would say, when the judges were non-plussed. Her first reply on this subject is remarkable and shows that dark and terrible forebodings were already beginning to mingle with her hopes.

Asked, what she had to say about the woman's dress that had been offered to her, to hear mass in: she answered, that she would not take it yet, not until the Lord pleased; but that if it were necessary to lead her out to be executed, and if she should then have to be undressed, she required of the Lords of the Church that they would give her the grace to have a long chemise, and a kerchief for her head; that she would prefer to die rather than to alter what our Lord had directed her to do, and that she firmly believed our Lord would not let her descend so low, but that she should soon be helped by God and by a miracle. She was then asked, if what she did in respect to the man's costume was by command of God, why she asked for a woman's chemise in case of death? answered, It is enough that it should be long.

The effect of these words in which so much was implied, must have made a supreme sensation among the handful of men gathered round the helpless girl in her prison, bringing the stake in all its horror before the eyes of the judges as before her own. No other thing could have been suggested by that piteous prayer. The stake, the scaffold, the fire—and the shrinking figure all maidenly, helpless, exposed to every evil gaze, must have showed themselves at least for a moment against that dark background of prison wall. It was enough that it should be long—to hide her as much as was possible from those dreadful staring eyes.

The interrogatory goes on wildly after this about the age and the dress of the saints. But a tone of fate had come into it, and Jeanne herself, it was evident, was very serious; her mind turned to more weighty thoughts. Presently they asked if the saints hated the English, to which she replied that they hated what God hated and loved what He loved. She was then asked if God hated the English. She replied that of the love or hate that God had for the English, or what God did for their souls, she knew nothing; but she knew well that they should be driven out of France, except those who died there; and that God would send victory to the French against the English. Asked, if God was for the English so long as they were prosperous in France: she answered, that she knew not whether God hated the French, but believed He had allowed them to be beaten because of their sins.

Jeanne was then brought to a test which, had she been a great statesman or a learned doctor, would have been as dangerous, as the question concerning John the Baptist was to the priests and scribes. "If we shall say: From heaven, he will say, Why then believed ye him not? but if we shall say of men we fear the people." And she was only a peasant girl and the event of which they spoke had been before her little time.

Asked, if she thought and believed firmly that her King did well to kill Monseigneur de Bourgogne, she answered that IT WAS A GREAT MISFORTUNE FOR THE KINGDOM OF FRANCE: but that however it might be among themselves, God had sent her to the succour of the King.

One or two other questions of some importance followed amid perpetual changes of the subject: one of which called forth as follows her last deliverance on the subject of the Pope.

Asked, if she had said to Monseigneur de Beauvais that she would answer as exactly to him and to his clerks as she would have done before our Holy Father the Pope, although at several points in the trial she would have had to refuse to answer, if she did not answer more plainly than before Monseigneur de Beauvais—she said that she had answered as much as she knew, and that if anything came to her memory that she had forgotten to say, she would say it willingly. Asked, if it seemed to her that she would be bound to answer the plain truth to the Pope, the vicar of God, in all he asked her touching the faith and her conscience, she replied that she desired to be taken before him, and then she would answer all that she ought to answer.

Here we seem to perceive dimly that there was beginning to be a second party among those examiners, one of which was covertly but earnestly attempting to lead Jeanne into an appeal to the Pope, which would have conveyed her out of the hands of the English at least, and gained time, probably deliverance for her, could Jeanne have been made to understand it.

This, however, was by no means the wish of Cauchon, whose spy and whisperer, L'Oyseleur, was working against it in the background. Jeanne evidently failed to take up what they meant. She did not understand the distinction between the Church militant and the Church triumphant: that God alone was her judge, and that no tribunal could decide upon the questions which were between her Lord and herself, was too firmly fixed in her mind: and again and again the men whose desire was to make her adopt this expedient, were driven back into the ever repeated questions about St. Catherine and St. Margaret.

One other of her distinctive sayings fell from her in the little interval that remained, in a series of useless questions about her standard. Was it true that this standard had been carried into the Cathedral at Rheims when those of the other captains were left behind? "It had been through the labour and the pain," she said, "there was good reason that it should have the honour."

This last movement of a proud spirit, absolutely disinterested and without thought of honour or advancement in the usual sense of the word, gives a sort of trumpet note at the end of these wonderful wranglings in prison, in which, however, there is a softening of tone visible throughout, and evident effect of human nature bringing into immediate contact divers human creatures day after day. Jeanne is often at her best, and never so frequently as during these less formal sittings utters those flying words, simple and noble and of absolute truth to nature, which are noted everywhere, even in the most rambling records.

The private examination, concluding with that last answer about the banner, came to an end on the 17th March, the day before Passion Sunday. Several subsequent days were occupied with repeated consultations in the Bishop's palace, and the reading over of the minutes of the examinations, to the judges first and afterwards to Jeanne, who acknowledged their correctness, with one or two small amendments. It is only now that Cauchon reappears in his own person. On the morning of the following Sunday, which was Palm Sunday, he and four other doctors with him had a conversation with Jeanne in her prison, very early in the morning, touching her repeated application to be allowed to hear mass and to communicate. The Bishop offered her his ultimatum: if she consented to resume her woman's dress, she might hear mass, but not otherwise; to which Jeanne replied, sorrowfully, that she would have done so before now if she could; but that it was not in her power to do so. Thus after the long and bitter Lent her hopes of sharing in the sacred feast were finally taken from her. It remains uncertain whether she considered that her change of dress would be direct disobedience to God, which her words seem often to imply; or whether it would mean renunciation of her mission, which she still hoped against hope to be able to resume; or if the fear of personal insult weighed most with her. The latter reason had evidently something to do with it, but, as evidently, not all.

The background to these curious sittings, afterwards revealed to us, casts a hazy side-light upon them. Probably the Bishop, never present, must have been made aware by his spies of an intention on the part of those most favourable to Jeanne to support an appeal to the Pope; and L'Oyseleur, the traitor, who was all this time admitted to her cell by permission of Cauchon, and really as his tool and agent, was actively employed in prejudicing her mind against them, counselling her not to trust to those clerks, not to yield to the Church. How he managed to explain his own appearance on the other side, his official connection with the trial, and constant presence as one of her judges, it is hard to imagine. Probably he gave her to believe that he had sought that position (having got himself liberated from the imprisonment which he had represented himself as sharing) for her sake, to be able to help her.

On the other hand her friends, whose hearts were touched by her candour and her sufferings, were not inactive. Jean de la Fontaine and the two monks— l'Advenu and Frère Isambard—also succeeded in gaining admission to her, and pressed upon her the advantage of appealing to the Church, to the Council of Bâle about to assemble, or to the Pope himself, which would have again changed the venue, and transferred her into less prejudiced hands. It is very likely that Jeanne in her ignorance and innocence might have held by her reference to the supreme tribunal of God in any case; and it is highly unlikely that of the English authorities, intent on removing the only thing in France of which their forces were afraid, should have given her up into the hands of the

Pope, or allowed her to be transferred to any place of defence beyond their reach; but at least it is a relief to the mind to find that all these men were not base, as appears on the face of things, but that pity and justice and human feeling sometimes existed under the priest's gown and the monk's cowl, if also treachery and falsehood of the blackest kind. The Bishop, who remained withdrawn, we know not why, from all these private sittings in the prison (probably busy with his ecclesiastical duties as Holy Week was approaching), heard with fury of this visit and advice, and threatened vengeance upon the meddlers, not without effect, for Jean de la Fontaine, we are told—who had been deep in his councils, and indeed his deputy, as chief examiner— disappeared from Rouen immediately after, and was heard of no more.

CHAPTER XV — RE-EXAMINATION. MARCH-MAY, 1431.

Upon all these contentions followed the calm of Palm Sunday, a great and touching festival, the first break upon the gloom of Lent, and a forerunner of the blessedness of Easter. We have already told how—a semblance of charity with which the reader might easily be deceived—the Bishop and four of his assessors had gone to the prison to offer to the Maid permission to receive the sacrament if she would do so in a woman's dress: and how after pleading that she might be allowed that privilege as she was, in her male costume, and with a pathetic statement that she would have yielded if she could, but that it was impossible—she finally refused; and was so left in her prison to pass that sacred day unsuccoured and alone. The historian Michelet, in the wonderful sketch in which he rises superior to himself, and which amidst all after writings remains the most beautiful and touching memorial of Jeanne d'Arc, has made this day a central point in his tale, using with the skill of genius the service of the Church appropriate to the day, in heart-rending contrast with those doors of the prison which did not open, and the help of God which did not come to the young and solitary captive. Le beau jour fleuri passed over her in darkness and desertion: her agony and passion lay before her like those of the Divine Sufferer, to whom every day of the succeeding week is specially consecrated. There is almost indeed a painful following of the Saviour's steps in these dark days, the circumstances lending themselves in a wonderful way to the comparison which French writers love to make, but which many of us must always feel, however spotless the sufferer, to have a certain irreverence in them. But if ever martyr were worthy of being called a partaker of the sufferings of Christ it was surely this girl, free, if ever human creature was, from self-seeking, or thought of reward, or ambitious hope, in whose heart there had never been any motive but the service of God and the deliverance of her country, who had neither looked before nor after, nor put her own interests into consideration in any way. Silently the feast passed with no holy privileges of religion, no blessed token of the spring, no remembrance of the waving palms and scattered blossoms over which her Lord rode into Jerusalem to die. She had not that sweet fallacious triumph; but the darker ordeal remained for her to follow.

On Tuesday the 27th of March, her troubles began again. Before Palm Sunday, the report of the trial had been read to her. She had now to hear the formal reading of the articles founded upon it, to give a final response if she had any to give, or explanation, or addition, if she thought proper. The sitting was held in the great hall of the Castle of Rouen before a band of more than forty, all assembled for this final test. The Bishop made a prefactory speech to the prisoner, pointing out to her how benign and merciful were the judges now assembled, that they had no wish to punish, but rather to instruct and lead her in the right way; and requesting her at this late period in the proceedings to choose one or more from among them to help her. To which Jeanne replied; "In the first place concerning my good and our faith, I thank you and all the company. As for the counsellor you offer me I thank you also, but I have no need to depart from our Lord as my counsellor."

The articles, in which the former questions put to her and answered by her, were now repeated in the form of accusations, were then read to her one by one; her sorcery, sacrilege, etc., being taken as facts. To a few she repeated, with various forcible and fine turns of phrase, her previous answers, with here and there a new explanation; but to the great majority she referred simply to her former replies, or denied the charge, as follows: "The second article concerning sortilège, superstitious acts and divination, she denied, and in respect to adoration (i.e. allowing herself to be adored) said: If any kissed her hands or her garments, it was not by her will, and that she kept herself from it as much as she could; and the rest of the article she denies." This is a specimen of the manner in which she responded, with a clear-headed and undisturbed intelligence, point after point—ipsa Johanna negat, is the usual refrain: or else she referred with dignity to previous replies as her sole answer. But sometimes the girl was moved to indignation, sometimes added a word in her own defence: "As for fairies she knew not what they were, and as for her education she had been well and duly instructed what to believe, as a good child should." This was her answer to the article in which all the folk-lore of Domremy, all the fairy tales, had been collected into a solemn statement of heresy. The matter of dress was once more treated in endless detail, with many interjected questions and reports of what she had already said: and at the end, answering the statement that woman's dress was most fit for woman's work, Jeanne added the quick mot: "As for the usual work of women, there are enough of other women to do it." On another occasion when the report ran that she claimed to have done all things by the counsel of God, she interrupted and said "that it ought to be, all that I have done well." To her former answer that she had yielded to the desire of the French knights in attacking Paris, she added the fine words, "It seemed to me that it was their duty to attack their adversaries." In respect to her visions she added to her former answer, "that she had not asked advice of bishop, curé, or any other before believing her revelations, but had many times prayed God to reveal them to others of her party." About calling her saints when she required their aid she added, that she asked God and Our Lady to send her council and comfort, and immediately her heavenly visitors came; and that this was the prayer she made:

"Gentle God, in honour of Your passion, I pray You, if You love me, that You would reveal to me how I ought to answer these people of the Church. I know well by what command it was that I took this dress, but I know not in what manner I ought to give it up. For this may it please You to teach me."

In respect to the reproach that she had been a general in the war (chef de guerre), she explained that if she were, it was to drive out the English, repelling the accusation that she had assumed this title in pride; and to that which accused her of preferring to live among men, she explained that when she was in a lodging she generally had a woman with her; but that when engaged in war she lived in her clothes whenever there was not a woman present. In respect to her hope of escaping from prison, she was asked if her council had thrown any light on that question, and replied, "I have yet to tell you." Manchon, the clerk, makes a note upon his margin at these words, "Proudly answered"—superbe responsum.

This re-examination lasted for two long days, the 27th and 28th of March. On several points Jeanne requested that she might be allowed to give an answer on Saturday, and accordingly, on Saturday, the last day of March, Easter Eve, she was visited in prison by the Bishop and seven or eight assessors. She was then asked if she would submit to the judgment of the Church on earth all that she had done and said, specially in things that concerned her trial. She answered that she would submit to the judgment of the Church militant, provided that it did not enforce anything that was impossible. She explained that what she called impossible was to acknowledge that the visions and revelations came otherwise than from God, or that what she had done was not on the part of God: these she would never deny or revoke for any power on earth: and that which our Lord had commanded or should command, she would not give up for any living man, and this would be impossible to her. And in case the Church should command her to do anything contrary to the command given her by God she would not do it for any reason whatsoever. Asked whether she would submit to the Church if the Church militant pronounced that her revelations were delusions or from the devil, or superstitious, or evil things, she answered that she would refer everything to our Lord, whose command she always obeyed; and that she knew well that everything had come to her by the commandment of God; and that what she had affirmed during this trial to have been done by the commandment of God it would be impossible for her to deny. And in case the Church militant commanded her to go against God, she would submit herself to no man in this world but to our Lord, whose good commandment she had always obeyed. She was asked if she did not believe that she was subject to the Church on earth, that is, to our Holy Father the Pope, the Cardinals, Bishops, and other prelates of the Church. She answered, "Yes, our Lord being served first." Asked if she had directions from her voices not to submit to the Church militant which is on earth, nor to its judgment, she replied that she does not answer according to what comes into her head, but that when she replies it is by commandment; and that she has never been told not to obey the Church, our Lord being served first (noster Sire premier servi).

Other less formal particulars come to us long after, from various witnesses at the procès de rehabilitation, in which a lively picture is given of this scene. Frère Isambard had apparently managed, as was his wont, to get close to the prisoner, and to whisper to her to appeal to the Council of Bâle. "What is this Council of Bâle?" she asked in the same tone. Isambard replied that it was the "congregation of the whole Church, Catholic and Universal, and that there would be as many there on her side as on that of the English." "Ah!" she cried, "since there will be some of our party in that place, I will willingly yield and submit to the Council of Bâle, to our Holy Father the Pope, and to the sacred Council." And immediately—continues the deposition—the Bishop of Beauvais cried out, "Silence, in the devil's name!" and told the notary to take no notice of what she said, that she would submit herself to the Council of Bâle; whereupon a second cry burst from the bosom of Jeanne, "You write what is against me, but you will not write what is for me." "Because of these things, the English and their officers threatened terribly the said Frère Isambard, warning him that if he did not hold his peace he would be thrown in the Seine." No notice whatever is taken of any such interruption in the formal record. It must have been before this time that Jean de la Fontaine disappeared. He left Rouen secretly and never returned, nor does he ever appear again. Frère Isambard is said to have taken temporary refuge in his convent; they scattered, de par l'diable, according to the Christian adjuration of Mgr. De Beauvais; though l'Advenu would seem to have held his ground, and served as Confessor to Jeanne in her agony, at which Frère Isambard was also present. We are told that the Deputy Inquisitor Lemâitre, he who had been got to lend the aid of his presence with such difficulty, fiercely warned the authorities that he would have no harm done to those two friars, from which we may infer that he too had leanings towards the Maid; and these honest and loyal men, well deserving of their country and of mankind, should not lose their record when the tragic story of so much human treachery and baseness has to be told.

After this there came a long pause, full of much business to the judges, councillors, and clerks who had to reduce the seventy articles to twelve, in order to forward a summary of the case to the University of Paris for their judgment. Jeanne in the meantime had been left, but not neglected, in her prison. The great Feast of Easter had passed without any sacred consolation of the Church; but Monseigneur de Beauvais, in his kindness, sent her a carp to keep the feast withal, if not any spiritual food. It was quite congenial to the spirit of the time to imagine that the carp had been poisoned, and such a thought seems to have crossed the mind of Jeanne, who was very ill after eating of it, and like to die. But it was not thus, poisoned in prison, that it would have suited any of her persecutors to let her die. As a matter of fact, as soon as it was known that she was ill, the best doctors procurable were sent to the prison with peremptory orders to prolong her life and cure her at any cost. But for a little time we lose sight of the sick-bed on which the unfortunate Maid lay fully dressed, never relinquishing the garb which was her protection, with her feet chained to her uneasy couch. Even at the moment when her life hung in the balance we read of no indulgence granted in this respect, no unlocking of the infamous chain, nor substitution of a gentler nurse for the attendanthouspillers, who were her guards night and day.

When the Bishop and his court had completed their business and sent off to Paris the important document on which so much depended, they found themselves at leisure to return to Jeanne, to inquire after her health and to make her "a charitable admonition." It was on the 18th of April, after the silence of more than a fortnight, that their visit was made with this benevolent purpose. Seven of her judges attended the Bishop into the sick-chamber. They had come, he assured her, charitably and familiarly, to visit her in her sickness and to carry her comfort and consolation. Most of these men were indeed familiar enough: she had seen their faces already through many a dreadful day, though there were one or two which were new and strange, come to stare at her in the depths of her distress. Cauchon reminded her how much and how carefully she had been questioned by the most wise and learned men; and that those there present were ready to do anything for the salvation of her soul and body in every possible way, by instructing or advising her. He added, however, that if she still refused to accept advice, and to act according to the counsel of the Church, she was in the greatest danger—to which she replied:

"It seems to me, being so ill as I am, that I am in great danger of death. And if it is thus that God pleases to decide for me, I ask of you to be allowed to confess and receive my Saviour, and to be laid in holy ground."

"If you desire to have the rites and sacraments of the Church," said Cauchon, "you must do as good Catholics ought to do, submit to Holy Church." She answered, "I can say no other thing to you." She was then told that if she was in fear of death through sickness she ought all the more to amend her life; but that she could not have the privileges of the Church as a Catholic, if she did not submit to the Church. She answered: "If my body dies in prison, I hope that you will bury me in consecrated ground: yet if not, I still hope in our Lord."

She was then reminded that she had said in her trial—if anything had been said or done by her against our Christian faith ordained by our Lord, that she would not stand by it. She answered, "I refer to the answer I made, and to our Lord."

It was then asked of her, since she believed herself to have had many revelations from God by St. Michael, St. Catherine, and St. Margaret, whether if there should appear some good creature (sic) who professed to have had a revelation from God in respect to her, she would believe that? She answered that there was no Christian in the world who could come to her professing to have had a revelation, of whom she should not know whether he spoke the truth or not: she would know it through St. Catherine and St. Margaret.

Asked, if she could not imagine that God might reveal something to a good creature who might be unknown to her, she answered: "Yes; but I would not believe either man or woman without a sign."

Asked, if she believed that the Holy Scripture was revealed by God, she answered, "You know that I do, and it is good to know."

The last answer she made in respect to submission to Holy Church was this, "Whatever may happen to me I will neither do nor say anything else, for I have answered before, during the trial."

She was then "exhorted powerfully by the venerable doctors present" (four are mentioned by name) to submit to our Mother the Church, with many authorities and examples drawn from the Holy Scriptures; and finally, Magister Nicolas Midi made her an exhortation from Matthew xviii.: "If your brother trespass against you," and what follows, "If he will not hear the Church, let him be to you as a heathen man and a publican." This was expounded to Jeanne in the French tongue and, finally, she was told that if she would not obey and submit to the Church she must be given up as if she was a Saracen. To which Jeanne replied that she was a good Christian and well baptised, and that she desired to die as a Christian. She was then asked whether, since she begged leave of the Church to receive her Saviour, she would submit to the Church if it were promised to her that she should receive. She answered that she would say no more than she had said; that she loved God, served Him, and was a good Christian, and would aid and uphold the

Holy Church with all her power. Asked if she wished that a beautiful procession should be made for her to restore her to health, she answered that she would be glad if the Church and the Catholics would pray for her.

For another fortnight Jeanne was sent back into the silence, and to her own thoughts, which must have grown heavier and heavier as the weary days went on, and no sound of approaching deliverance came, no rumour of help at hand. All was quiet and safe at Rouen; amid the babble of the courtyard which she might hear fitfully when her guardians were quieter than usual, there was not one word which brought the hope of a French army at hand, or of any movement to rescue her. All was silent in the world around, not a breath of hope, not the whisper of a friend. It was not till the 2d of May that the dreadful blank was again broken, and she was called to the great hall of the castle for another interview with her tormentors. When she was led into the hall it was full, as in the first sitting, sixty-three judges in all being present. The interest had flagged or the pity had grown as the trial dragged its slow length along; but now, when every day the verdict was expected from Paris, the interest had risen again. On her way from her prison to the hall, it was necessary to pass the door of the castle chapel: and here once or twice Massieu, the officer of the court, had permitted her to pause and kneel down as she passed. This was all the celebration of the Paschal Feast that was permitted to Jeanne. The compassionate official, however, was discovered in this small service of charity, and sternly reprimanded and threatened. Henceforward she had to pass without even a longing look through the door at the altar on which was the holy sacrament.

She came in on the renewed sitting of the 2d May to find the assembled priests settling themselves, after the address which had been made to them, to hear another address which John de Chasteillon, Archdeacon, had prepared for herself, in which he said much that was good both for body and soul, to which she consented. He had a list of twelve articles in his hands, and explained and expounded them to her, as they were the occasion of the sitting. He then "admonished her in charity," explaining that those who were faithful to Christ hold firmly and closely to the Christian creed, and adjuring her to consent and to amend her ways. To this Jeanne answered: "Read your book," meaning the schedule held by Monseigneur the Archdeacon, "and then I will answer you. I refer myself to God my master in all things; and I love Him with all my heart."

To read this book, however, was precisely what Monseigneur the Archdeacon had no intention of doing. She was never allowed to hear the twelve articles upon which the verdict against her was founded; but the speaker gave her a long discourse by way of explanation, following more or less the schedule which he held. This "monition general," however, elicited no detailed reply from Jeanne, who answered briefly with some impatience, "I refer myself to my judge, who is the King of Heaven and earth." The "Lord Archdeacon" then proceeded to "monitions particulares."

It was then once more explained to her that this reference to God alone was a refusal to submit to the Church militant, and she was instructed in the authority of the Church, which it was the duty of every Christian to believe—unam sanctam Ecclesiam always guided by the Holy Spirit and which could not err, to the judgment of which every question should be referred. She answered: "I believe in the Church here below; but my doings and sayings, as I have already said, I refer and submit to God. I believe that the Church militant cannot err or fail; but as for my deeds and words I put them all before God, who has made me do that which I have done"; she also said that she submitted herself to God, her Creator, who had made her do everything, and referred everything to Him, and to Him alone.

She was then asked, if she would have no judge on earth and if our Holy Father the Pope were not her judge; she answered: "I will tell you nothing more. I have a good master, that is our Lord, on whom I depend for everything, and not an any other."

She was then told that if she would not believe the Church and the article Ecclesiam sanctam Catholicam, that she might be reckoned as a heretic and punished by burning: to which she answered: "I can say nothing else to you; and if I saw the fire before me, I should say only that which I say, and could do nothing else." (Once more at this point the clerk writes on his margin, "Proud reply"—Superba responsio—but whether in admiration or in blame it would be hard to say.)

Asked, if the Council General, or the Holy Father, Cardinals, etc., were there —whether she would submit to them. "You shall have no other answer from me," she said.

Asked, if she would submit to our Holy Father the Pope: she answered, "Take me to him and I will answer him," but would say no more.

Questioned in respect to her dress, she answered, that she would willingly accept a long dress and a woman's hood to go to church to receive her Saviour, provided that, as she had already said, she were allowed to wear it on that occasion only, and then to take back that which she at present wore. Further, when it was set before her that she wore that dress without any need, being in prison, she answered, "When I have done that for which I was sent by God, I will then take back a woman's dress." Asked, if she thought she did well in being dressed like a man, she answered, "I refer every thing to our Lord."

Again, after the exhortation made to her, namely, that in saying that she did well and did not sin in wearing that dress, and in the circumstances which concerned her assuming and wearing it, and in saying that God and the saints made her do so—she blasphemed, and as is contained in this schedule, erred and did evil: she answered that she never blasphemed God or the saints.

She was then admonished to give up that dress, and no longer to think it was right, and to return to the garb of a woman; but answered that she would make no change in this respect.

Concerning her revelations: she replied in regard to them, that she referred everything to her judge, that is God, and that her revelations were from God, without any other medium.

Asked concerning the sign given to the King if she would refer to the Archbishop of Rheims, the Sire de Boussac, Charles de Bourbon, La Tremouille, and La Hire, to them or to any one of them, who, according to what she formerly said, had seen the crown, and were present when the angel brought it, and gave it to the Archbishop; or if she would refer to any others of her party who might write under their seals that it was so; she answered, "Send a messenger, and I will write to them about the whole trial": but otherwise she was not disposed to refer to them.

In respect to her presumption in divining the future, etc., she answered, "I refer everything to my judge who is God, and to what I have already answered, which is written in the book."

Asked, if two or three or four knights of her party were to be brought here under a safe conduct, whether she would refer to them her apparitions and other things contained in this trial; answered, "Let them come and then I will answer:" but otherwise she was not willing to refer to anyone.

Asked whether, at the Church of Poitiers where she was examined, she had submitted to the Church, she answered, "Do you hope to catch me in this way, and by that draw advantage to yourselves?"

In conclusion, "afresh and abundantly," she was admonished to submit herself to the Church, on pain of being abandoned by the Church; for if the Church left her she would be in great danger of body and of soul; and she might well put herself in peril of eternal fire for the soul, as well as of temporal fire for the body, by the sentence of other judges. "You will not do this which you say against me, without doing injury to your own bodies and souls," she said.

Asked, whether she could give a reason why she would not submit to the Church: but to this she would make no additional reply.

Again a week passed in busy talk and consultation without, in silence and desertion within. On the 9th of May the prisoner was again led, this time to the great tower, apparently the torture chamber of the castle, where she found nine of her judges awaiting her, and was once more adjured to speak the truth, with the threat of torture if she continued to refuse. Never was her attitude more calm, more dignified and lofty in its simplicity, than at this grim moment.

"Truly," she replied, "if you tear the limbs from my body, and my soul out of it, I can say nothing other than what I have said; or if I said anything different, I should afterwards say that you had compelled me to do it by force." She added that on the day of the Holy Cross, the 3d of May past, she had been comforted by St. Gabriel. She believed that it was St. Gabriel: and she knew by her voices that it was St. Gabriel. She had asked counsel of her voices whether she should submit to the Church, because the priests pressed her so strongly to submit: but it had been said to her that if she desired our Lord to help her she must depend upon Him for everything. She added that she knew well that our Lord had always been the master of all she did, and that the Enemy had nothing to do with her deeds. Also she had asked her voices if she should be burned, and the said voices had replied to her that she was to wait for the Lord and He would help her.

Afterwards in respect to the crown which had been handed by the angel to the Archbishop of Rheims, she was asked if she would refer to him. She answered: "Bring him here, that I may hear what he says, and then I shall answer you; he will not dare to say the contrary of that which I have said to you."

The Archbishop of Rheims had been her constant enemy; all the hindrances that had occurred in her active life, and the constant attempts made to balk her even in her brief moment of triumph, came from him and his associate La Trémouille. He was the last person in the world to whom Jeanne naturally would have appealed. Perhaps that was the admirable reason why he was suggested in this dreadful crisis of her fate.

A few days later, it was discussed among those dark inquisitors whether the torture should be applied or not. Finally, among thirteen there were but two (let not the voice of sacred vengeance be silent on their shame though after four centuries and more), Thomas de Courcelles, first of theologians, cleverest of ecclesiastical lawyers, mildest of men, and Nicolas L'Oyseleur, the spy and traitor, who voted for the torture. One man most reasonably asked why she should be put to torture when they had ample material for judgment without it? One cannot but feel that the proceedings on this occasion were either intended to beguile the impatience of the English authorities, eager to be done with the whole business, or to add a quite gratuitous pang to the sufferings of the heroic girl. As the men were not devils, though probably possessed by this time, the more cruel among them, by the horrible curiosity, innate alas! in human nature, of seeing how far a suffering soul could go, it is probable that the first motive was the true one. The English, Warwick especially, whose every movement was restrained by this long-pending affair, were exceedingly impatient, and tempted at times to take the matter into their own hands, and spoil the perfectness of this well constructed work of art, conducted according to all the rules, the beautiful trial which was dear to the Bishop's heart—and destined to be, though perhaps in a sense somewhat different to that which he hoped, his chief title to fame.

Ten days after, the decision of the University of Paris arrived, and a great assembly of counsellors, fifty-one in all, besides the permanent presidents, collected together in the chapel of the Archbishop's house, to hear that document read, along with many other documents, the individual opinions of a host of doctors and eminent authorities. After an explanation of the solemn care given by the University to the consideration of every one of the twelve articles of the indictment, that learned tribunal pronounced its verdict upon each. The length of the proceedings makes it impossible to reproduce these. First as to the early revelations given to Jeanne, described in the first and second articles, they are denounced as "murderous, seductive, and pernicious fictions," the apparitions those of "malignant spirits and devils, Belial, Satan, and Behemoth." The third article, which concerned her recognition of the saints, was described more mildly as containing errors in faith; the fourth, as to her knowledge of future events, was characterised as "superstitious and presumptuous divination." The fifth, concerning her dress, declared her to be "blasphemous and contemptuous of God in His Sacraments." The sixth, by which she was accused of loving bloodshed, because she made war against those who did not obey the summons in her letters bearing the name Jhesus Maria, was declared to prove that she was cruel, "seeking the shedding of blood, seditious, and a blasphemer of God." The tenor is the same to the end: Blasphemy, superstition, pernicious doctrine, impiety, cruelty, presumption, lying; a schismatic, a heretic, an apostate, an idolator, an invoker of demons. These are the conclusions drawn by the most solemn and weighty tribunal on matters of faith in France. The precautions taken to procure a full and trustworthy judgment, the appeal to each section in turn, the Faculty of Theology, the Faculty of Law, the "Nations," all separately and than all together passing every item in review—are set forth at full length. Every formality had been fulfilled, every rule followed, every detail was in the fullest order, signed and sealed and attested by solemn notaries, bristling with well-known names. A beautiful judgment, equal to the trial, which was beautiful too—not a rule omitted except those of justice, fairness, and truth! The doctors sat and listened with every fine professional sense satisfied.

"If the beforesaid woman, charitably exhorted and admonished by competent judges, does not return spontaneously to the Catholic faith, publicly abjure her errors, and give full satisfaction to her judges, she is hereby given up to the secular judge to receive the reward of her deeds."

The attendant judges, each in his place, now added their adhesion. Most of them simply stated their agreement with the judgment of the University, or with that of the Bishop of Fecamp, which was a similar tenor; a few wished that Jeanne should be again "charitably admonished"; many desired that on this selfsame day the final sentence should be pronounced. One among them, a certain Raoul Sauvage (Radulphus Silvestris), suggested that she should be brought before the people in a public place, a suggestion afterwards carried out. Frère Isambard desired that she should be charitably admonished again and have another chance, and that her final fate should still be in the hands of "us her judges." The conclusion was that one more "charitable admonition" should be given to Jeanne, and that the law should then take its course. The suggestion that she should make a public appearance had only one supporter.

This dark scene in the chapel is very notable, each man rising to pronounce what was in reality a sentence of death,—fifty of them almost unanimous, filled no doubt with a hundred different motives, to please this man or that, to win favour, to get into the way of promotion,—but all with a distinct consciousness of the great yet horrible spectacle, the stake, the burning:—though perhaps here and there was one with a hope that perpetual imprisonment, bread of sorrow and water of anguish, might be substituted for that terrible death. Finally, it was decided that—always on the side of mercy, as every act proved—the tribunal should once more "charitably admonish" the prisoner for the salvation of her soul and body, and that after all this "good deliberation and wholesome counsel" the case should be concluded.

Again there follows a pause of four days. No doubt the Bishop and his assessors had other things to do, their ecclesiastical functions, their private business, which could not always be put aside because one forsaken soul was held in suspense day after day. Finally on the 24th of May, Jeanne again received in her prison a dignified company, some quite new and strange to her (indeed the idea may cross the reader's mind that it was perhaps to show off the interesting prisoner to two new and powerful bishops, the first, Louis of Luxembourg, a relative of her first captor, that this last examination was held), nine men in all, crowding her chamber—exponuntur Johannæ defectus sui, says the record—to expound to Jeanne her faults. It was Magister Peter Morice to whom this office was confided. Once more the "schedule" was gone over, and an address delivered laden with all the bad words of the University. "Jeanne, dearest friend," said the orator at last, "it is now time, at the end of the trial, to think well what words these are." She would seem to have spoken during this address, at least once—to say that she held to everything she had said during the trial. When Morice had finished she was once more questioned personally.

She was asked if she still thought and believed that it was not her duty to submit her deeds and words to the Church militant, or to any other except

God, upon which she replied, "What I have always said and held to during the trial, I maintain to this moment"; and added that if she were in judgment and saw the fire lighted, the faggots burning, and the executioner ready to rake the fire, and she herself within the fire, she could say nothing else, but would sustain what she had said in her trial, to death.

Once more the scribe has written on his margin the words Responsio Johannæ superba—the proud answer of Jeanne. Her raised head, her expanded breast, something of a splendour of indignation about her, must have moved the man, thus for the third time to send down to us his distinctly human impression of the worn out prisoner before her judges. "And immediately the promoter and she refusing to say more, the cause was concluded," says the record, so formal, sustained within such purely abstract limits, yet here and there with a sort of throb and reverberation of the mortal encounter. From the lips of the Inquisitor too all words seemed to have been taken. It is as when amid the excited crowd in the Temple the officers of the Pharisees approaching to lay hands on a greater than Jeanne, fell back, not knowing why, and could not do their office. This man was silenced also. Two bishops were present, and one a great man full of patronage; but not for the richest living in Normandy could Peter Morice find any more to say.

These are in one sense the words of Jeanne; the last we have from her in her prison, the last of her consistent and unbroken life. After, there was a deeper horror to go through, a moment when all her forces failed. Here on the verge of eternity she stands heroic and unyielding, brave, calm, and steadfast as at the outset of her career, the Maid of France. Were the fires lighted and the faggots burning, and she herself within the fire, she had no other word to say.

CHAPTER XVI — THE ABJURATION. MAY 24, 1431.

On the 23d of May Jeanne was taken back to her prison attended by the officer of the court, Massieu, her frame still thrilling, her heart still high, with that great note of constancy yet defiance. She had been no doubt strongly excited, the commotion within her growing with every repetition of these scenes, each one of which promised to be the last. And the fire and the stake and the executioner had come very near to her; no doubt a whole murmuring world of rumour, of strange information about herself, never long inaudible, never heard outside of the Castle of Rouen, rose half-comprehended from the echoing courtyard outside and the babble of her guards within. She would hear even as she was conveyed along the echoing stone passages something here and there of the popular expectation:—a burning! the wonderful unheard of sight, which by hook or by crook everyone must see; and no doubt among the

English talk she might now be able to make out something concerning this long business which had retarded all warlike proceedings but which would soon be over now, and the witch burnt. There must have been some, even among those rude companions, who would be sorry, who would feel that she was no witch, yet be helpless to do anything for her, any more than Massieu could, or Frère Isambard: and if it was all for the sake of certain words to be said, was the wench mad? would it not be better to say anything, to give up anything rather than be burned at the stake? Jeanne, notwithstanding the wonderful courage of her last speech, must have returned to her cell with small illusion possible to her intelligent spirit. The stake had indeed come very near, the flames already dazzled her eyes, she must have felt her slender form shrink together at the thought. All that long night, through the early daylight of the May morning did she lie and ponder, as for far less reasons so many of us have pondered as we lay wakeful through those morning watches. God's promises are great, but where is the fulfilment? We ask for bread and he gives us, if not a stone, yet something which we cannot realise to be bread till after many days. Jeanne's voices had never paused in their pledge to her of succour. "Speak boldly, God will help you—fear nothing"; there would be aid for her before three months, and great victory. They went on saying so, though the stake was already being raised. What did they mean? what did they mean? Could she still trust them? or was it possible——?

Her heart was like to break. At their word she would have faced the fire. She meant to do so now, notwithstanding the terrible, the heartrending ache of hope that was still in her. But they did not give her that heroic command. Still and always, they said God will help you, our Lord will stand by you. What did that mean? It must mean deliverance, deliverance! What else could it mean? If she held her head high as she returned to the horrible monotony of that prison so often left with hope, so often re-entered in sadness, it must soon have dropped upon her tired bosom. Slowly the clouds had settled round her. Over and over again had she affirmed them to be true—these voices that had guided her steps and led her to victory. And they had promised her the aid of God if she went forward boldly, and spoke and did not fear. But now every way of salvation was closing; all around her were fierce soldiers thirsting for her blood, smooth priests who admonished her in charity, threatening her with eternal fire for the soul, temporal fire for the body. She felt that fire, already blowing towards her as if on the breath of the evening wind, and her girlish flesh shrank. Was that what the voices had called deliverance? was that the grand victory, the aid of the Lord?

It may well be imagined that Jeanne slept but little that night; she had reached the lowest depths; her soul had begun to lose itself in bitterness, in the horror of a doubt. The atmosphere of her prison became intolerable, and the noise of her guards keeping up their rough jests half through the night, their stamping and clamour, and the clang of their arms when relieved. Early next morning a party of her usual visitors came in upon her to give her fresh instruction and advice. Something new was about to happen to-day. She was to be led forth, to breathe the air of heaven, to confront the people, the raging sea of men's faces, all the unknown world about her. The crowd had never been unfriendly to Jeanne. It had closed about her, almost wherever she was visible, with sweet applause and outcries of joy. Perhaps a little hope stirred her heart in the thought of being surrounded once more by the common folk, though probably it did not occur to her to think of these Norman strangers as her own people. And a great day was before her, a day in which something might still be done, in which deliverance might yet come. L'Oyseleur, who was one of her visitors, adjured her now to change her conduct, to accept whatever means of salvation might be offered to her. There was no longer any mention of Pope or Council, but only of the Church to which she ought to yield. How it was that he preserved his influence over her, having been proved to be a member of the tribunal that judged her, and not a fellow-prisoner, nor a fellow-countryman, nor any of the things he had professed to be, no once can tell us; but evidently he had managed to do so. Jeanne would seem to have received him without signs of repulsion or displeasure. Indeed she seems to have been ready to hear anyone, to believe in those who professed to wish her well, even when she did not follow their counsel.

It would require, however, no great persuasion on L'Oyseleur's part to convince her that this was a more than usually important day, and that something decisive must be done, now or never. Why should she be so determined to resist her only chance of safety? If she were but delivered from the hands of the English, safe in the gentler keeping of the Church, there would be time to think of everything, even to make her peace with her voices who would surely understand if, for the saving of her life, and out of terror for the dreadful fire, she abandoned them for a moment. She had disobeyed them at Beaurevoir and they had forgiven. One faltering word now, a mark of her hand upon a paper, and she would be safe—even if still all they said was true; and if indeed and in fact, after buoying her up from day to day, such a dreadful thing might be as that they were not true——

The traitor was at her ear whispering; the cold chill of disappointment, of disillusion, of sickening doubt was in her heart.

Then there came into the prison a better man than L'Oyseleur, Jean Beaupère, her questioner in the public trial, the representative of all these notabilities. What he said was spoken with authority and he came in all seriousness, may not we believe in some kindness too? to warn her. He came with permission of the Bishop, no stealthy visitor. "Jean Beaupère entered alone into the prison of the said Jeanne by permission, and advertised her that she would straightway be taken to the scaffold to be addressed (pour y être preschée), and that if she was a good Christian she would on that scaffold place all her acts and words under the jurisdiction of our Holy Mother, the Church, and specially of the ecclesiastical judges." "Accept the woman's dress and do all that you are told," her other adviser had said. When the car that was to convey her came to the prison doors, L'Oyseleur accompanied her, no doubt with a show of supporting her to the end. What a change from the confined and gloomy prison to the dazzling clearness of the May daylight, the air, the murmuring streets, the throng that gazed and shouted and followed! Life that had run so low in the prisoner's veins must have bounded up within her in response to that sunshine and open sky, and movement and sound of existence—summer weather too, and everything softened in the medium of that soft breathing air, sound and sensation and hope. She had been three months in her prison. As the charrette rumbled along the roughly paved streets drawing all those crowds after it, a strange object appeared to Jeanne's eyes in the midst of the market-place, a lofty scaffold with a stake upon it, rising over the heads of the crowd, the logs all arranged ready for the fire, a car waiting below with four horses, to bring hither the victim. The place of sacrifice was ready, everything arranged—for whom? for her? They drove her noisily past that she might see the preparations. It was all ready; and where then was the great victory, the deliverance in which she had believed?

In front of the beautiful gates of St. Ouen there was a different scene. That stately church was surrounded then by a churchyard, a great open space, which afforded room for a very large assembly. In this were erected two platforms, one facing the other. On the first sat the court of judges in number about forty, Cardinal Winchester having a place by the side of Monseigneur de Beauvais, the president, with several other bishops and dignified ecclesiastics. Opposite, on the other platform, were a pulpit and a place for the accused, to which Jeanne was conducted by Massieu, who never left her, and L'Oyseleur, who kept as near as he could, the rest of the platform being immediately covered by lawyers, doctors, all the camp followers, so to speak, of the black army, who could find footing there. Jeanne was in her usual male dress, the doublet and hose, with her short-clipped hair—no doubt looking like a slim boy among all this dark crowd of men. The people swayed like a sea all about and around— the throng which had gathered in her progress through the streets pushing out the crowd already assembled with a movement like the waves of the sea. Every step of the trial all through had been attended by preaching, by discourses and reasoning and admonishments, charitable and otherwise. Now she was to be "preached" for the last time.

It was Doctor Guillaume Érard who ascended the pulpit, a great preacher, one whom the "copious multitude" ran after and were eager to hear. He himself had not been disposed to accept this office, but no doubt, set up there on that height before the eyes of all the people, he thought of his own reputation, and of the great audience, and Winchester the more than king, the great English Prince, the wealthiest and most influential of men. The preacher took his text from a verse in St. John's Gospel: "A branch cannot bear fruit except it remain in the vine." The centre circle containing the two platforms was surrounded by a close ring of English soldiers, understanding none of it, and anxious only that the witch should be condemned.

It was in this strange and crowded scene that the sermon which was long and eloquent began. When it was half over, in one of his fine periods admired by all the people, the preacher, after heaping every reproach upon the head of Jeanne, suddenly turned to apostrophise the House of France, and the head of that House, "Charles who calls himself King." "He has," cried the preacher, stimulated no doubt by the eye of Winchester upon him, "adhered, like a schismatic and heretical person as he is, to the words and acts of a useless woman, disgraced and full of dishonour; and not he only, but the clergy who are under his sway, and the nobility. This guilt is thine, Jeanne, and to thee I say that thy King is a schismatic and a heretic."

In the full flood of his oratory the preacher was arrested here by that clear voice that had so often made itself heard through the tumult of battle. Jeanne could bear much, but not this. She was used to abuse in her own person, but all her spirit came back at this assault on her King. And interruption to a sermon has always a dramatic and startling effect, but when that voice arose now, when the startled speaker stopped, and every dulled attention revived, it is easy to imagine what a stir, what a wonderful, sudden sensation must have arisen in the midst of the crowd. "By my faith, sire," cried Jeanne, "saving your respect, I swear upon my life that my King is the most noble Christian of all Christians, that he is not what you say."

The sermon, however, was resumed after this interruption. And finally the preacher turned to Jeanne, who had subsided from that start of animation, and was again the subdued and silent prisoner, her heart overwhelmed with many heavy thoughts. "Here," said Èrard, "are my lords the judges who have so often summoned and required of you to submit your acts and words to our Holy Mother the Church; because in these acts and words there are many things which it seemed to the clergy were not good either to say or to sustain."

To which she replied (we quote again from the formal records), "I will answer you." And as to her submission to the Church she said: "I have told them on that point that all the works which I have done and said may be sent to Rome, to our Holy Father the Pope, to whom, but to God first, I refer in all. And as for my acts and words I have done all on the part of God." She also said that no one was to blame for her acts and words, neither her King nor any other; and if there were faults in them, the blame was hers and no other's.

Asked, if she would renounce all that she had done wrong; answered, "I refer everything to God and to our Holy Father the Pope."

It was then told her that this was not enough, and that our Holy Father was too far off; also that the Ordinaries were judges each in his diocese, and it was necessary that she should submit to our Mother the Holy Church, and that she should confess that the clergy and officers of the Church had a right to determine in her case. And of this she was admonished three times.

After this the Bishop began to read the definitive sentence. When a great part of it was read, Jeanne began to speak and said that she would hold to all that the judges and the Church said, and obey in everything their ordinance and will. And there in the presence of the above-named and of the great multitude assembled she made her abjuration in the manner that follows:

And she said several times that since the Church said her apparitions and revelations should not be sustained or believed, she would not sustain them; but in everything submit to the judges and to our Mother the Holy Church.

In this strange, brief, subdued manner is the formal record made. Manchon writes on his margin: At the end of the sentence Jeanne, fearing the fire, said she would obey the Church. Even into the bare legal document there comes a hush as of awe, the one voice responding in the silence of the crowd, with a quiver in it; the very animation of the previous outcry enhancing the effect of this low and faltering submission, timens igneum—in fear of the fire.

The more familiar record, and the recollections long after of those eye-witnesses, give us another version of the scene. Èrard, from his pulpit, read the form of abjuration prepared. But Jeanne answered that she did not know what abjuration meant, and the preacher called upon Massieu to explain it to her. "And he" (we quote from his own deposition), "after excusing himself, said that it meant this: that if she opposed the said articles she would be burnt; but he advised her to refer it to the Church universal whether she should abjure or not. Which thing she did, saying to Èrard, 'I refer to the Church universal whether I should abjure or not.' To which Èrard answered, 'You shall abjure at once or you will be burnt.' Massieu gives further particulars in another part of the Rehabilitation process. Èrard, he says, asked what he was saying to the prisoner, and he answered that she would sign if the schedule was read to her; but Jeanne said that she could not write, and then added that she wished it to be decided by the Church, and ought not to sign unless that was done: and also required that she should be placed in the custody of the Church, and freed from the hands of the English. The same Èrard answered that there had been ample delay, and that if she did not sign at once she should be burned, and forbade Massieu to say any more."

Meanwhile many cries and entreaties came, as far as they dared, from the crowd. Some one, in the excitement of the moment, would seem to have promised that she should be transferred to the custody of the Church. "Jeanne, why will you die? Jeanne, will you not save yourself?" was called to her by many a bystander. The girl stood fast, but her heart failed her in this terrible climax of her suffering. Once she called out over their heads, "All that I did was done for good, and it was well to do it:"—her last cry. Then she would seem to have recovered in some measure her composure. Probably her agitated brain was unable to understand the formula of recantation which was read to her amid all the increasing noises of the crowd, but she had a vague faith in the condition she had herself stated, that the paper should be submitted to the Church, and that she should at once be transferred to an ecclesiastical prison. Other suggestions are made, namely, that it was a very short document upon which she hastily in her despair made a cross, and that it was a long one, consisting of several pages, which was shown afterwards with Jehanne scribbled underneath. "In fact," says Massieu, "she abjured and made a cross with the pen which the witness handed to her:" he, if any one must have known exactly what happened.

No doubt all this would be imperfectly heard on the other platform. But the agitation must have been visible enough, the spectators closing round the young figure in the midst, the pleadings, the appeals, seconded by many a cry from the crowd. Such a small matter to risk her young life for! "Sign, sign; why should you die!" Cauchon had gone on reading the sentence, half through the struggle. He had two sentences all ready, two courses of procedure, cut and dry: either to absolve her—which meant condemning her to perpetual imprisonment on bread and water: or to carry her off at once to the stake. The English were impatient for the last. It is a horrible thing to acknowledge, but it is evidently true. They had never wished to play with her as a cat with a mouse, as her learned countrymen had done those three months past; they had desired at once to get her out of their way. But the idea of her perpetual imprisonment did not please them at all; the risk of such a prisoner was more than they chose to encounter. Nevertheless there are some things a churchman cannot do. When it was seen that Jeanne had yielded, that she had put her mark to something on a paper flourished forth in somebody's hand in the sunshine, the Bishop turned to the Cardinal on his right hand, and asked what he was to do? There was but one answer possible to Winchester, had he been English and Jeanne's natural enemy ten times over. To admit her to penitence was the only practicable way.

Here arises a great question, already referred to, as to what it was that Jeanne signed. She could not write, she could only put her cross on the document hurriedly read to her, amid the confusion and the murmurs of the crowd. The cédule to which she put her sign "contained eight lines:" what she is reported to have signed is three pages long, and full of detail. Massieu declares certainly that this (the abjuration published) was not the one of which mention is made in the trial; "for the one read by the deponent and signed by the said Jeanne was quite different." This would seem to prove the fact that a much enlarged version of an act of abjuration, in its original form strictly confined to the necessary points and expressed in few words—was afterwards published as that bearing the sign of the penitent. Her own admissions, as will be seen, are of the scantiest, scarcely enough to tell as an abjuration at all.

When the shouts of the people proved that this great step had been taken, and Winchester had signified his conviction that the penitence must be accepted, Cauchon replaced one sentence by another and pronounced the prisoner's fate. "Seeing that thou hast returned to the bosom of the Church by the grace of God, and hast revoked and denied all thy errors, we, the Bishop aforesaid, commit thee to perpetual prison, with the bread of sorrow and water of anguish, to purge thy soul by solitary penitence." Whether the words reached her over all those crowding heads, or whether they were reported to her, or what Jeanne expected to follow standing there upon her platform, more shamed and downcast than through all her trial, no one can tell. There seems even to have been a moment of uncertainty among the officials. Some of them congratulated Jeanne, L'Oyseleur for one pressing forward to say, "You have done a good day's work, you have saved your soul." She herself, excited and anxious, desired eagerly to know where she was not to go. She would seem for the moment to have accepted the fact of her perpetual imprisonment with complete faith and content. It meant to her instant relief from her hideous prison-house, and she could not contain her impatience and eagerness. "People of the Church—gens de' Église—lead me to your prison; let me be no longer in the hands of the English," she cried with feverish anxiety. To gain this point, to escape the irons and the dreadful durance which she had suffered so long, was all her thought. The men about her could not answer this appeal. Some of them no doubt knew very well what the answer must be, and some must have seen the angry looks and stern exclamation which Warwick addressed to Cauchon, deceived like Jeanne by this unsatisfactory conclusion, and the stir among the soldiers at sight of his displeasure. But perhaps flurried by all that had happened, perhaps hoping to strengthen the victim in her moment of hope, some of them hurried across to the Bishop to ask where they were to take her. One of these was Pierre Miger, friar of Longueville. Where was she to be taken? In Winchester's hearing, perhaps in Warwick's, what a question to put! An English bishop, says this witness turned to him angrily and said to Cauchon that this was a "fauteur de ladite Jeanne," "this fellow was also one of them." Miger excused himself in alarm as St. Peter did before him, and Cauchon turning upon him commanded grimly that she should be taken back whence she came. Thus ended the last hope of the Maid. Her abjuration, which by no just title could be called an abjuration, had been in vain.

Jeanne was taken back, dismayed and miserable, to the prison which she had perilled her soul to escape. It was very little she had done in reality, and at that moment she could scarcely yet have realised what she had done, except that it had failed. At the end of so long and bitter a struggle she had thrown down her arms—but for what? to escape those horrible gaolers and that accursed room with its ear of Dionysius, its Judas hole in the wall. The bitterness of the going back was beyond words. We hear of no word that she said when she realised the hideous fact that nothing was changed for her; the bitter waters closed over her head. Again the chains to be locked and double locked that bound her to her dreadful bed, again the presence of those men who must have been all the more odious to her from the momentary hope that she had got free from them for ever.

The same afternoon the Vicar-Inquisitor, who had never been hard upon her, accompanied by Nicole Midi, by the young seraphic doctor, Courcelles, and L'Oyseleur, along with various other ecclesiastical persons, visited her prison. The Inquisitor congratulated and almost blessed her, sermonising as usual, but briefly and not ungently, though with a word of warning that should she change her mind and return to her evil ways there would be no further place for repentance. As a return for the mercy and clemency of the Church, he required her immediately to put on the female dress which his attendants had brought. There is something almost ludicrous, could we forget the tragedy to follow, in the bundle of humble clothing brought by such exalted personages, with the solemnity which became a thing upon which hung the issues of life or death. Jeanne replied with the humility of a broken spirit. "I take them willingly," she said, "and in everything I will obey the Church." Then silence closed upon her, the horrible silence of the prison, full of hidden listeners and of watching eyes.

Meantime there was great discontent and strife of tongues outside. It was said that many even of the doctors who condemned her would fain have seen Jeanne removed to some less dangerous prison: but Monseigneur de Beauvais had to hold head against the great English authorities who were out of all patience, fearing that the witch might still slip through their fingers and by her spells and incantations make the heart of the troops melt once more within them. If the mind of the Church had been as charitable as it professed to be, I doubt if all the power of Rome could have got the Maid now out of the English grip. They were exasperated, and felt that they too, as well as the prisoner, had been played with. But the Bishop had good hope in his mind, still to be able to content his patrons. Jeanne had abjured, it was true, but the more he inquired into that act, the less secure he must have felt about it. And she might relapse; and if she relapsed there would be no longer any place for repentance. And it is evident that his confidence in the power of the clothes was boundless. In any case a few days more would make all clear.

They did not have many days to wait. There are two, to all appearance, well-authenticated stories of the cause of Jeanne's "relapse." One account is given by Frère Isambard, whom she told in the presence of several others, that she had been assaulted in her cell by a Millourt Anglois, and barbarously used, and in self-defence had resumed again the man's dress which had been left in her cell. The story of Massieu is different: To him Jeanne explained that when she asked to be released from her bed on the morning of Trinity Sunday, her guards took away her female dress which she was wearing, and emptied the sack containing the other upon her bed. She appealed to them, reminding them that these were forbidden to her; but got no answer except a brutal order to get up. It is very probable that both stories are true. Frère Isambard found her weeping and agitated, and nothing is more probable than this was the occasion on which Warwick heard her cries, and interfered to save her. Massieu's version, of which he is certain, was communicated to him a day or two after when they happened to be alone together. It was on the Thursday before Trinity Sunday that she put on the female dress, but it would seem that rumours on the subject of a relapse had begun to spread even before the Sunday on which that event happened: and Beaupère and Midi were sent by the Bishop to investigate. But they were very ill-received in the Castle, sworn at by the guards, and forced to go back without seeing Jeanne, there being as yet, it appeared, nothing to see. On the morning of the Monday, however, the rumours arose with greater force; and no doubt secret messages must have informed the Bishop that the hoped-for relapse had taken place. He set out himself accordingly, accompanied by the Vicar-Inquisitor and attended by eight of the familiar names so often quoted, triumphant, important, no doubt with much show of pompous solemnity, to find out for himself. The Castle was all in excitement, report and gossip already busy with the new event so trifling, so all-important. There was no idea now of turning back the visitors. The prison doors were eagerly thrown open, and there indeed once more, in her tunic and hose, was Jeanne, whom they had left four days before painfully contemplating the garments they had given her, and humbly promising obedience. The men burst in upon her with an outcry of astonishment. What she had changed her dress again? "Yes," she replied, "she had resumed the costume of a man." There was no triumph in what she said, but rather a subdued tone of sadness, as of one who in the most desperate strait has taken her resolution and must abide by it, whether she likes it or not. She was asked why she had resumed that dress, and who had made her do so. There was no question of anything else at first. The tunic and gippon were at once enough to decide her fate.

She answered that she had done it by her own will, no one influencing her to do so; and that she preferred the dress of a man to that of a woman.

She was reminded that she had promised and sworn not to resume the dress of a man. She answered that she was not aware she had ever sworn or had made any such oath.

She was asked why she had done it. She answered that it was more lawful to wear a man's dress among men, than the dress of a woman; and also that she had taken it back because the promise made to her had not been kept, that she should hear the mass, and receive her Saviour, and be delivered from her irons.

She was asked if she had not abjured that dress, and sworn not to resume it. She answered that she would rather die than be left in irons; but if they would allow her to go to mass and take her out of her irons and put her in a gracious prison, and a woman with her, she would be good, and do whatever the Church pleased.

She was then asked suddenly, as if there had been no condemnation of her voices as lying fables, whether since Thursday she had heard them again. To this she answered, recovering a little courage, "Yes."

She was asked what they said to her; she answered that they said God had made known to her by St. Catherine and St. Margaret the great pity there was of the treason to which she had consented by making abjuration and revocation in order to save her life: and that she had earned damnation for herself to save her life. Also that before Thursday her voices had told her that she should do what she did that day, that on the scaffold they had told her to answer the preachers boldly, and that this preacher whom she called a false preacher had accused her of many things she never did. She also added that if she said God had not sent her she would damn herself, for true it was that God had sent her. Also that her voices had told her since, that she had done a great sin in confessing that she had sinned; but that for fear of the fire she had said that which she had said.

She was asked (all over again) if she believed that these voices were those of St. Catherine and St. Margaret. She answered, Yes, they were so; and from God. And as for what had been said to her on the scaffold that she had spoken lies and boasted concerning St. Catherine and St. Margaret, she had not intended any such thing. Also she said that she never intended to deny her apparitions, or to say that they were not St. Catherine and St. Margaret. All that she had done was in fear of the fire, and she had denied nothing but what was contrary to truth; and she said that she would like better to make her penitence all at one time—that is to say, in dying, than to endure a long penitence in prison. Also that she had never done anything against God or the faith whatever they might have made her say; and that for what was in the schedule of the abjuration she did not know what it was. Also she said that she never intended to revoke anything so long as it pleased our Lord. At the end she said that if her judges would have her do so, she might put on again her female dress; but for the rest she would do no more.

"What need we any further witness; for we ourselves have heard of his own mouth." Jeanne's protracted, broken, yet continuous apology and defence, overawed her judges; they do not seem to have interrupted it with questions. It was enough and more than enough. She had relapsed; the end of all things had come, the will of her enemies could now be accomplished. No one could say she had not had full justice done her; every formality had been fulfilled, every lingering formula carried out. Now there was but one thing before her, whose sad young voice with many pauses thus sighed forth its last utterance; and for her judges, one last spectacle to prepare, and the work to complete which it had taken them three long months to do.

CHAPTER XVIII — THE SACRIFICE. MAY 31, 1431.

It is not necessary to be a good man in order to divine what in certain circumstances a good and pure spirit will do. The Bishop of Beauvais had entertained no doubt as to what would happen. He knew exactly, with a perspicuity creditable to his perceptions at least, that, notwithstanding the effect which his theatrical mise en scène had produced upon the imagination of Jeanne, no power in heaven or earth would induce that young soul to content itself with a lie. He knew it, though lies were his daily bread; the children of this world are wiser in their generation than the children of light. He had bidden his English patrons to wait a little, and now his predictions were triumphantly fulfilled. It is hard to believe of any man that on such a certainty he could have calculated and laid his devilish plans; but there would seem to have existed in the mediæval churchman a certain horrible thirst for the blood of a relapsed heretic which was peculiar to their age and profession, and which no better principle in their own minds could subdue. It was their appetite, their delight of sensation, in distinction from the other appetites perhaps scarcely less cruel which other men indulged with no such horrified denunciation from the rest of the world. Others, it is evident, shared with Cauchon that sharp sensation of dreadful pleasure in finding her out; young Courcelles, so modest and unassuming and so learned, among the rest; not L'Oyseleur, it appears by the sequel. That Judas, like the greater traitor, was struck to the heart; but the less bad man who had only persecuted, not betrayed, stood high in superior virtue, and only rejoiced that at last the victim was ready to drop into the flames which had been so carefully prepared.

The next morning, Tuesday after Trinity Sunday, the witnesses hurried with their news to the quickly summoned assembly in the chapel of the Archbishop's house; thirty-three of the judges, having been hastily called together, were there to hear. Jeanne had relapsed; the sinner escaped had been re-caught; and what was now to be done? One by one each man rose again and gave his verdict. Once more Egidius, Abbot of Fécamp, led the tide of opinion. There was but one thing to be done: to give her up to the secular justice, "praying that she might be gently dealt with." Man after man added his voice "to that of Abbot of Fécamp aforesaid"—that she might be gently dealt with! Not one of them could be under any doubt what gentle meaning would be in the execution; but apparently the words were of some strange use in salving their consciences.

The decree was pronounced at once without further formalities. In point of view of the law, there should have followed another trial, more evidence, pleadings, and admonitions. We may be thankful to Monseigneur de Beauvais that he now defied law, and no longer prolonged the useless ceremonials of that mockery of justice. It is said that in coming out of the prison, through the courtyard full of Englishmen, where Warwick was in waiting to hear what news, the Bishop greeted them with all the satisfaction of success, laughing and bidding them "Make good cheer, the thing is done." In the same spirit of satisfaction was the rapid action of the further proceedings. On Tuesday she was condemned, summoned on Wednesday morning at eight 'clock to the Old Market of Rouen to hear her sentence, and there, without even that formality, the penalty was at once carried out. No time, certainly, was lost in this last stage.

All the interest of the heart-rending tragedy now turns to the prison where Jeanne woke in the early morning without, as yet, any knowledge of her fate. It must be remembered that the details of this wonderful scene, which we have in abundance, are taken from reports made twenty years after by eye-witnesses indeed, but men to whom by that time it had become the only policy to represent Jeanne in the brightest colours, and themselves as her sympathetic friends. There is no doubt that so remarkable an occurrence as her martyrdom must have made a deep impression on the minds of all those who were in any way actors in or spectators of that wonderful scene. And every word of all these different reports is on oath; but notwithstanding, a touch of unconscious colour, a more favourable sentiment, influenced by the feeling of later days, may well have crept in. With this warning we may yet accept these depositions as trustworthy, all the more for the atmosphere of truth, perfectly realistic, and in no way idealised, which is in every description of the great catastrophe; in which Jeanne figures as no supernatural heroine, but as a terrified, tormented, and often trembling girl.

On the fatal morning very early, Brother Martin l'Advenu appeared in the cell of the Maid. He had a mingled tale to tell—first "to announce to her her approaching death, and to lead her to true contrition and penitence; and also to hear her confession, which the said l'Advenu did very carefully and charitably." Jeanne on her part received the news with no conventional resignation or calm. Was it possible that she had been deceived and really hoped for mercy? She began to weep and to cry at the sudden stroke of fate. Notwithstanding the solemnity of her last declaration, that she would rather bear her punishment all at once than to endure the long punishment of her prison, her heart failed before the imminent stake, the immediate martyrdom. She cried out to heaven and earth: "My body, which has never been corrupted, must it be burned to ashes to-day!" No one but Jeanne knew at what cost she had kept her perfect purity; was it good for nothing but to be burned, that young body not nineteen years old? "Ah," she said, "I would rather be beheaded seven times than burned! I appeal to God against all these great wrongs they do me." But after a while the passion wore itself out, the child's outburst was stilled; calming herself, she knelt down and made her confession to the compassionate friar, then asked for the sacrament, to "receive her Saviour" as she had so often prayed and entreated before. It would appear that this had not been within Friar Martin's commission. He sent to ask the Bishop's leave, and it was granted "anything she asked for"—as they give whatever he may wish to eat to a condemned convict. But the Host was brought into the prison without ceremony, without accompanying candles or vestment for the priest. There are always some things which are insupportable to a man. Brother Martin could bear the sight of the girl's anguish, but not to administer to her a diminished rite. He sent again to demand what was needful, out of respect for the Holy Sacrament and the present victim. And his request had come, it would seem, to some canon or person in authority whose heart had been touched by the wonderful Maid in her long martyrdom. This nameless sympathiser did all that a man could do. He sent the Host with a train of priests chanting litanies as they went through the streets, with torches burning in the pure early daylight; some of these exhorted the people who knelt as they passed, to pray for her. She must have heard in her prison the sound of the bell, the chant of the clergy, the pause of awe, and then the rising, irregular murmur of the voices, that sound of prayer never to be mistaken. Pray for her! At last the city was touched to its heart. There is no sign that it had been sympathetic to Jeanne before; it was half English or more. But she was about to die: she had stood bravely against the world and answered like a true Maid; and they had now seen her led through their streets, a girl just nineteen. The popular imagination at least was subjugated for the time.

Thus Jeanne for the first time, after all the feasts were over, received at last "her Saviour" as she said, the consecration of that rite which He himself had instituted before He died. But she was not permitted to receive it in simplicity and silence as becomes the sacred commemoration. All the time she was still preschée and admonished by the men about her. A few days after her death the

Bishop and his followers assembled, and set down in evidence their different parts in that scene. How far it is to be relied upon, it is difficult to say. The speakers did not testify under oath; there is no formal warrant for their truth, and an anxious attempt to prove her change of mind is evident throughout; still there seem elements of truth in it, and a certain glimpse is afforded of Jeanne in the depths, when hope and strength were gone. The general burden of their testimony is that she sadly allowed herself to have been deceived, as to the liberation for which all along she had hoped. Peter Morice, often already mentioned, importuning her on the subject of the spirits, endeavouring to get from her an admission that she had not seen them at all, and was herself a deceiver: or if not that, at least that they were evil spirits, not good,—drew from her the impatient exclamation: "Be they good spirits, or be they evil, they appeared to me." Even in the act of giving her her last communion, Brother Martin paused with the consecrated Host in his hands.

"Do you believe," he said, "that this is the body of Christ?" Jeanne answered: "Yes, and He alone can free me; I pray you to administer." Then this brother said to Jeanne: "Do you believe as fully in your voices?" Jeanne answered: "I believe in God alone and not in the voices, which have deceived me." L'Advenu himself, however, does not give this deposition, but another of the persons present, Le Camus, who did not live to revise his testimony at the Rehabilitation.

The rite being over, the Bishop himself bustled in with an air of satisfaction, rubbing his hands, one may suppose from his tone. "So, Jeanne," he said, "you have always told us that your 'voices' said you were to be delivered, and you see now they have deceived you. Tell us the truth at last." Then Jeanne answered: "Truly I see that they have deceived me." The report is Cauchon's, and therefore little to be trusted; but the sad reply is at least not unlike the sentiment that, even in records more trustworthy, seems to have breathed forth in her. The other spectators all report another portion of this conversation. "Bishop, it is by you I die," are the words with which the Maid is said to have met him. "Oh Jeanne, have patience," he replied. "It is because you did not keep your promise." "If you had kept yours, and sent me to the prison of the Church, and put me in gentle hands, it would not have happened," she replied. "I appeal from you to God." Several of the attendants, also according to the Bishop's account, heard from her the same sad words: "They have deceived me"; and there seems no reason why we should not believe it. Her mind was weighed down under this dreadful unaccountable fact. She was forsaken—as a greater sufferer was; and a horror of darkness had closed around her. "Ah, Sieur Pierre," she said to Morice, "where shall I be to-night?" The man had condemned her as a relapsed heretic, a daughter of perdition. He had just suggested to her that her angels must have been devils. Nevertheless perhaps his face was not unkindly, he had not meant all the harm he did. He ought to have answered, "In Hell, with the spirits you have trusted"; that would have been the only logical response. What he did say was very different. "Have you not good faith in the Lord?" said the judge who had doomed her. Amazing and notable speech! They had sentenced her to be burned for blasphemy as an envoy of the devil; they believed in fact that she was the child of God, and going straight in that flame to the skies. Jeanne, with the sound, clear head and the "sane mind" to which all of them testified, did she perceive, even at that dreadful moment, the inconceivable contradiction? "Ah," she said, "yes, God helping me, I shall be in Paradise."

There is one point in the equivocal report which commends itself to the mind, which several of these men unite in, but which was carefully not repeated at the Rehabilitation: and this was that Jeanne allowed "as if it had been a thing of small importance," that her story of the angel bearing the crown at Chinon was a romance which she neither expected nor intended to be believed. For this we have to thank L'Oyseleur and the rest of the reverend ghouls assembled on that dreadful morning in the prison.

Jeanne was then dressed, for her last appearance in this world, in the long white garment of penitence, the robe of sacrifice: and the mitre was placed on her head which was worn by the victims of the Holy Office. She was led for the last time down the echoing stair to the crowded courtyard where her "chariot" awaited her. It was her confessor's part to remain by her side, and Frère Isambard and Massieu, the officer, both her friends, were also with her. It is said that L'Oyseleur rushed forward at this moment, either to accompany her also, or, as many say, to fling himself at her feet and implore her pardon. He was hustled aside by the crowd and would have been killed by the English, it is said, but for Warwick. The bystanders would seem to have been seized with a sudden disgust for all the priests about, thinking them Jeanne's friends, the historians insinuate—more likely in scorn and horror of their treachery. And then the melancholy procession set forth.

The streets were overflowing as was natural, crowded in every part: eight hundred English soldiers surrounded and followed the cortège, as the car rumbled along over the rough stones. Not yet had the Maid attained to the calm of consent. She looked wildly about her at all the high houses and windows crowded with gazers, and at the throngs that gaped and gazed upon her on every side. In the midst of the consolations of the confessor who poured pious words in her ears, other words, the plaints of a wondering despair fell from her lips, "Rouen! Rouen!" she said; "am I to die here?" It seemed incredible to her, impossible. She looked about still for some sign of disturbance, some rising among the crowd, some cry of "France! France!" or glitter of mail. Nothing: but the crowds ever gazing, murmuring at her, the soldiers roughly clearing the way, the rude chariot rumbling on. "Rouen,

Rouen! I fear that you shall yet suffer because of this," she murmured in her distraction, amid her moanings and tears.

At last the procession came to the Old Market, an open space encumbered with three erections—one reaching up so high that the shadow of it seemed to touch the sky, the horrid stake with wood piled up in an enormous mass, made so high, it is said, in order that the executioner himself might not reach it to give a merciful blow, to secure unconsciousness before the flames could touch the trembling form. Two platforms were raised opposite, one furnished with chairs and benches for Winchester and his court, another for the judges, with the civil officers of Rouen who ought to have pronounced sentence in their turn. Without this form the execution was illegal: what did it matter? No sentence at all was read to her, not even the ecclesiastical one which was illegal also. She was probably placed first on the same platform with her judges, where there was a pulpit from which she was to be preschée for the last time. Of all Jeanne's sufferings this could scarcely be the least, that she was always preschée, lectured, addressed, sermonised through every painful step of her career.

The moan was still unsilenced on her lips, and her distracted soul scarcely yet freed from the sick thought of a possible deliverance, when the everlasting strain of admonishment, and re-enumeration of her errors, again penetrated the hum of the crowd. The preacher was Nicolas Midi, one of the eloquent members of that dark fraternity; and his text was in St. Paul's words: "If any of the members suffer, all the other members suffer with it." Jeanne was a rotten branch which had to be cut off from the Church for the good of her own soul, and that the Church might not suffer by her sin; a heretic, a blasphemer, an impostor, giving forth false fables at one time, and making a false penitence the next. It is very unlikely that she heard anything of that flood of invective. At the end of the sermon the preacher bade her "Go in peace." Even then, however, the fountain of abuse did not cease. The Bishop himself rose, and once more by way of exhorting her to a final repentance, heaped ill names upon her helpless head. The narrative shows that the prisoner, now arrived at the last point in her career, paid no attention to the tirade levelled at her from the president's place. "She knelt down on the platform showing great signs and appearance of contrition, so that all those who looked upon her wept. She called on her knees upon the blessed Trinity, the blessed glorious Virgin Mary, and all the blessed saints of Paradise." She called specially—was it with still a return towards the hoped for miracle? was it with the instinctive cry towards an old and faithful friend?—"St. Michael, St. Michael, St. Michael, help!" There would seem to have been a moment in which the hush and silence of a great crowd surrounded this wonderful stage, where was that white figure on her knees, praying, speaking—sometimes to God, sometimes to the saintly unseen companions of her life, sometimes in broken phrases to those about her. She asked the priests, thronging all round, those who had churches, to say a mass for her soul. She asked all whom she might have offended to forgive her. Through her tears and prayers broke again and again the sorrowful cry of "Rouen, Rouen! Is it here truly that I must die?" No reason is given for the special pang that seems to echo in this cry. Jeanne had once planned a campaign in Normandy with Alençon. Had there been perhaps some special hope which made this conclusion all the more bitter, of setting up in the Norman capital her standard and that of her King?

There have been martyrs more exalted above the circumstances of their fate than Jeanne. She was no abstract heroine. She felt every pang to the depth of her natural, spontaneous being, and the humiliation and the deep distress of having been abandoned in the sight of men, perhaps the profoundest pang of which nature is capable. "He trusted in God that he would deliver him: let him deliver him if he will have him." That which her Lord had borne, the little sister had now to bear. She called upon the saints, but they did not answer. She was shamed in the sight of men. But as she knelt there weeping, the Bishop's evil voice scarcely silenced, the soldiers waiting impatient—the entire crowd, touched to its heart with one impulse, broke into a burst of weeping and lamentation, "à chaudes larmes" according to the graphic French expression. They wept hot tears as in the keen personal pang of sorrow and fellow-feeling and impotence to help. Winchester—withdrawn high on his platform, ostentatiously separated from any share in it, a spectator merely—wept; and the judges wept. The Bishop of Boulogne was overwhelmed with emotion, iron tears flowed down the accursed Cauchon's cheeks. The very world stood still to see that white form of purity, and valour, and faith, the Maid, not shouting triumphant on the height of victory, but kneeling, weeping, on the verge of torture. Human nature could not bear this long. A hoarse cry burst forth: "Will you keep us here all day; must we dine here?" a voice perhaps of unendurable pain that simulated cruelty. And then the executioner stepped in and seized the victim.

It has been said that her stake was set so high, that there might be no chance of a merciful blow, or of strangulation to spare the victim the atrocities of the fire; perhaps, let us hope, it was rather that the ascending smoke might suffocate her before the flame could reach her: the fifteenth century would naturally accept the most cruel explanation. There was a writing set over the little platform which gave footing to the attendants below the stake, upon which were written the following words:

JEANNE CALLED THE MAID, LIAR, ABUSER OF THE PEOPLE, SOOTHSAYER, BLASPHEMER OF GOD, PERNICIOUS, SUPERSTITIOUS, IDOLATROUS, CRUEL, DISSOLUTE, INVOKER OF DEVILS, APOSTATE, SCHISMATIC, HERETIC.

This was how her countrymen in the name of law and justice and religion branded the Maid of France—one half of her countrymen: the other half, silent, speaking no word, looking on.

Before she began to ascend the stake, Jeanne, rising from her knees, asked for a cross. No place so fit for that emblem ever was: but no cross was to be found. One of the English soldiers who kept the way seized a stick from some one by, broke it across his knee in unequal parts, and bound them hurriedly together; so, in the legend and in all the pictures, when Mary of Nazareth was led to her espousals, one of her disappointed suitors broke his wand. The cross was rough with its broken edges which Jeanne accepted from her enemy, and carried, pressing it against her bosom. One would rather have that rude cross to preserve as a sacred thing, than the highest effort of art in gold and silver. This was her ornament and consolation as she trod the few remaining steps and mounted the pile of the faggots to her place high over all that sea of heads. When she was bound securely to her stake, she asked again for a cross, a cross blessed and sacred from a church, to be held before her as long as her eyes could see. Frère Isambard and Massieu, following her closely still, sent to the nearest church, and procured probably some cross which was used for processional purposes on a long staff which could be held up before her. The friar stood upon the faggots holding it up, and calling out broken words of encouragement so long that Jeanne bade him withdraw, lest the fire should catch his robes. And so at last, as the flames began to rise, she was left alone, the good brother always at the foot of the pile, painfully holding up with uplifted arms the cross that she might still see it, the soldiers crowding, lit up with the red glow of the fire, the horrified, trembling crowd like an agitated sea around. The wild flames rose and fell in sinister gleams and flashes, the smoke blew upwards, by times enveloping that white Maid standing out alone against a sky still blue and sweet with May—Pandemonium underneath, but Heaven above. Then suddenly there came a great cry from among the black fumes that began to reach the clouds: "My voices were of God! They have not deceived me!" She had seen and recognised it at last. Here it was, the miracle: the great victory that had been promised—though not with clang of swords and triumph of rescuing knights, and "St. Denis for France!"—but by the sole hand of God, a victory and triumph for all time, for her country a crown of glory and ineffable shame.

Thus died the Maid of France—with "Jesus, Jesus," on her lips—till the merciful smoke breathing upwards choked that voice in her throat; and one who was like unto the Son of God, who was with her in the fire, wiped all memory of the bitter cross, wavering uplifted through the air in the good monk's trembling hands—from eyes which opened bright upon the light and peace of that Paradise of which she had so long thought and dreamed.

CHAPTER XVIII — AFTER.

The natural burst of remorse which follows such an event is well known in history; and is as certainly to be expected as the details of the great catastrophe itself. We feel almost as if, had there not been fact and evidence for such a revulsion of feeling, it must have been recorded all the same, being inevitable. The executioner, perhaps the most innocent of all, sought out Frère Isambard, and confessed to him in an anguish of remorse fearing never to be pardoned for what he had done. An Englishman who had sworn to add a faggot to the flames in which the witch should be burned, when he rushed forward to keep his word was seized with sudden compunction—believed that he saw a white dove flutter forth from amid the smoke over her head, and, almost fainting at the sight, had to be led by his comrades to the nearest tavern for refreshment, a life-like touch in which we recognise our countryman; but he too found his way that afternoon to Frère Isambard like the other. A horrible story is told by the Bourgeois de Paris, whose contemporary journal is one of the authorities for this period, that "the fire was drawn aside" in order that Jeanne's form, with all its clothing burned away, should be visible by one last act of shameless insult to the crowd. The fifteenth century believed, as we have said, everything that is cruel and horrible, as indeed the vulgar mind does at all ages; but such brutal imaginings have seldom any truth to support them, and there is no such suggestion in the actual record. Isambard and Massieu heard from one of the officials that when every other part of her body was destroyed the heart was found intact, but was, by the order of Winchester, flung into the Seine along with all the ashes of that sacrifice. It was wise no doubt that no relics should be kept.

Other details were murmured abroad amid the excited talk that followed this dreadful scene. "When she was enveloped by the smoke, she cried out for water, holy water, and called to St. Michæl; then hung her head upon her breast and breathing forth the name of Jesus, gently died." "Being in the flame her voice never ceased repeating in a loud voice the holy name of Jesus, and invoking without cease the saints of paradise, she gave up her spirit, bowing her head and saying the name of Jesus in sign of the fervour of her faith." One of the Canons of Rouen, standing sobbing in the crowd, said to another: "Would that my soul were in the same place where the soul of that woman is at this moment"; which indeed is not very different from the authorised saying of Pierre Morice in the prison. Guillaume Manchon, the reporter, he who wrote superba responsio on his margin, and had written down every word of her long examination—his occupation for three months,—says that he "never wept so much for anything that happened to himself, and that for a whole month he could not recover his calm." This man adds a very characteristic touch, to wit, that "with part of the pay which he had for the trial, he bought a missal, that he might have a reason for praying for her." Jean Tressat, "secretary to the King of England" (whatever that office may have been), went home from the execution crying out, "We are all lost, for we have burned a saint." A priest, afterwards bishop, Jean Fabry, "did not believe that there was any man who could restrain his tears."

The modern historians speak of the mockeries of the English, but none are visible in the record. Indeed, the part of the English in it is extraordinarily diminished on investigation; they are the supposed inspirers of the whole proceedings; they are believed to be continually pushing on the inquisitors; still more, they are supposed to have bought all that large tribunal, the sixty or seventy judges, among whom were the most learned and esteemed Doctors in France; but of none of this is there any proof given. That they were anxious to procure Jeanne's condemnation and death, is very certain. Not one among them believed in her sacred mission, almost all considered her a sorceress, the most dangerous of evil influences, a witch who had brought shame and loss to England by her incantations and evil spells. On that point there could be no doubt whatever. She alone had stopped the progress of the invaders, and broken the charm of their invariable success. But all that she had done had been in favour of Charles, who made no attempt to serve or help her, and who had thwarted her plans, and hindered her work so long as it was possible to do so, even when she was performing miracles for his sake. And Alençon, Dunois, La Hire, where were they and all the knights? Two of them at least were at Louvins, within a day's march, but never made a step to rescue her. We need not ask where were the statesmen and clergy on the French side, for they were unfeignedly glad to have the burden of condemning her taken from their hands. No one in her own country said a word or struck a blow for Jeanne. As for the suborning of the University of Paris en masse, and all its best members in particular, that is a general baseness in which it is impossible to believe. There is no appearance even of any particular pressure put upon the judges. Jean de la Fontaine disappeared, we are told, and no one ever knew what became of him: but it was from Cauchon he fled. And nothing seems to have happened to the monks who attended the Maid to the scaffold, nor to the others who sobbed about the pile. On the other side, the Doctors who condemned her were in no way persecuted or troubled by the French authorities when the King came to his own. There was at the time a universal tacit consent in France to all that was done at Rouen on the 31st of May, 1431.

One reason for this was not far to seek. We have perhaps already sufficiently dwelt upon it. It was that France was not France at that dolorous moment. It was no unanimous nation repulsing an invader. It was two at least, if not more countries, one of them frankly and sympathetically attaching itself to the invader, almost as nearly allied to him in blood, and more nearly by other bonds, than any tie existing between France and Burgundy. This does not account for the hostile indifference of southern France and of the French monarch to Jeanne, who had delivered them; but it accounts for the hostility of Paris and the adjacent provinces, and Normandy. She was as much against them as against the English, and the national sentiment to which she, a patriot before her age, appealed,—bidding not only the English go home, or fight and be vanquished, which was their only alternative—but the Burgundians to be converted and to live in peace with their brothers,—did not exist. Neither to Burgundians, Picards, or Normans was the daughter of far Champagne a fellow countrywoman. There was neither sympathy nor kindness in their hearts on that score. Some were humane and full of pity for a simple woman in such terrible straits; but no more in Paris than in Rouen was the Maid of Orleans a native champion persecuted by the English; she was to both an enemy, a sorceress, putting their soldiers and themselves to shame.

I have no desire to lessen our guilt, whatever cruelty may have been practised by English hands against the Heavenly Maid. And much was practised—the iron cage, the chains, the brutal guards, the final stake, for which may God and also the world, forgive a crime fully and often confessed. But it was by French wits and French ingenuity that she was tortured for three months and betrayed to her death. A prisoner of war, yet taken and tried as a criminal, the first step in her downfall was a disgrace to two chivalrous nations; but the shame is greater upon those who sold than upon those who bought; and greatest of all upon those who did not move Heaven and earth, nay, did not move a finger, to rescue. And indeed we have been the most penitent of all concerned; we have shrived ourselves by open confession and tears. We have quarrelled with our Shakespeare on account of the Maid, and do not know how we could have forgiven him, but for the notable and delightful discovery that it was not he after all, but another and a lesser hand that endeavoured to befoul her shining garments. France has never quarrelled with her Voltaire for a much fouler and more intentional blasphemy.

The most significant and the most curious after-scene, a pendant to the remorse and pity of so many of the humbler spectators, was the assembly held on the Thursday after Jeanne's death, how and when we are not told. It consisted of "nos judices antedicti," but neither is the place of meeting named, nor the person who presided. Its sole testimonial is that the manuscript is in the same hand which has written the previous records: but whereas each page in that record was signed at the bottom by responsible notaries, Manchon and his colleagues, no name whatever certifies this. Seven men, Doctors and persons of high importance, all judges on the trial, all concerned in that last scene in the prison, stand up and give their report of what happened there— part of which we have quoted—their object being to establish that Jeanne at the last acknowledged herself to be deceived. According to their own showing it was exactly such an acknowledgment as our Lord might have been supposed to make in the moment of his agony when the words of the psalm, "My God, my God, why hast thou forsaken me?" burst from his lips. There seems no reason that we can see, why this evidence should not be received as substantially true. The inference that any real recantation on Jeanne's part was then made, is untrue, and not even asserted. She was deceived in respect to her deliverance, and felt it to the bottom of her heart. It was to her the bitterness of death. But the flames of her burning showed her the truth, and with her last breath she proclaimed her renewed conviction. The scene at the stake would lose something of its greatness without that momentary cloud which weighed down her troubled soul.

Twenty years after the martyrdom of Jeanne, long after he had, according to her prophecy, regained Paris and all that had been lost, it became a danger to the King of France that it should be possible to imagine that his kingdom had been recovered for him by means of sorcery; and accordingly a great new trial was appointed to revise the decisions of the old. In the same palace of the Archbishop at Rouen, which had witnessed so many scenes of the previous tragedy, the depositions of witnesses collected with the minutest care, and which it had taken a long time to gather from all quarters, were submitted for judgment, and a full and complete reversal of the condemnation was given. The procès was a civil one, instituted (nominally) by the mother and brothers of Jeanne, one of the latter being now a knight, Pierre de Lys, a gentleman of coat armour—against the heirs and representatives of Cauchon, Bishop of Beauvais, and Lemaître, the Deputy Inquisitor—with other persons chiefly concerned in the judgment. Some of these men were dead, some, wisely, not to be found. The result was such a mass of testimony as put every incident of the life of the Maid in the fullest light from her childhood to her death, and in consequence secured a triumphant and full acquittal of herself and her name from every reproach. This remarkable and indeed unique occurrence does not seem, however, to have roused any enthusiasm. Perhaps France felt herself too guilty: perhaps the extraordinary calm of contemporary opinion which was still too near the catastrophe to see it fully: perhaps that difficulty in the diffusion of news which hindered the common knowledge of a trial—a thing too heavy to be blown upon the winds,—while it promulgated the legend, a thing so much more light to carry: may be the cause of this. But it is an extraordinary fact that Jeanne's name remained in abeyance for many ages, and that only in this century has it come to any sort of glory, in the country of which Jeanne is the first and greatest of patriots and champions, a country, too, to which national glory is more dear than daily bread.

In the new and wonderful spring of life that succeeded the revolution of 1830, the martyr of the fifteenth century came to light as by a revelation. The episode of the Pucelle in Michelet's History of France touched the heart of the world, and remains one of the finest efforts of history and the most popular picture of the saint. And perhaps, though so much less important in point of art, the maiden work of another maiden of Orleans—the little statue of Jeanne, so pure, so simple, so spiritual, made by the Princess Marie of that house, the daughter of the race which the Maid held in visionary love, and which thus only has ever attempted any return of that devotion—had its part in reawakening her name and memory. It fell again, however, after the great work of Quicherat had finally given to the country the means of fully forming its opinion on the subject which Fabre's translation, though unfortunately not literal and adorned with modern decorations, was calculated to render popular. A great crop of statues and some pictures not of any great artistic merit have since been dedicated to the memory of the Maid: but yet the public enthusiasm has never risen above the tide mark of literary applause.

There has been, however, a great movement of enthusiasm lately to gain for Jeanne the honour of canonisation; but it seems to have failed, or at least to have sunk again for the moment into silence. Perhaps these honours are out of date in our time. One of the most recent writers on the subject, M. Henri Blaze de Bury, suggests that one reason which retards this final consecration is "England, certainly not a negligible quantity to a Pope of our time." Let no such illusion move any mind, French or ecclesiastical. Canonisation means to us, I presume, and even to a great number of Catholics, simply the highest honour that can be paid to a holy and spotless name. In that sense there is no distinction of nation, and the English as warmly as the French, both being guilty towards her, and before God on her account—would welcome all honour that could be paid to one who, more truly than any princess of the blood, is Jeanne of France, the Maid, alone in her lofty humility and valour, and in everlasting fragrance of modesty and youth.